October 12, 1974

Dear Dad,
  Hope you have a very happy birthday today — and a very good year ahead.

[Automatic renewal of these wishes on each following October 12!]

  Love,
  Beverly

INVISIBLE HORIZONS
True Mysteries of the Sea

INVISIBLE HORIZONS
True Mysteries of the Sea

by Vincent Gaddis

CHILTON BOOK COMPANY
Philadelphia   New York   London

CONTENTS

Chapter 1

OVER THE HORIZON, 1

HOW DOES THE MARINER "SMELL" LAND? · SUPERSENSORY PERCEPTION · GEO-RHYTHMS AND BIO-RHYTHMS · BOTTINEAU · AND HIS PREDICTION OF ARRIVAL OF SHIPS AT THE ISLAND OF MAURITIUS · AUTHORITIES JEER, THEN CHEER · BOTTINEAU TRIES TO EXPLAIN ABILITY · GOES TO FRANCE BUT THE SAVANTS WILL NOT LISTEN · HIS "ART" LOST BUT HIS STORY SAVED · NAUSCOPIE—WHAT WAS IT?

Chapter 2

VANISHING ISLANDS, 13

A LARGE POPULATED ISLAND, LONG KNOWN, APPARENTLY DISAPPEARS · DISAPPEARING ISLANDS OF THE PACIFIC · NEW ISLANDS · PEEK-A-BOO ISLANDS · THE BELCHER ISLANDS · EARLY SLIPSHOD CARTOGRAPHY · BOUVET ISLAND FINALLY MAKES IT · IS DOUGHERTY ISLAND? · NAMED BUT UNFOUND ISLANDS BY THE DOZENS · A PARADISE THAT EXISTED · THE VANISHED TUANAKIS · $300,000 SPENT ON A MIRAGE · JUST WHAT ARE MIRAGES? · PALAEO-CRYSTIC ICE-RAFTS · WHAT HAPPENED TO MAYDA?

Chapter 3

BOTTLES, CASKS, AND CASKETS, 35

MESSAGES IN BOTTLES THAT LEAD TO LOVE AND HATE · PHONY MESSAGES · COLUMBUS' MESSAGE · UNNEEDED MESSAGES · LAST MESSAGES · THE SCIENTIFIC STUDY OF OCEAN CURRENTS BY THE USE OF BOTTLES · COINCIDENCE · HOMING MESSAGES · THE HOMING COFFIN: THE STORY OF CHARLES COGHLAN.

Chapter 4

THE WATCHERS AND THE AVENGERS, 42

COINCIDENCE? · THE CASE OF THE ALANTHUS · WAS IT CHANCE TO THE RESCUE? · THE INCREDIBLE STORY OF THE FIVE SHIPWRECKS AND THE PAYOFF · MOTHER AND SON · OFF ONE SHIP AND ONTO ANOTHER · OFF YOUR OWN SHIP AND BACK AGAIN · RESCUED ON A HUNCH · SAVED BY A VISION AND A MOONBEAM · SAVED FROM A REEF BY PREMONITION · THE SHIP THAT SAVED HER CREW · SHIPS THAT LOVED MEN · THE AVENGING FRIGORIFIQUE.

Chapter 5

THE JINXED AND THE DAMNED, 62

THE HELL-STORY OF THE GERMAN CRUISER SCHARNHORST · *THE SHIP WITH THE GRAVEYARD BALLAST · THE* CARL FRITZEN *AND THE* BRATT · *THE ALBATROSS JINX · THE FABULOUS* GREAT EASTERN · *THE SKELETONS*

CONTENTS

CONTENTS

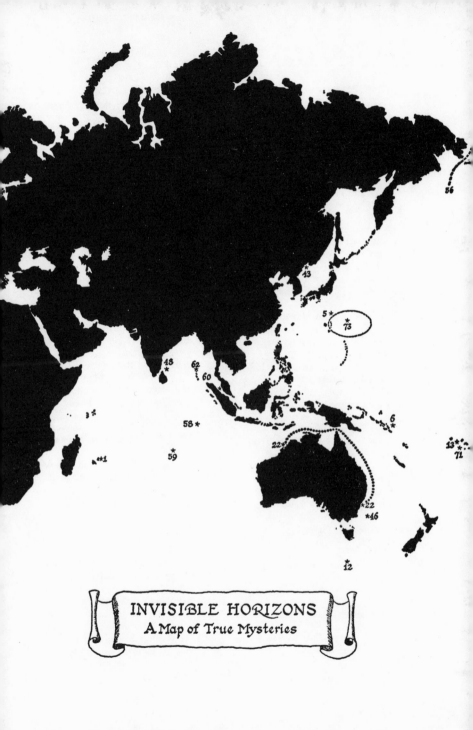

INVISIBLE HORIZONS
A Map of True Mysteries

MAP LEGEND

There may be no obvious change in the appearance of the sea and the sky, no variation of wave, wind or temperature, yet, the seafarer or the person born to the sea "smells" coming storms, a change in the weather, or his approach to land. How is this possible?

Our conscious minds deceive us. We are led to believe that all our awareness, all our knowledge, is derived through the five senses. But consciousness is only the surface of a great mental well that drops deep into the unknown—the outer light of a spectrum that radiates far into the infra-red of the subconscious and the ultra-violet of the superconscious.

All of our senses are limited in scope. A dog, for example, hears sounds inaudible to humans, and there is even evidence that it can occasionally see things which we cannot. Animals react not only to auditory and visual vibrations beyond our comprehension, but also, it seems more than likely, to changes in magnetism and atmospheric pressure. Some apparently "foretell" earthquakes and avalanches. Many definitely possess a homing instinct.

Some of these abilities extend to primitive peoples. There are Eskimos and Arabs with an astonishing directional sense. Explorers have told of following the former across trackless ice, and the latter across sand, without a compass. Despite the absence of landmarks, they never once swerved from their directions. As primitive peoples cease to be primitive, the need for these abilities end and they fade into disuse. Here is a fascinating ability that is rapidly disappearing.

If mariners of old, subconsciously reacting to drops in atmospheric pressure, could "smell" an approaching storm, this talent was not required after the Italian physicist Torricelli invented the barometer in 1643. But the talent seemingly remains as a latent ability that can still come to the fore in certain individuals whose environment encourages its use.

Our subconscious minds can detect far more with our physical senses than the conscious mind. We glance at a scene and focus our attention on one aspect of it. The subconscious records every detail of the total scene. The conscious forgets; the subconscious remembers. This is evident in hypnosis.

Professor George H. Estabrooks, of Colgate University, in his book *Hypnotism*,[1] gives us some remarkable cases of subconscious perception.* For example, the operator may show the subject twenty perfectly blank white calling cards and state that they are photographs. He picks up one of the cards, saying: "Look. Here is a picture of your mother. Do you recognize it?"

"Certainly," the subject replies.

"Will you recognize it again?"

"Of course."

The hypnotist makes a slight mark on the back of this card so he will be able to pick it out again. After a time the cards are shuffled and handed to the subject, face down. "Now pick out your mother's picture," the operator asks. The subject looks over the cards and selects the same card previously designated.

Estabrooks explains that when the subject knows he is supposed to remember that particular card, he memorizes some very trifling difference in the edge of the card, picks out some tiny flaw in its surface or some slight difference in texture.

Coming events cast their shadows before—often in subtle ways. Subconsciously a seafarer might detect a slight change in water color, a deepening of the sky ahead, a change in atmospheric pressure, or of magnetism. The subconscious communicates its observation to the conscious as a premonition.

Recent research, however, has opened the doors to a far greater concept.

Almost all plants and animals have cycles of behavior called bio-rhythms. Man, too, is influenced by cycles. His temperature and his blood pressure rise and fall at regular intervals. His energy and moods follow regular swings.

Each living organism is permeated by its own permanent electromagnetic force field. Sensitive measuring devices have demonstrated that these force fields enveloping living bodies change in strength and polarity in response to internal (biologic) and external (cosmologic) events. These responses are called "field profiles."

---

* Superior numbers refer to notes which will be found at the end of the book, beginning on page 227. Notes marked with other symbols will appear at the bottom of the page.

Under the direction of Dr. Harold S. Burr (Yale School of Medicine) and his associates, 30,000 field profiles from 430 people, some tested daily for a year, were analyzed. It was found that during the winter the field is strongest and positive. During the spring equinox, the field fluctuates erratically, then its strength declines through spring and summer until the polarity is reversed. During autumn the field returns to the positive high winter level.

Superimposed on the seasonal cyclic change are regular diurnal rhythms—semi-monthly and monthly changes related to the phases of the moon, and fluctuations that seem to be connected with changes in the earth's magnetic field.[2]

Oysters open and close their shells with the rising and falling of the tides. Dr. Frank A. Brown, Jr., of Northwestern University, Evanston, Illinois, took some oysters from a sound near New Haven, Connecticut, and placed them in a tank of salt water at Evanston. The temperature was kept constant, the water on an even level, and the room was illuminated with a dim, steady light.

For two weeks the oysters opened and closed their shells in time with the tides in New Haven. This indicated that the rhythm was inherited.

After fourteen days the rhythm ended. Hours passed by. Then a new rhythm began. The oysters opened their shells when the full moon stood at zenith over Evanston, when there would have been high tide in Evanston if the city had been on the sea coast.[3]

It was the moon's position that influenced the oysters, but what signal, what intermediary force, caused the four-hour change in rhythms?

These studies suggest that bio-rhythms are not only influenced by the moon and the earth's magnetic field, but also by fluctuations in barometric pressure, the gravitational field, and atmospheric electricity. These forces, in turn, are affected by forces from both inner and outer space that bombard the earth—cosmic and gamma rays, sunspot radiation, and other electromagnetic waves. And some of these forces influence our weather.

Dr. Burr says that what establishes the pattern and regulates and controls a particular human brain is actually a complex magnetic field. With ten billion cells offering countless circuits, the human brain is a superb receptor of electromagnetic energies.

"It is quite possible," writes Rutherford Platt, "that in a manner not yet discovered, earthly magnetic fields may influence human behavior, their rhythmic ebb and flow producing within our brains cyclical changes in feeling, alertness, and sensibility; perhaps even stirring the memory or inciting ideas."

If all this is true, it is quite possible that the highly-discerning subconscious mind can interpret subtle changes, such as barometric pressures and atmospheric electrical flux, and transmit a message to the consciousness enabling the seafarer to "smell" the coming storm.

And it is also possible that in this realm of research many more puzzling mysteries (and what Charles Fort[4] called "wild talents") will be found. Man, along with all other creatures, responds to cosmic rhythms emanating from the stellar mainland beyond. He is influenced by innumerable invisible forces that, in turn, respond to the ceaseless ebb and flow of the universe. This research is only beginning. Who can say what greater discoveries lie in the future?

There was once a man who lived on the island of Mauritius (also known as Île de France) in the Indian Ocean who had a "wild talent."

He could foretell the arrival of ships at the island long before they appeared over the horizon. With his mysterious gift, he could determine whether one ship, or more, was approaching, and how long it would be before it, or they, came in sight. When on board a ship, he could tell the distance and bearing of the land when it lay far below the visible horizon.

This ability, which he called the art or science of "Nauscopie," was attributed to his observation of effects in the atmosphere which he claimed were caused by the existence of land or moving vessels. He said he could teach other persons to develop this ability and he tried unsuccessfully to sell his secret to the French government.

The man was a Frenchman named Bottineau.

With the exception of brief references in the *Gazette de France* and by Sir David Brewster and the Abbe des Fontains, we would have almost no knowledge of this unusual man and his strange discovery today if Madame Guilleminot (sister-in-law to the General of that name) had not made a hobby of collecting documents signed by noted men of her day. Her collection survived the French Revolution and some of the material was brought to England early in the nineteenth century.

The seven documents relating to Bottineau were acquired by

Captain A. B. Becher, R.N., who founded *The Nautical Magazine* in 1832. Under the title "Original Papers," he published the documents in the magazine's March, 1834, issue.

Almost a century later, Lieutenant Commander Rupert T. Gould, R.N. (Ret.), found the story while reading a file of the magazine. In his book *Oddities: A Book of Unexplained Facts*, he has a chapter on Bottineau and reproduces the documents. This book, published in London in 1928, is long out of print and very scarce, especially in the United States.[5]

After twenty years on Mauritius, Bottineau returned to France in 1784 hoping to sell his discovery to the government. But it was the time of political turmoil that preceded the French Revolution, and he was ignored despite the impressive certificates he brought with him. He did, however, interest Jean Paul Marat, later one of the three most powerful men during the Reign of Terror, in his cause. One of the documents is a letter written about 1785 by Marat and addressed to an unidentified Mr. Daly in England.

Marat states that Bottineau has "experienced every kind of disappointment," and that if he can obtain the money he plans to go to London "where he is likely to meet with more success." Later Marat adds that "my poor friend looks very ill; I am afraid he will not be able to visit England, the only resource . . . that is left to him."

Along with Marat's letter is the following account of his discovery written by Bottineau:

> As early as the year 1762, holding then an inferior situation in the King's navy, it appeared to me that a vessel approaching land must produce a certain effect upon the atmosphere, and cause the approach to be discovered by a practiced eye even before the vessel itself was visible. After making many observations, I thought I could discover a particular appearance before the vessel came in sight: sometimes I was right, but more frequently wrong; so that at the time I gave up all thoughts of success.
>
> In 1764, I was appointed to a situation in the Île de France; while there, having much leisure time, I again betook myself to my favorite observations.
>
> Here the advantages I possessed were much greater than before. First, the clear sky and pure atmosphere . . . were favorable to my studies, and as fewer vessels came to the island, I was less liable to error than was the case off the coast of France, where vessels are continually passing, some of which may never arrive in sight . . . I had

not been more than six months upon the island when I became confident that my discovery was certain, and that all that was requisite was to acquire more experience, and then *Nauscopie* would become a real science.

As the officers in the island led an idle life, they were frequently on the shore looking through their glasses to discover when a vessel was arriving from Europe. I frequently laid wagers that a vessel was arriving one, two, and even three days before she was actually in sight, and as I was very seldom wrong, I gained a considerable sum of money.

The officers attributed my success to a particular power of vision I possessed; but then again, they were quite puzzled on reflecting that although they used glasses, I never employed any.

In 1780 I wrote to the Minister of Marine, Marechal de Castries, announcing my discovery. In his answer, he instructed the Governor of the island to enter my announcements of arrivals in a private register for two years at least. On the 15th of May, 1782, my observations commenced.

On the 16th of May I announced to the Governor, Viscount de Souillac, that three vessels were near the island. Orders were immediately given to the official watchmen; their glasses were turned to the direction which I had pointed out. Their declaration was "No vessel in sight." On the 17th the watchmen informed the Governor that a ship had just appeared above the horizon. On the 18th a second came in sight, and on the 26th a third was visible to the naked eye.

The Governor sent for me on the last-named day, and made me an offer of 10,000 livres, and a pension of 1,200 livres a year, on the part of the Government, if I would disclose my secret; but not conceiving the remuneration sufficient, I declined accepting the offer.

The Governor, some months after, wrote to M. de Castries: he stated that I had made the surprising discovery of a new art—that of being able to observe the arrival of vessels 100, 150, and even 200 leagues distant; that for more than fifteen years I had regularly predicted the arrival of vessels, sometimes three or four days before they could be seen with a glass; that the register kept by order of the Minister showed that I had almost always been right in my predictions; and that even when I had announced the approach of a vessel which did not actually arrive, it was proved beyond a doubt that the vessel or vessels in question were foreign ones that had come within two or three days' sail of the island, and had proceeded to their destination without touching at the Île of France.

"Upon one occasion [Bottineau here is quoting from the Governor's letter] he asserted that a fleet of eleven vessels were approaching the island; the announcement caused great alarm, as we anticipated an attack from the English. A sloop of war was instantly dispatched to look out; but before she returned, M. Bottineau (said) that the signs in the atmosphere had disappeared, and that the fleet had taken a different direction. Later a vessel arrived here from the East Indies and reported that she had seen a fleet of eleven vessels sailing towards Fort St. William. In fine, that from the year 1778 till 1782, he had announced the arrival of 575 vessels, many of them four days before they became visible."

The letter terminated thus—"However incredible this discovery may appear, myself and a great many officers, naval and military, must bear testimony to the announcements made by M. Bottineau. We cannot treat him as an imposter or as a visionary. We have had ocular demonstration for so many years, and in no instance has any vessel reached the island, the approach of which he has not predicted; those which did approach, but did not touch the island, were in most cases proved to be foreign vessels."

A short time after this letter had been dispatched, I determined to return to my native country, and accordingly took my passage on board one of His Majesty's vessels, commanded by Captain Dufour. I felt somewhat anxious to ascertain whether the effect produced on the atmosphere, when a vessel approaches (land), would be somewhat similar as regards the approach of one vessel towards another. To my great delight I perceived it to be the same, although less powerful; but my eyes now became so practiced that not once during the voyage did I make a mistake.

I announced to Captain Dufour the approach of 27 vessels while proceeding to our destination. What afforded me more heartfelt satisfaction (was) certain appearances in the skies when a vessel approaches land . . . in my opinion, to be able to discover land from a vessel long before it is in sight is . . . of infinitely greater advantage to navigation.

Upon one occasion, I told Captain Dufour that we were not more than thirty leagues from some land. This he denied to be possible; however, upon looking to his reckoning, he was compelled to acknowledge his error and immediately altered his course. I discovered land three times during the voyage; once at a distance of 150 leagues.

On the 13th of June, 1784, I landed at L'Orient and proceeded to Paris. My applications to the Minister to obtain an audience were not attended to; and the only answer I obtained from the Officer of Marine was that my memorial (sic) was under consideration.

Abbe Fontenay, editor of the *Mercure de France,* having heard of my "pretended" discovery, without even asking to see my certificates signed by the Governor of the Ile de France and all the officers of the garrison there, thought proper to turn my discovery into ridicule, and affirmed that it was not "ships at sea, but castles in the air" I had found out.

In this state the affair remains. All I can add is, that should vexation and disappointment terminate my existence before I can explain my discovery, the world will probably be deprived for some time of an art that would have done honor to the eighteenth century.

Unfortunately this final prediction of Bottineau did come true. He died shortly before the dawn of the French Revolution and his secret died with him. He joined, as Gould says, all the other poor and friendless men who have made discoveries that happened to get on the blind side of officialdom.

Four of the surviving documents are the certificates (actually detailed statements) attesting to Bottineau's ability and signed by the island's governor, attorney-general, infantry colonel, and commissary-general of the navy.

The governor, in part, wrote that Bottineau "sees in Nature signs that indicate the presence of vessels as we assert that fire exists in places where we see the smoke . . . but only those who can read the signs are able to judge of the distances, and this art, he asserts, is an extremely laborious study. . . . What we can certify is that M. Bottineau was almost always right."

Melis, the commissary-general, wrote in his statement that he, personally, had Bottineau inform him in writing of his predictions. During a six-month period, Bottineau forecast the arrival of 109 vessels from one to four days in advance of sighting by watchmen. Only twice was he mistaken, and this could be explained by contrary winds or currents.

"We have also to acknowledge," Melis wrote, "and not without great astonishment, that his art extends so far as to inform him whether there was one, or there were several in the vicinity of the isle, and if they were together or separated."

The final document translated and published by Captain Becher in 1834 is Bottineau's own explanation of his ability, although he refrains from giving a clear description of the atmospheric effects he said he detected.

His plea that he be excused from explaining how a vessel causes such an effect is justified. A discovery is one thing, its explanation another, as recognized by Bacon in his "Interpreters of Nature." As Gould says, "to gird at a discoverer because he has not hit upon the true explanation of his observations is not far removed from the sin of Ham."

One other thought: We must never deny the existence of talents or phenomena because of the explanations, however popular.

This has been the great barrier that has prevented many orthodox scientists from approaching that vast realm of occurrences now known as parapsychology. There can be more than one, sometimes many, tentative explanations of a phenomenon; only the steady increase of knowledge may bring the correct explanation to light. Bottineau's own statement follows:

Nauscopie is the art of ascertaining the approach of vessels, or, being in a vessel, the approach to land, at a very great distance. The knowledge neither results from the undulation of the waves, nor from quick sight, nor from a particular sensation, but simply from observing the horizon, which bears upon it certain signs indicative of the approach of vessels or land.

When a vessel approaches land, or another vessel, a *meteor* (the word in this usage means atmospheric effect or aberration) appears in the atmosphere, of a particular nature, visible to every eye without any difficult effort; it is not by the effect of a fortuitous occurrence that this meteor makes its appearance in such circumstances; it is, on the contrary, the necessary result of the approach of one vessel towards another or towards land. The existence of this meteor, and the knowledge of its different modifications, constitute the certainty and the precision of my announcements.

If I am asked how it is possible that the approach of a vessel towards land can cause any meteor to be engendered in the atmosphere, and what affinity exists between two effects so removed; I reply that I must be excused giving an account of the *why* and the *wherefore;* that it is sufficient I have discovered the fact, without being obliged to explain the principle.

However, the study of twenty years seems to have given me a right to reason upon (this) subject and the following is my opinion.

The vast expanse of water forms an immense abyss into which substances of all kinds are continually entering. The enormous number of animals, fishes, birds, vegetable and mineral productions are decomposed in the vast body of water, producing a continual fermentation of matter. The presence of these gases is sufficiently apparent from the smell and disagreeable taste of sea water. These gases, closely united with the sea water, remain stationary so long as the waters are quiet and not disturbed.

But when the water is put in motion by stormy weather, or by an active mass which passes over its surface with violence and rapidity (a vessel for instance), then the volatile vapors that are enclosed within the bosom of the deep escape, and rise (like) smoke composing a vast envelope around the vessel. As she advances, the envelope advances with her, increased every moment by fresh emanations. These emanations are like so many clouds, which, by degrees, joining each other, form a kind of cloud that projects forward, one extremity touching the vessel while the other advances to a considerable distance.

This train of vapors is not on that account visible; it escapes observation by the transparency of its parts. It is lost among the other fluids that compose the atmosphere. But as soon as the vessel reaches a situation in which it meets with other homogeneous vapors, such as those which escape from the earth, one perceives that cloud until then so limpid and subtle, acquire consistence and color by the mixing of the two opposed columns.

The change commences at the prolonged extremities, which unite by contact, and are thus strengthened and colored; and then, every minute as the vessel advances, the change is graduated, gains the center, and at length the *engrainement* being complete, the phenomenon becomes more manifest and the vessel appears.

Whatever the cause of this phenomenon, it is quite certain that it is the infallible satellite of a vessel; and because of its prolonged form, it manifests itself to the eyes one, three and even six days before the vessel itself, according to the state of the weather and the nature of the obstacles it meets.

When the vessel sails with a fair wind and meets with no obstacle, the phenomenon possesses its greatest celerity; and arriving several days before the vessel, it affords the observer the means of announcing the presence of a vessel at a considerable distance. But when the vessel meets with contrary winds, it will be understood that this circumstance must have a great influence on the progress of the phenomenon. On this account, I state that the phenomenon sometimes appears four or five days before the vessel, and sometimes only one day.

It will naturally be supposed that there may be weather when the phenomenon cannot show itself before the vessel; for instance, in a violent gale which appears capable of carrying away the phenomenon. This, however, is not the case. The most impetuous wind only retards the phenomenon without destroying it. When the vessel has reached a certain distance from land, then the phenomenon has acquired so much consistence that it overcomes the efforts of the strongest winds, which, though they agitate it, still leave some part which they cannot wholly disperse.

The whole of my science consists in being able to follow the apparition of this meteor, and distinguish its character, in order not to confound it with the other clouds in the atmosphere. In order to make these observations neither telescopes nor mathematical instruments are required; the eyes alone are sufficient.

The cloudy mass does not present itself suddenly. The first appearance is equivocal and serves to put the observer upon his guard. By degrees the forms are developed, the colors assume a certain tone, the volume acquires consistence, so that the *nauscopist* can no longer doubt that a vessel is behind; because these forms and these developments are such that they can only belong to these kind of vapors.

As the vessel advances, the meteor extends and becomes consistent. From the moment I became familiar with this singular analogy, I never failed seeing my announcements followed by complete success. This punctuality caused the great astonishment mentioned in my certificates from the Governor, officers and inhabitants. Convinced of the effect, but not understanding the cause, they could not conceive that a science existed which could give to man a foreknowledge of events so distant with respect to time and place.

The people attributed these events to the power of magic; the better informed ascribed them to chance. Nothing, however, is more natural than this principle which has astonished everyone, and concerning which so much incredulity will be manifested throughout Europe.

Bottineau

What was the secret of the wizard of Mauritius?

Sir David Brewster, in his *Letters on Natural Magic*,[6] suggests that Bottineau saw mirages. But the conditions that produce mirages would not be consistent day after day for twenty years. Moreover, we can be sure that, after the island's governor offered the substantial reward that Bottineau refused, there were many others who tried unsuccessfully to see the alleged "meteors."

Gould suggests that the *nauscopist* had "trained himself to see some very faint appearance, like an extremely attenuated cloud, somewhere near the sea horizon, and he found, by experience, that this heralded the advent of a ship.

"He speaks of the 'form' and 'color' of such clouds and of their acquiring 'consistency'; but there can be little doubt that even when most fully developed this appearance must have been far from easy to see. . . . Bottineau's own statements support this; he remarks that a person practicing his 'science' must undergo a short period of education; sure proof that his 'meteor' did not leap to the eye."

If Gould is correct in his suggestion, Bottineau may have been assisted by unusually keen vision. Cases of almost incredible sight are to be found in medical records. In 1954 the London Refraction Hospital reported eyesight tests with Mrs. Janet Hitchman, thirty-seven, of Newmarket, Suffolk, England, whose "eyes are among the most remarkable in the world."[7]

Mrs. Hitchman, whose eyes had deep brown irises, could read

a newspaper ten feet away, see the facial expression on her daughter when the child was three-quarters of a mile away, and see the phases of the planet Venus and other astronomical sights usually requiring a telescope.

Again, there is the matter of knowing what to look for and where to look. Asaph Hall discovered the satellites of Mars in 1877 with the 26-inch Washington telescope, but they can be observed with a 12-inch telescope now that we know they exist!

"It seems likely that Bottineau," Gould comments, "saw what others failed to see simply because he had trained his eye to detect indications which were invisible to an ordinary observer who did not know what they looked like."

Finally, Gould suggests that an observer along a clear sea coast who took a series of photographs of the horizon at short intervals over a considerable period of time and checked them against a register of shipping movements within a 200-mile radius might be able to confirm if Bottineau's "meteor" had any real existence.

There is, however, one other possible explanation—that Bottineau's observations were not objective but subjective; that his "meteors" were projections from his own mind. In support of this view, I emphasize two facts: first, that in all the centuries that countless men have watched the sea horizons only Bottineau has reported such "meteors"; second, that Bottineau never taught his secret to another person. Obviously, he believed he could do so, but if he had succeeded in selling his secret he might have found out that his gift was unique.

Bottineau may have been unconsciously clairvoyant—his precognition limited to the arrival of ships at Mauritius. He consciously sought, however, a physical interpretion, and this came in the form of faint images that only he could see, projected outward upon the atmosphere like visions in a crystal.

Someday we may know more about the true nature of that mysterious dimension we call time. If so, we may rediscover the secret that Bottineau carried to his tomb, and at the same time find some plausible explanations for a number of other presently inexplicable matters, to which I shall now turn.

At high noon on a summer day in 1928 the captain of a 20,000-ton round-the-world tourist ship mounted to the bridge to check his bearings. At his side were two British Naval Reserve officers who joined him daily to keep in practice. Using his sextant, the captain made his determinations and turned to his chart.

His eyes widened in astonishment.

Working independently, the two naval officers checked the ship's position. Then all three men compared their calculations. All agreed there could be no doubt about their results. Bewildered, they glanced at the empty spinning horizon around the vessel. Then the captain made his way to the radio room and the news was flashed to the world.

Easter Island had vanished!

The strange lonely island of the southeast Pacific where the huge statues of a prehistoric people had gazed at the sea was gone. The enigma of Easter and its stone giants of antiquity had been covered by the waters of the world's greatest ocean.

A gunboat was sent from Valparaiso, Chile, to investigate the report. Ten days later the island was sighted. It was at its charted latitude and longitude. The ancient gods were intact—still brooding over blue infinity. There had been no earthquake, no tidal wave. The peak of Rano Raraku still rose 12,000 feet above the floor of the ocean. Its position was unchanged. The crew of the gunboat shook their heads and returned home.

The report of the tourist ship was only the latest in a series of puzzling observations in an area where phantom islands have been reported for almost three centuries. Robert Casey, in his book *Easter Island*,[1] tells of the preceding incident, and discusses in detail the appearing and disappearing islands of the southeast Pacific.

Back in 1687 the English pirate Captain Edward Davis discovered an island with "a long sandy beach and cocoanut palms." The location was given as latitude 27° S, and about five hundred miles west of the South American coast. Another island with high peaks was observed approximately twelve leagues away to the west.

Davis was in a hurry and he decided not to land since he had ample provisions. Since he was known to be an experienced, trustworthy navigator, his report was accepted and for fifty years the charts of the sea showed the location of "Davis Land." There was one big problem, however. No one could find it.

While searching for it in 1722, the Dutch Admiral Roggeveen discovered Easter Island on Easter Sunday and gave his land-fall its holiday name. But the admiral said that Easter could not be Davis Land. Easter was 2,000 miles from the mainland and the nearest land is the rocks of Sala-y-Gomez 250 miles to the east.

In 1802 a Captain Gwyn reported that the rocks of Sala-y-Gomez had been erroneously charted. He had found that the rocks were three hundred miles *west* and fifty miles south of Easter Island. Mariners made a search. The rocks were found at their charted location, while there was no trace of rocks at the location given by Gwyn.

A small uninhabited island was reported by Juan Fernandez in 1576 off the South American coast, observed while he was on a voyage from Callao to Valparaiso. It was never found, but in 1809 the ship *Guinevere* found a reef in the general area that may have been the remains of an island.

Captain Pinocchio, in 1879, announced his discovery of Podesta Island, which he named after his vessel. Its location was given as 870 miles due west of Valparaiso, Chile, a lonely part of the sea far from shipping lanes.

The Italian captain said the island was oval in shape, about three-quarters of a mile in circumference and forty feet in height. The Italian Hydrographic Office claimed that the captain's navigation could not have been in error more than a few miles. It might have been Davis Land, although there was no other island nearby.

But the island has not been found since the original report, and it was removed from charts in 1935.

Again, in 1912, the S.S. *Glewalon,* a large English vessel, steamed into Valparaiso harbor with the news that land had been sighted off the coast and not far from Easter Island. All officers aboard had checked the calculations which were turned over to harbor authorities.

Apparently a new island had arisen from the sea, but the training ship *Baquedano* searched for the new land for three weeks without success. Soundings in the region revealed a depth of around ten thousand feet.

Finally, northwest of this area and just north of the Equator, there was Sarah Ann Island. It would have been in the path of totality during the solar eclipse of June 8, 1937, and astronomers were anxious to establish an observation post there since there were no other nearby islands.

During the summer of 1932 vessels of the U.S. Navy Pacific Fleet searched for Sarah Ann, but finally gave up. Once again an island was removed from the charts.[2]

If you are planning to flee from turmoil and tension to a Pacific island, be certain you choose a paradise with a good history of stability. Otherwise you may find yourself cradled in the deep with legendary Mu or Lemuria.

This warning may be timely in view of the increased volcanic submarine activity in the Pacific during recent years. Skirmishes in the eternal battle between land and sea for supremacy have created peekaboo islands—land masses that appear and disappear like cards during a sleight-of-hand performance.

In 1955 the U.S. Navy's Hydrographic Office in Honolulu reported that military pilots flying to Wake Island had sighted a land mass with breaking surf 385 miles west of Honolulu. Within a few weeks the island disappeared, leaving only sulphurous streaks visible on the surface.

But in other areas west of Hawaii there were more signs of volcanic activity—smoke and yellow and orange lines across long stretches of water. Observers on ships and planes reported rising columns of steam and masses of sulphur scum.

Navy hydrographic officers pointed out that these observations were made along surface and air traffic lanes, and there were probably other disturbances in out-of-the-way areas. "It seems to be a part of the stepped-up pattern of underwater activity around the Pacific," they added. (See AP dispatch from Honolulu, September 24, 1955.)

Earlier, in February, 1946, the crew of a British warship witnessed the birth of twins in the prolific Pacific, two hundred miles south of Tokyo. The two cones rose to a height of fifty feet and spread out over an area of about a square mile.

The British Admiralty decided the land mass was a single entity and named it Urania Island after the destroyer H.M.S. *Urania* which had discovered it.

Two months later the twins had dissolved into a shoal considerably larger than their initial size. They had followed the pattern of other upstart volcanic isles that play hide and seek with geographers. As large heaps of volcanic ash thrown up from submarine craters, they are subject to rapid erosion by waves, storms, tides, and currents.[3]

Volcanic fires long ago punctured the ocean floor and built up many of the stable islands rising from submarine ridges. Some of them have been above water for millions of years. But today the mis-named Pacific remains encircled by a volcanic "ring of fire" accompanied by earthquake faults.

One of the most interesting facts about these volcanic islands, past and present, is that they do not spring out of any array of shallows, but push their way upward from the very bottom of the sea. The short-lived land mass of 1955 west of Hawaii was located where charts mark the depth at 16,000 feet!

Professor Karl Versteeg, of the Department of Geology, College of Wooster, wrote that Urania was situated in the *"vicinity* [i.e., on the rim] of the Rampo Deep, where the floor of the Pacific drops down to 34,626 feet, a matter of some six miles."[4]

It's not surprising that volcanologists suggest there are catastrophes to come. In Hawaii, Dr. Gordon MacDonald says activities in recent years "point out the fact that we could get an eruption on Kauai or Oahu." The latter island with its capital of Honolulu is home for most of Hawaii's population. MacDonald adds that while the possibility is remote, even the long-dormant crater of Diamond Head at Waikiki could turn into something more spectacular than a tourist attraction.[5] And Professor Thomas A. Jaggar, of the University of Hawaii, has forecast tremendous explosive eruptions in Hawaii and Japan, followed by earthquakes and tidal waves which may strike along the California coast.[6]

Scientists, you see, remember Krakatoa.

This volcanic island in the East Indies blew up in 1883 in history's greatest explosion. The blast was heard 3,000 miles away, tidal waves swept beaches for 8,000 miles, and clouds of dust dimmed the sun for almost a year. The loss of life was estimated at 36,000. Since then Krakatoa's crater has appeared and ducked out of sight twice. Above the remains of the island a geyser still spouts ashes and steam. Nobody knows when hell may break loose again—on Krakatoa or elsewhere.[7]

In addition to temporary volcanic islands, there are jack-in-the-box isles that rise and fall with the years in more shallow regions. Examples are Bogoslof in the Aleutians near Alaska, and Falcon in the Tonga group.

Bogoslof first appeared above the Bering Sea in 1796, rising from a wide shoal to a height of about two hundred feet in four years. Since then it has been constantly changing its shape. It appears to be the top of a volcano, although its nose has never emerged.

Falcon was born in 1885 when an eruption raised a shoal 290 feet above the ocean surface. During the following thirteen years its two-mile-diameter mass disappeared. It was reborn in 1927, and today is about one hundred feet in height. Metis Island, seventy-five miles from Falcon, popped up in 1875, vanished in 1899.

Expedition Island is now under forty-two feet of water. Torca, once a well-populated island in the Indian Ocean, vanished in explosion and flame in 1683. Thus islands are born, live and die.

The solid earth beneath our feet is in fact constantly changing—responding to the rhythms of tides, and being subjected to tremendous pressures. As ages pass mountains are forced skyward, then dissolve under the attacks of rain and wind. Earthquakes and volcanoes are the most spectacular manifestations of these changes; and, they are the swiftest in action. Large and even enormous masses of rock may rise, fall, or shift in a matter of *minutes,* not years or millennia.

With 70 per cent of the earth's surface covered with water and both surface and air travel lanes well defined, perhaps it is not surprising that some islands on the charts refuse to stay where they belong or disappear permanently. Compass variations, volcanic or earthquake disturbances, and mirages are complicating factors.

There are numerous little-known areas on the seas. The reader who sees a nautical chart for the first time will be astonished at the number of spots marked E.D. (existence doubtful) or P.D. (position doubtful). Each year hundreds of rocks, shoals, and reefs are reported at various locations. Some are confirmed; others cannot be found later by surveying ships and other vessels.

Lieutenant Commander Gould, in his book *Oddities: A Book of Unexplained Facts*, wrote: "Until we know considerably more about the geography of our planet than we do now, there will always be doubtful islands distinguished on the . . . charts.

"It may seem curious, in these days of over-civilization, that we should still be in this state of uncertainty. But, in sober fact, we still know less about the round world than is generally supposed, and a small departure from the beaten track may still, in certain parts of the great oceans and even nearer home, transform the ordinary mariner into a discoverer."

As an example, Gould refers to the case of the Belcher Islands in Hudson Bay. Since 1610 the bay (or rather, inland sea) has been known and traveled, and the Hudson's Bay Company for centuries has operated trading posts on its shores. Yet it was not until 1915 that a group of islands was discovered in the bay and, incredibly, almost within sight of land. More astonishing still, they are large islands. Several are more than seventy miles long, and they have a total area of about 5,000 square miles.

"Strictly speaking," Gould explains, "they were not absolutely a new discovery. Old charts showed, in their vicinity, one or two little clusters of tiny islets, proving that in times gone by some vessel or vessels had sighted them; but their actual size, extent, and position had remained unknown and unguessed-at. Obviously, they were not of recent formation; they merely happen to lie off the ordinary trade route of vessels navigating the bay, and in a region which, until 1915, had never been properly examined."[8]

We should keep two facts in mind. First, in the early days of cartography, prior to the beginning of the seventeenth century, many map-makers failed to have a sense of responsibility. For political reasons, or to compliment a patron, relative, or friend, they placed imaginary islands on their charts. Since these charts were copied by later draftsmen, these fictitious or mythical islands, especially when placed in unfrequented parts of the ocean, remained on charts for many years.

Second, while seamen have always been able to determine latitude by means of astronomical observations, the finding of longitude remained an unsolved problem until shortly after the middle of the eighteenth century when John Harrison, an English carpenter, invented the chronometer.

As we shall see, however, many of our found and lost islands were reported during the past 150 years during which time navigation has been developed into a fairly exact science.

Difficulties in navigational calculations were responsible for causing the Solomon Islands to be lost for two centuries. The Solomons, so important in World War II, were first discovered in 1567. Unable to find them for two hundred years, mariners regarded the first report as false. Finally, in 1767, they were rediscovered.[9]

A more startling performance in the oceanic game of hide-and-seek was given by Bouvet Island. Pierre des Loziers Bouvet, the first Antarctic explorer, found the island in 1739 approximately 1,500 miles southwest of the Cape of Good Hope. He described it as about five miles in diameter and partly covered by a glacier.

Unsuccessful searches for the island were conducted by Captain James Cook in 1772 and 1775, and by Captain Furneaux in the H.M.S. *Adventure* in 1774. But in 1808 two sealing vessels, the *Snow Swan* and the *Otter,* reported sighting Bouvet. And in 1822 Captain Benjamin Morrell of an American whaler claimed he landed on the island and killed a number of seals.

Three years later two whalers, the *Sprightly* and the *Lively,* arrived at Bouvet. At the same time Captain George Norris, of the *Sprightly,* discovered Thompson Island, situated northeast of Bouvet near three rocky islets that he called the "Chimneys." A larger rock about three miles distant from Thompson he named Liverpool Island.

The British Admiralty decided to investigate. Sir James C. Ross, R.N., searched the region in 1843, but failed to sight any land. To settle the matter once for all, Lieutenant T. E. L. Moore, R.N., followed with a second expedition in 1845. He agreed with Ross that the islands must be phantoms, and they were removed from charts.

Thirty-three years passed, then Captain Williams of the *Golden West,* followed in 1882 by Captain Church of the *Delia Church,* reported seeing Bouvet. And in 1893 Captain Joseph Fuller of the whaler *Francis Allen* not only sighted Bouvet but made six sketches of Thompson Island.

The German oceanographic vessel *Valdivia* definitely located Bouvet in 1898—and in the same position given 154 years before. Thompson and its rocky satellites, however, could not be found.

The location of Bouvet was confirmed by the German research ship *Meteor* in 1926, the R.R.S. *Discovery* in 1926, and the Norwegian vessel *Norvegia* in 1927.

Bouvet is now known to definitely exist and has been correctly marked in charts since 1917. But all of these surveying ships have failed to locate Thompson Island and its nearby rocks. The water in the area reported by Norris and Fuller as their location, is over 750 fathoms in depth.

The existence of Dougherty Island remains a mystery.

At the turn of the last century an American whaler under the command of Captain Swain of Nantucket sighted an island at lat. 59 degrees south and "Long. about 90 to 100 West," approximately 1,800 miles west by south of Cape Horn. (Longitudes at the time were still largely determined by chronometers, which, being mechanical devices, could deviate appreciably over long periods of time.)

The island was described as about eight miles long, two to three miles wide, eighty feet at its highest point, and covered with ice and snow. Hundreds of seals and flocks of birds were observed.

Dougherty, as it was later named, was again sighted a few years later by Gardiner and Macy, whaler captains. Macy said the water around the island was "dark-colored and contained much rockweed or kelp." No attempts were made to land.

Then in 1830 two American vessels, captained by two brothers, N. B. and A. S. Palmer, set out to confirm the island's position and explore it. They couldn't find it. But eleven years later Captain Dougherty, of the whaler *James Stewart*, passed it at three hundred yards and kept it in sight for the better part of a day. Dougherty fixed its location as lat. 59° 20′ S., and long. 120° 20′ W. He described the island in detail down to a small iceberg grounded on its northern shore.

In 1859 Captain Keates of England confirmed Dougherty's location and description, and his chronometer later was found to be in error less than a quarter of a mile. With this additional evidence, the island was placed on the charts.

There were more observations. Captains Whitson, in 1885, and William Stannard, in 1886 and again in 1890, sighted the island. Stannard made a sketch of the island but, while he may have been a good navigator, he was a poor artist. Lieutenant Commander Gould describes his sketch as "a cross between a disreputable iceberg and a dissipated saw."

Finally, in 1893, Captain White, of New Zealand, sailed around the island, and his description tallied closely with those of previous navigators.

Then the island vanished.

The *Ruapehu,* a research vessel, searched four times for Dougherty in favorable weather between the years 1894 and 1910 without success. Captain Scott, of Antarctic fame, passed over the island's reported position and made soundings of 2,588 fathoms where seven ships had reported land.

Additional unsuccessful surveys were made in 1910 by the *Nimrod,* in 1915 by the yacht *Carnegie,* and in 1930 by the yacht *Discovery* and the Norwegian exploring ship *Norvega.* The island was removed from the charts in 1932.

But, like Bouvet, Dougherty may actually exist. No nation has ever claimed it. In lonely isolation, it may still be awaiting rediscovery.

Saxemberg, if it ever existed, is another such isolated island, far from the trade-routes. Lindeman, a Dutch navigator, found it in 1670 about six hundred miles northwest of Tristan de Cunha in the South Atlantic, describing it as a low-lying island with a high peak near the center.

It was sighted in 1804 by Captain Galloway of the American schooner *Fanny,* who reported that he had the island in view for four hours and commented on the peaked hill in the center. Again, in 1816, Captain Head of the English ship *True Briton* reported having Saxemberg in view for almost six hours.

The island was never seen again. A Captain Cornwallis sailed over the location in 1821, followed several years later by Captain Horsburgh. Soundings at the location have revealed a depth of 2,000 fathoms.

Then there are the Auroras, a group of three islands said to lie in the South Atlantic about halfway between the Falklands and South Georgia. They were first reported in 1762 by the whaler *Aurora.* Later sightings were logged by the vessels *San Miguel* in 1769, again by the *Aurora* in 1774, by the *Pearl* in 1779, and by the *Dolores* and *Princess* in 1790.

The Spanish surveying ship *Atrevida* fixed their position in 1794 and its officers made detailed charts and sketches of the three islands. But searches conducted in 1820 and 1822 and by exploring vessels since have all failed to uncover any trace of the islands that were the scene of Edgar Allen Poe's story "Arthur Gordon

Pym." The last report of them was an observation made in 1856 by the brig *Helen Baird*.

Several phantom islands were once charted in the area four hundred to five hundred miles south of Tasmania. One group, the Royal Company Islands, were eliminated from charts in 1904. In this same area, Nimrod Island was discovered in 1828 by Captain Eilbech and named after his ship.

Three years later Captain John Biscoe found marine vegetation and numerous birds at the location given, but no islands. Two antarctic explorers, Shackleton in 1909 and Scott in 1913, made unsuccessful searches, and soundings disclosed a two mile depth. Nimrod was dropped from charts in 1922.

In 1860 the U.S.S. *Levant* sailed from Hawaii for Panama and vanished in the area bounded by the 133rd to the 138th meridians west and the 15th to 20th parallels north. Within this 30,000 square-mile region, the warship was believed to have been wrecked on an uncharted island. A search by the U.S.S. *Albatross* and the cruiser *Tacoma* failed to reveal any trace of the warship or of islands.

In this area, however, whalers had reported islands named Bunker, New, Sultan, Eclipse, Roca and others unnamed. One of the unnamed islands was reported by a British mariner, DeGreaves, in 1859 as located twelve hundred miles southeast of Honolulu. Not one of these islands has been found by exploring vessels.

Other phantom islands in the South Pacific never found include Sprague, Monks, Favorite, Duke of York, Dangerous, Grand Duke Alexander, Little Paternosters, Marqueen, Massacre, and Mortlock.

The U.S. government in 1858 listed over a dozen islands in the South Pacific as "pertaining to the United States under the act of Aug. 18, 1856." Not one of these islands has ever been found!

Accounts of most of the phantom islands we have been considering will be found in Gould's *Oddities*, referred to earlier, and in Karl Baarslag's *Islands of Adventure*.

It is Baarslag, moreover, who tells us about Onaneuse or Hunter Island, a perfect isle, if it could be found, for escapists from civilization. Its alleged location is lat. 15° 31′ S.; long. 176° 11′ W., and the nearest land is Niaufou or "tin can" island.

Hunter was discovered in 1823 by Captain Hunter of the *Donna Carmelita*. The captain said it was inhabited by intelligent and cultivated Polynesians who had the curious custom of amputating the little finger of the left hand at the second joint. He added that the land was fertile, with plenty of cocoanut palms and breadfruit. Hunter should have remained in his paradise; no one else has been able to find it.

Well over a century ago Father Santa Clara, at the Rosario Mission near St. Francis Bay, California, told Captain Charles Morrell about the St. Vincent Islands where the priest had resided for a time. They had been discovered by Antonio Martinus in 1789 at lat. 7° 21′ N. and long. 127° 4′ W., while on a voyage from Panama to China. Father Clara said they were inhabited, well-wooded, and with good harbors.

Morrell made his search in 1825. At the location given all he found was discolored water 120 fathoms deep. There are no other islands within hundreds of miles, and Morrell searched the area for over a month. But the St. Vincents had vanished.[10]

There is pathos in the story of the Tuanaki Islands, a part of the Cook group in the South Pacific, that disappeared around the middle of the last century. They were three low-lying adjoining islands of tropical beauty located southeast of Rarotonga, about halfway to Mangaia.

The Tuanakis were inhabited by Polynesians unspoiled by the white man's avarice, afflictions, and anomalies. However, according to the Rev. William Gill (*Gems of the Coral Islands,* 1865), missionaries were en route to the islands in 1844 when their schooner failed to locate them.

In the *Rarotongan Records* of the Rev. W. Wyatt Gill, published in Honolulu in 1916 by the Polynesian Society, the account of a sailor of Aitutaki who visited the islands in 1842 is given. It is an echo from the abyss of yesterday, a voice from the past about an island that has vanished forever:

> Two years have passed since I saw that island. We went thither by way of Rurutu Island, and, when we found it, our captain . . . lowered a boat into which we descended. There were seven of us. No one was on the beach. I was sent inland and saw the house of the *Ariki,* or high chief, full of men; I told the chief I came from Araura [an old name of Aitutaki].
>
> There were no women inside, as they had a separate house. "We do not kill men; we only know how to dance and sing; we know nothing of war," said the chief. The captain afterwards went inland, and we slept there that night, taking some food—fowls, pigs, yams and bananas. We were six days ashore there.

Their water is scraped up in a bowl or in the leaf of the giant taro. Their dialect is that of Mangaia, and they wear the *tiputa* [or poncho], and use the same kind of fans as at Mangaia. It takes one night and a day to reach Tuanaki from Mangaia.

The story of the Tuanakis is told by Professor H. Macmillan Brown in his book *The Riddle of the Pacific,* and is repeated from this source by Lewis Spence in his work *The Problem of Lemuria.*

Destruction must have come to these enchanting islands between 1842 and 1844. And it must have come suddenly since the Polynesians are expert sailors and no survivors appeared at other islands.

Several former inhabitants of the Tuanaki Islands, who left in their youth, died at Rarotonga during the present century.

But time and tide are relentless, and even island paradises are transient. Other islands will appear—and vanish. *Terra* is not always *firma,* especially among the protean islands dotting our great seas.[11]

And far from the lanes of commercial and tourist travel, chilled by ice and snow, or warm and fragrant beneath the sun, there may still be islands waiting in solitude to be discovered.

The American Museum of Natural History once spent $300,000 and lost a ship on an expedition sent out to explore a mirage.

The story is told by the late Roy Chapman Andrews, the noted explorer and director of the museum for many years. It appeared in an article he wrote on mirages, published in the Baltimore *Sunday Sun* November 13, 1938, and reprinted in *Readers Digest,* December, 1938.

In his 1906 Arctic expedition, Robert E. Peary reported that twice he had seen "the white summits of a distant land above the ice horizon." He named the new land mass Crocker Land. The museum organized an expedition to explore it under the direction of Donald MacMillan, but the ship was wrecked on the voyage north.

Later MacMillan traveled over the ice beyond where Crocker Land should have been. It wasn't there. Suspicious, MacMillan returned to the point where Peary had seen the land.

"The day was clear," MacMillan wrote, "and there the land was. Our glasses brought it out so clearly that we might have staked our lives on its existence."

Peary had been deceived by a type of mirage known as *looming*. It is most frequent upon the water and it makes objects appear to be raised above their natural elevations. Phantom lakes as seen on deserts and plains are called *inferior* mirages. Usually these two types vary with atmospheric conditions, but a few are permanent and are identical day after day.

Obviously, some of our vanishing islands may have been mirages, especially when they were observed on the edges of the Arctic and Antarctic regions. And they may have been permanent or repeating mirages.

"Most mirages occur when layers of air of different density are superimposed," Andrews wrote. "Also, somewhere on the earth's surface, perhaps a few miles, a hundred or even a thousand miles away, there must be objects similar to those we see in the mirage. The light waves are bent and refracted irregularly instead of traveling a normal course as they pass from these objects through the layers of air."

This principle can be illustrated by placing a stick into clear water. The stick below the surface appears to be bent because water is denser than air. The light waves are bent as they pass through the unequal media.

A *superior* mirage causes objects, either erect or inverted, to be seen above the horizon; a ship may be seen apparently sailing in the sky. A *lateral* mirage makes objects appear to be displaced sideways; a vessel may seemingly divide into two identical craft that sail away in opposite directions. A *towering* mirage distorts objects into abnormal length or size; a rowboat may appear to be a large vessel.

In 1944 an American submarine several hundred miles south of Formosa Strait observed a convoy of ships that the crew suspected were Japanese. They were puzzled since intelligence had reported no enemy convoys near the area. As the submarine moved on an attack course, the ships suddenly vanished. Later it was found that the nearest convoy was a hundred miles away.[12]

Most mirages of cities are easily identified, but there are several repeating mirages that are puzzles. They seem to be cities of the past. Perhaps they are reflections from the same strange realm that projects visions to sensitive observers of buildings that no longer exist and battles fought long ago.

One is known as Fata Morgana and it has been seen since the sixteenth century in the Straits of Messina, between Sicily and the

Italian mainland. Apparently it is a harbor city with white walls, glistening palaces, and inhabitants. A popular legend is that the city is the kingdom of King Arthur's sister, Morgan Le Fay, who was a fairy, and that it lies on the bottom of the strait.[18]

Another is the "Phantom City of Alaska."

Known to the Alaskan Indians for generations, its repeated appearances in the vicinity of the Muir Glacier indicate a fixed position somewhere, but it cannot be identified with any city now existing on earth.

"Whether this city exists in some unknown world on the other side of the North Pole or not," states a report written in 1897, "it is a fact that this wonderful mirage occurs from time to time yearly . . . (it is) like some immense city of the past."

Willoughby, an early pioneer, learned of the mirage from the Indians. He unsuccessfully attempted to photograph it in 1887. Another witness, C. W. Thornton of Seattle, wrote: "It required no effort of the imagination to liken it to a city, but was so distinct that it required, instead, faith to believe that it was not in reality a city."

Alexander Badlam, in his book *Wonders of Alaska,* tells of two prospectors near the glacier who saw a reflection of the mysterious city in a pan of quicksilver.

In 1889 L. R. French, of Chicago, succeeded in photographing the mirage near Mt. Fairweather. He wrote: "We could see plainly houses, well-defined streets and trees. Here and there rose tall spires over large buildings, which appeared to be ancient mosques or cathedrals . . . It did not look like a modern city, but more like an ancient European city."

Another explanation for phantom islands may be floating islands. Although they occasionally appear in lakes, they are almost unknown on the seas. Small islets of decayed vegetation, sometimes bearing small trees, appear on the Indian Ocean during the monsoon season, but elsewhere the mariner is as likely to see a sea serpent as a floating island.

There is one exception to this statement, and it's a big one if we regard icebergs and huge ice formations in the Antarctic and Arctic regions as islands. They sometimes look like islands and they have been mistaken for islands. For example, Eskimos in 1931 found and photographed Takpuk Island in the Beaufort Sea. But it floated and melted away.

Large rafts of ice that have broken away from the Ellesmere

Glacier have been used by U.S. Air Force observation teams as manned stations. These ice islands have rocks and earth, fresh water ponds and mosses. They travel a circular course in the Arctic basin.

American scientists took a 250-mile ride on one of these islands for six months in 1961. It was two miles in diameter, featured a silt-floored lake and eleven species of plants. It bore evidence that musk oxen, lemmings, and other land animals had roamed over its surface.[14]

There have also been reports by explorers of large, apparently permanent, land masses in the Arctic that later could not be found. Examples are Bradley Land about one hundred miles from the North Pole allegedly observed by Dr. Frederick A. Cook in 1908; Presidents Land reported by Captain Charles F. Hall in the Lincoln Sea in 1871; uncharted land in the Beaufort Sea, seen by Captain John Keenan; and Sannikov Land north of Asiatic Siberia found by Russian explorers.

Thousands of square miles of Arctic vastness remain unexplored. Polar air routes are well-defined. Northeast Command reconnaissance planes cannot study the topography through the mist and haze that hovers continually over the surface.

"In many respects the region between the North Pole and Ellesmere Land is still a mystery," writes Colonel Joseph Fletcher, commander of the Air Force task group that surveyed the Polar ice cap for three years. "While we have learned a great deal in the last decade, our understanding is far from complete."[15]

It was Colonel Fletcher as skipper of the 58th Reconnaissance Squadron; his wife Caroline; and Captain Lawrence S. Koenig, the squadron meteorologist, who solved the mystery of the origin of the huge ice islands later used as mobile observation stations.

On August 14, 1946, a U.S. Air Force patrol plane picked up by radar the outline of an island while flying through heavy fog three hundred miles north of Point Barrow, Alaska. The island, about eighteen miles long and fifteen miles wide, larger than Guam, would obviously be important in military strategy.

Fog continued to blanket the region for several days, and later flights began reporting that the island was several miles east of its last position. When the fog finally cleared, the airmen were astonished to discover that the island was a vast slab of ice of almost three hundred square miles. Its height varied from thirty to two hundred feet, which meant it was from two hundred and forty to sixteen hundred feet thick. Its texture and pale-blue color revealed that it was fresh-water ice.

This "iceberg" was designated "T-1," and its course was charted for three years as it traveled fifteen hundred miles in the current of the Beaufort Eddy. In October, 1949, the patrol planes lost the T-1 north of Greenland.

But where did this vast raft of ice come from?

Huge bergs are common enough in Antarctica where they break off from the glacial Ross Ice Shelf and drift north. Gould tells of one, sixty by forty miles in size, that wrecked a ship in 1866. He believes the record is held by a berg sighted in the 1920's near the South Shetland Islands by a Norwegian whaler. It was over a hundred miles long and obviously many miles in width.

But the land around the Arctic Ocean is relatively flat. No known glaciers in Europe, Asia, or America were large enough to produce a berg the size of the T-1.

Colonel and Mrs. Fletcher and Captain Koenig began a study of the reports of Arctic explorers. They found that Admiral Robert Peary in 1906 had discovered a huge glacial formation on the coast of Ellesmere Island, close to the North Pole. This discovery had been confirmed in 1947 by a joint U.S.-Canadian expedition that had photographed a fresh-water ice formation in the sea off the same island.

The two Air Force officers flew to the island and found the glacier. Its surface was similar to that of the T-1. Then, in May, 1950, the Pentagon ordered a search of the Arctic to see if any more floating islands existed and to see if the lost T-1 could be located.

Two months later a patrol found T-2 near the Pole. It was about twenty by twenty miles in size, larger than T-1. Caroline Fletcher found that its ridges matched those of the ice formation photographed by the 1947 expedition. Several weeks later T-3 was found far to the north of Siberia. It was nine by four and a half miles in dimensions. For two more summers the search continued, but only one more tiny island was found.

In August, 1951, T-1 was rediscovered along the shore of Ellesmere Island. It seems evident that the glacier on this island is the origin of these ice islands, but the glacier's progress is so slow that it requires several centuries to produce one. The youngest berg is at least two hundred years old; the oldest possibly thousands of years.

Moreover, they are maintaining their size. They make up in winter what they lose by melting in summer. They should continue to exist for many more centuries.

They have a military value. Landing fields can easily be built on their almost flat surfaces and they are so thick that they would be impervious to non-nuclear bombs or torpedoes. They are several hundred miles closer to Russia than our nearest land bases.

And they also have a scientific value. They are floating platforms from which the Arctic can be explored and measurements in the study of weather, currents, the ocean floor, and magnetic force fields can be made.[16]

Bound for London from New Orleans, the United States freighter *American Scientist,* on August 22, 1948, slowed to quarter-speed at lat. 46° 23′ N., long. 37° 20′ W., approximately 550 miles northwest of the Azores. *The charts showed a depth of 2,400 fathoms.*

But this was the legendary location of an island considered a myth by modern geographers and historians—once known as Mayda and later as Asmaida—the treasure island of the seven cities.

Under the captain's direction, the echo-sounder was brought into operation. It registered only twenty fathoms! As the ship slowly proceeded, the sounding device traced the shape of an island about 120 feet below the surface for twenty minutes.

The freighter was turned around for another run over the location. This time the depth was fifteen fathoms, but as the vessel continued back over its course for thirty-five minutes the depth varied from fifteen to thirty-five fathoms before it again revealed the usual mid-Atlantic depths. This apparently confirmed the legend that the island was twenty-eight miles in length.

The *American Scientist* radioed a report of its discovery, and the message was picked up by another U.S. freighter, the S.S. *Southland,* steaming along the same course two days behind the *Scientist.* The captain of the second freighter decided to check the report. He got readings of twenty-nine to thirty-five fathoms, and in what may have been the island's harbor, a sounding of ninety fathoms.

The reports of these two vessels are listed in the U.S. Hydrographic Office Notices to Mariners as No. 32 (4352) and No. 42 (5592).

There is an orthodox history of men and events, and there is a hidden history embodied in myth and legend. With scholarship and the spade, truth is frequently brought out of the shadows. Troy, for example, was considered a myth until Heinrich Schliemann, who could not forget "the surge and thunder of the Odyssey," brought once more into the light of the sun the ancient walls and towers of Ilium.

And so it may be with Mayda, the golden isle of refuge.

We are indebted to Lawrence D. Hills and his extensive research for this remarkable story. His article appeared in *Fate* magazine, June, 1958.

In A.D. 734 the Moors were conquering Spain and Portugal. As the Mohammedan hordes advanced, the Bishop of Oporto, Portugal, with six other bishops and chosen refugees, prepared to flee and preserve the Christian faith in exile. Provisions and water, livestock and seeds, were loaded on several vessels.

The ships set sail for the "Purples," now known as the Azores, as the Moorish cavalry entered the city. With only the sun for a compass, the vessels missed the then uninhabited Azores. At this point the refugees vanish from orthodox history. Some historians believe they were lost at sea, others that they may have reached the West Indies, but there is no evidence that they ever reached the New World.

Over seven centuries later—in 1447—a Portuguese freighter under the command of Captain Antonio Leone was bound for Lisbon from the Mediterranean when it was struck by a severe storm. With a broken mast, the helpless vessel was driven far to the west. When the gale had passed, Captain Leone tried to reach the Azores, but missed the islands, and the ship was blown to the northwest. At last he reached a low, crescent-shaped volcanic island "where the people spake the Portuguese tongue and asked if the Moors did yet trouble Spain."

On the twenty-eight-mile-long island there were seven communities, each with a bishop and "cathedral" built of basalt rocks mortared with burnt seashell lime. The island was well-populated—seven centuries includes twenty-eight generations. When the captain and his crew attended Mass, they were astonished to see large gold crucifixes and candlesticks and gold embroided altar cloths.

Captain Leone and his men were on the island for several weeks repairing their vessel. During this period white quartz sand was taken from the beach to scrub the decks. Later, after the vessel sailed for Lisbon, the origin of the island's gold was revealed when gold particles were discovered in the sand. Apparently the island's geological formation was similar to that of the Cape Verdes.

Despite the gold dust, little attention was paid by mariners to the discovery. After all, it was a self-contained island that provided no market and was inhabited by civilized Catholics who could hardly be converted and sold as slaves. But the island was placed on ocean charts, and since longitude could not be determined at that time except by dead-reckoning, it was placed at various spots along latitude 46 degrees north.

The island had apparently been sighted before Antonio Leone's visit. Arab sailors of the eleventh century had reported it, and Edrisi, the Moorish geographer, had it in his *Description of the World* written in 1154. He called the island "Mam." In addition, Bretons had noticed the island and called it "Mayda" or "Asmaida."

In 1474 the Florentine map maker, Toscanelli, sent a copy of his latest map to Columbus. It included the island. With the map was the following erroneous note: "From the island of Antillia, which you call the Seven Cities, to the most noble Island of Cipango (Japan) are 10 spaces which makes 2,500 miles."

Again, the island is clearly marked to the northeast of the Azores on one of the first globes made in 1492 by Martin Behaim of Nuremberg. Behaim had lived on the Azores for fourteen years. This last statement is important for two reasons: first, it is evidence against the later theory that Mayda was actually St. Miguel in the Azores; second, because the two American freighters in 1948 found the sunken island at the location marked on Behaim's globe.

In 1498—six years after the first voyage of Columbus to the New World—Pedro de Ayala, Spanish Ambassador to the court of Henry VII, told King Ferdinand that the sailors of Bristol, England, had "fitted out every year, two, three or four caravels in search of . . . the Seven Cities." Apparently they had no success, and one wonders if this is the origin of the legend of the "Seven Cities of Cibola" so long sought for in the New World.

The island, at this time, may have been slowly sinking. The Spanish geographer, Galvano, reported in 1555 that "this island is not now seen." From this time on charts still bore the name of Mayda, but it was listed as a rock or group of rocks. Hills says its last appearance under this name was on a map of the Atlantic published in New York in 1814 by E. M. Blunt.

The confusion that Mayda has produced among geographers is illustrated by Lieutenant Commander Gould in his book *Oddities*. Gould says that Mayda was "probably a distorted version of Bermuda, and was long a source of puzzlement to cartographers in general, (but it) turned up smilingly in the middle of the Bay of Biscay on a map published at Chicago so recently as 1906." The Bay of Biscay is off the coast of France.

Early in the nineteenth century the name of Mayda was dropped from charts after the vessel *Barenetha* was wrecked on a submerged rock at the location. This rock, probably the last of the island to sink beneath the surface, was thereafter marked on charts as Barenetha Rock. The rock was last reported above water in 1813 by the captain of the British ship *Crompton*.

To see if the rock still existed in 1873, Captain Urquhart of the American vessel *Trimountain* altered his course. This action brought him to the vicinity just in time to rescue the passengers and crew of the French liner *Ville de Paris* which was sinking after a collision with the British barque *Loch Earn*.

If Mayda had sunk slowly, it would seem the inhabitants would have prepared to escape. No survivors turned up at the Azores or elsewhere. More than likely it sank quickly during a submarine earthquake. There have been a number of severe shocks in this general area, including the historic one of 1638. There were six earthquakes in this region in the nineteenth century.

Mayda must have perished with all its citizens sometime during the sixteenth century.

"It is still there—out in the wide Atlantic," writes Lawrence Hills. "Its 28 mile length is still within the reach of aqualung divers, for the latest apparatus can take a free diver down to 50 fathoms. Today there are cameras that can make a mosaic picture, much like an aerial survey, of the sea floor . . . salvage is possible in that relatively small depth—in the right weather, for the right ship."[17]

That islands may sink below the waves is not in any way unbelievable or even extraordinary. Submarine archaeologists have mapped dozens of them along with many quite deeply sunken coastlines. Volcanic activity alone has accounted for many cases of submergence that have been properly and fully witnessed and examined. However, the "apparent" disappearance of a fairly substantial land mass like the Pacific Easter Island, with a fair population of people with an old culture, and its subsequent continued existence—in the right location—along with its inhabitants *after* it had been reported missing, is quite another matter. Similarly, the real (i.e., physical or material) or paraphysical (but susceptible to photography) appearances of islands and other land masses is yet another one. The former may indeed be pushed up by volcanic or other tectonic activity but they are just sterile masses of ash, mud, lava, ooze, or even seaweed-covered rocks, according to their origin or the depth from which they arose. But islands covered with typical sub-aerial topographic features, and even vegetation and signs of human activity, are still something else again. And when one comes to supra-marine phenomena like Fata Morgana, and mirages that can be photographed but in no way identified, we enter a realm that is outside our present understanding.

The whole matter of mirages is, as a matter of fact, distressing to say the least. The standard meteorological explanations of and for them just do not hold up in many circumstances. Apparently there are those that can be photographed and those that cannot. Also, some of the former have proved to be objects (including islands) that do not lie in the direct line of observation and cannot in any way be identified. The extraordinary mirages, so-called, reported as being seen throughout the ages off the coast of Sweden in the Baltic are alleged to display towns, castles, and even people in unidentified costumes. Mirages are supposed to be reflections; if so, reflections of just what, in such cases?

Monsieur Bottineau may have been able to see things in the skies over the sea that others normally can not; others may have seen other things in the sky that their colleagues could see; scenes may have appeared to dozens of people and been called mirages on the assumption that they were ships or islands or other things directly ahead, over the horizon. But what if a number of people see the same thing from different angles? And what if there is nothing known today anything like what a wide variety of eye-witnesses assert they see? Why can some be photographed and others not? Above all, why should the same unknowns appear in the same location and part of the sky year after year?

These questions are difficult enough but there are others just as hard to explain—especially when we are dealing with the sea. Perhaps there is some as yet unknown set of laws of nature that link them all together and which, when discovered, will explain them all. So permit me to start again with another apparently simple and pragmatic maritime matter and see where we end up.

BOTTLES, CASKS, AND CASKETS (3)

Bobbing with the waves or rolling with the swells of earth's seas are untold thousands of bottles, cans, and casks containing messages of hope, mischief, and tragedy. The finders may acquire a wife or husband, win money, or solve a maritime mystery.

Off the Australian coast a seaman on a British liner picked up a bottle and took it to the captain. Inside was the photograph of a handsome sailor and the following note:

"I am a mate on a freighter bound for the South Seas. I am a lonesome fellow and hope that fate will bring me a wife. Perhaps somewhere in the Commonwealth there is a girl not older than 30 who wants to write to me." A name and address followed.

The captain turned over the bottle and its contents to his attractive stewardess. Months later the captain lost a stewardess and the mate gained a wife.

While his ship was in the Mediterranean during the winter of 1955, Aarke Wiking of Goteburg, Sweden, wrote a note asking "all girls aged 16 to 20" to write to him if they wanted to marry a "handsome, blond Swede." He placed the note in a bottle which he tossed overboard.

In May, 1957, Sebastiano Puzzo, a Sicilian factory worker, found the bottle on a beach. He had the message translated and sent the Swedish sailor a picture of his eighteen-year-old daughter, Paolina. A correspondence followed, and a year later they were married in Syracuse, Sicily.

Wealthy cruise passengers sometimes throw "money-bottles" in the sea. They contain notes which promise to pay the finder a reward if the note is returned to the writer with a statement of where the bottle was found. In a publicity stunt by a radio program sponsor, a bottle containing a $1,000 reward to the finder was cast into New York harbor. It was found months later by a farm boy in the Azores.

While celebrating the historic flight of Lindbergh in the *Spirit of St. Louis* in 1927, an American tourist on board the *President Roosevelt* wrote "Hurrah for Lindbergh!" on a slip of paper, attached it to a large personal check, placed both papers in a wine bottle and flung the bottle from the deck. The bottle was found by a French modiste on the water front at Saffi, Morocco. She found the check was as good as gold.

But the purpose of bottle messages can be as varied as human interests. On the West Coast a minister collects liquor bottles, cleans them, and then casts them upon the deep. The finders, happily anticipating at least a few drops of potent refreshment, find tracts exhorting them to give up their sinful habits.[1]

The messages in many of these salt-encrusted bottles must be taken with a bit of salt.

After the liner S.S. *Waratah* vanished off the South African coast in July, 1909, with 211 persons aboard, five bottle messages were found washed ashore. All proved to be hoaxes.

"Every shipwreck, or any other catastrophe, brings out merrymakers," wrote Charles Fort. "The tragedy of the *Waratah* was enjoyed a long time. More than thirteen years later (November 21, 1922) another bottle, said to be a hoax, was found near Cape Town. Still, I am affected just the other way, and am taking on a new pessimism.

"Heretofore, I have thought cheerfully of bottles. But there's a depression from anything, once the humorists get ahold of it. I wonder how comes it that nobody has reported finding an old bottle, and in it a sea captain's account of an impending mutiny, signed 'Christopher Columbus.' "[2]

Columbus actually did place a message in a wooden cask off the West Indies in 1493, according to his ship's log. It simply described the fears of his men as their ship was being violently tossed about in a hurricane. But it's unlikely that a cask would remain on the surface for centuries.

It's usually easy to spot these hoax messages since carelessness accompanies the moronic mentalities of the senders. There are errors in the writing, and the latitude and longitude given often place the vessel on land or far from the ship's known course.

Sometimes authentic messages are false alarms.

Some years ago Major D. W. MacGregor was a passenger aboard the East India merchant vessel *Kent* when it caught fire at sea. While the ship was burning, he wrote a message and enclosed it in a bottle, throwing the bottle overboard. The ship was destroyed, but the survivors were rescued by the *Cambria* and taken to England. Eventually the bottle was found on a Barbados beach and Major MacGregor confirmed the fact that he had written the message.[3]

A Soviet fisherman found a small watertight container while in the Russian Arctic. The message inside, written in both English and Norwegian, read: "Five ponies and 150 dogs remaining. Desire hay, fish and 30 sledges. Must return early in August. Baffled." The message had been written by Evelyn Baldwin, the polar explorer, and had drifted in the water for forty-five years. The Baldwin expedition, however, had come through safely, and the explorer died of natural causes in 1933.[4]

Other messages are the last written words of doomed men.

In 1902 the S.S. *Huronian* left Glasgow, Scotland, but it never arrived at its destination of Newfoundland. Two months later, off Owl's Head, Nova Scotia, a bottle was found containing a note stating that survivors of the ship were in a lifeboat. If so, the survivors were never found. About a month after the first discovery, another bottle message was found on the coast of Ireland near Castlerock. It read: "*Huronian* sinking fast. Top-heavy. One side under water. Good-bye mother and sister. Charles McFall, greaser." This note was doubtless authentic, since McFall was a greaser on the vessel, and did have a mother and sister in Scotland.[5]

A scrawled S.O.S. sealed in a bottle, supposedly signed by two German pilots, was found in 1958 on the island of Majorca. The message, written on the back of a slip of paper giving instructions for inflating a life raft, read: "August, 1943, shipwrecked south of Espiritu Santo Island. S.O.S. Heil Hitler." It has never been determined if the two men whose signatures ended the message were rescued.

A wartime farewell message came to light in 1947 when two boys playing along the Maine coast found a corked beer bottle. Inside was a page torn from a notebook and bearing a tragic message: "Our ship is sinking. The S.O.S. won't help. I guess this is it. Good-bye now—maybe this will reach the good old USA." The signature was followed by the name and address of a loved one.

Several weeks later another bottle message was found on the same coast along with flotsam from a vessel. Investigating U.S. Naval Intelligence officials found that the bottle and debris had come from the destroyer U.S.S. *Beatty,* sunk *in the Mediter-ranean* in November, 1943. It had taken four years for these remnants of a lost warship to cross the Atlantic.

Apparently a number of passengers aboard the *Lusitania,* tor-pedoed early in World War I, spent their last moments writing messages to loved ones and consigning the bottles to the rising waters. One note that proved to be authentic gave this grim account of the vessel's end:

"I am still on deck with a few people. One is a child. The last boats have left. Now we are sinking fast. The orchestra is still playing bravely. Some men near me are praying with a priest. The end is near. Maybe this note will . . ." The message ended in mid-sentence.[6]

The largest number of wave-borne receptacles adrift in the seas have been launched for studies of the great ocean currents. Almost every nation with an extensive coastline, as well as many private scientific organizations, is engaged in these studies which are important in navigational, weather, climate, and geological research and may even indicate the routes in the migration of races.

As long ago as 300 B.C., the Greek philosopher Theophrastus used bottles and marked seaweed to prove that the Mediterranean receives most of its water from the Atlantic Ocean.

In more recent years Albert, Prince of Monaco, a marine re-search hobbyist, had ship captains drop bottles at certain lati-tudes and longitudes. From 1885 to 1888 about 1,700 bottles were released, and during the following ten years 227 were recovered.

Today, as man looks toward the stars, he is also peering into earth's deeps. Oceanography is a science of increasing impor-tance. In the pursuit of this new research, our nation's "Little Navy"—the U.S. Coast and Geodetic Survey's fleet of seventeen oceanographic vessels—is tossing thousands of message bottles into the sea in an effort to map the great currents. One vessel alone, the O.S.S. (Ocean Survey Ship) *Pioneer,* out of Oakland, Cali-fornia, had released more than 22,000 bottles up to May, 1964.

Records are kept of the time, date, and place each numbered bottle is dropped. The corked containers, about the size of soft-drink bottles, enclose forms printed in English, French, Spanish, and Japanese explaining the program and asking the finders to note where and when the bottle was found on a postcard attached to the form. The postcards are to be taken or mailed to any U.S.

Consul for forwarding to Washington, D.C., or may be mailed direct to Washington.[7]

The survey ships have dropped bottles in the Atlantic, Pacific, the Bering Sea, the Gulf of Mexico, and the Caribbean. Some have drifted thousands of miles to points along the coasts of Central and South America, Australia, New Zealand, and Europe.

An over-all average of an eight per cent return of the postcards is reported by the Coast and Geodetic Survey. The bottles are usually found between nine months to two years after they are thrown overboard.

The program has its human interest aspects.

A native of British Somaliland found a bottle off the coast. Unable to read any of the printed languages, he took the bottle and its contents to the nearest British agent who filled out the form and mailed it to Washington. Two months later the native returned to the agent's office with a letter from the hydrographer thanking him for his services. With the letter was a pilot chart of his native waters. The chart, the native insisted, was a payment from the U.S. Government. He demanded to know why the local bank refused to cash it.

A resident on Andros Island sent the following note along with the report card: "I got my home and everything what was in it burn up. I have tin kids. I am in sorrow and distress. Please, if only a few dollars to help me get my home, it would be very thoughtful."

In November, 1933, the S.S. *Saxilby* sailed from Newfoundland for Port Talbot, Wales, and vanished. Twenty-nine men were aboard.

Early in 1936 a cocoa tin drifted ashore near the Welsh village of Aberavon. Inside was a penciled message: "S.S. *Saxilby* sinking somewhere off the Irish coast. Love to sister, brothers and Dinah—Joe Okane."

Joe Okane was a member of the lost steamer's crew, his home town was Aberavon, and the message was addressed to his relatives in Aberavon. The tin had floated to shore within a mile of his family's home.[8]

The long arm of coincidence can stretch over seas and surprise us with its elasticity.

During World War II Marine Sergeant Wallace C. Stich, while stationed in the Southwest Pacific, shipped a wooden box to his wife living in Fairmont, North Carolina. It contained a wrist watch, a silk Japanese flag, a pocket Testament, and about one hundred letters. Exactly what happened to remove the box from the orthodox mails is not known, but apparently the vessel bringing the box to the States was sunk, then currents and waves took over.

Months later, on March 6, 1946, the box was found washed ashore by a shipyard guard two miles below Wilmington, North Carolina, and within one hundred miles of Fairmont. The guard turned it over to local authorities. When Sergeant Stich arrived at Camp Lejune, North Carolina, on March 30, the box was waiting for him.[9]

More startling is the experience of Ross Alexander. In 1952, while awaiting rescue from a troopship aground on a reef north of Darwin, Australia, he threw an S.O.S. note in a wine bottle overboard. In 1955, soon after he returned home to his ranch at Waverly, New Zealand, he was walking along the beach. At his feet was the bottle and note he had dispatched to the deep three years before.[10]

Back in 1934 Doyle Branscum sealed a picture of himself inside a bottle and threw it into a river in Arkansas. In 1958 Bill Headstream, of Largo, Florida, found the bottle on a beach near his home. Using the return address on the back, he mailed the photograph back to Branscum along with a long letter recalling earlier years.

Headstream and Branscum had been boyhood friends in Arkansas, but they hadn't heard from each other until the bottle incident.[11]

One of the most remarkable cases of the homing instinct affecting inanimate objects involves not a box or a bottle, but a coffin.

Charles Francis Coghlan was born on Prince Edward Island in 1841. He displayed exceptional dramatic ability as a boy and first appeared on the stage in London in 1860. In the years that followed he attained international fame as an actor and was considered one of the greatest Shakespearean performers of his day. In America he was a leading man in companies with Lily Langtry and Mrs. Harrison Fiske; and toured America with his own company for some years.

Prince Edward Island remained his home. Sir Johnston Forbes-Robertson, in his book *A Player Under Three Reigns,* says Coghlan was living on the island several years before his death when Sir Johnston had him come to London to play in a Shakespearean drama.

The actor was appearing in Galveston, Texas, when he died on November 27, 1899, after a short illness. His lead-lined coffin was placed in a granite vault in a Galveston cemetery.

On September 8, 1900, the great hurricane struck Galveston Island. Six thousand people—nearly a sixth of the city's population—died in the disaster. Four thousand buildings were reduced to heaps of brick or kindling. Property loss was estimated at $30 million.

The flood waters washed into the cemeteries and shattered vaults and disinterred the dead. The bodies of the long dead mingled with the newly dead. Coffins beat a dirge against uprooted tombstones, then floated out into the Gulf of Mexico to be scattered far and wide by the waves.

After the fury of the hurricane had been spent, a backwash carried the coffin of Charles Coghlan to the southeast. There it was caught by the West Indian current and carried into the Gulf Stream. It drifted around the tip of Florida and began moving north in the great oceanic river.

The Gulf Stream current moves rapidly, approximately seventy miles a day, and it is quite likely that the coffin moved with this current until it reached the vicinity of Newfoundland. There it was probably blown out of the current by a gale.

Once free of the Gulf Stream, it apparently drifted aimlessly off the eastern Canadian coast, subject to vagrant winds and waves. No one will ever know.

In October, 1908, after a series of gales, several fishermen left Prince Edward Island to set their nets in the Gulf of St. Lawrence. They noticed a large box lying low in the water and drifting toward shore. They towed it to the beach.

Encrusted with sea mollusks and barnacles, it was obvious the box had been in the water a long time. They chipped away the thick crust of shells. It was a coffin containing the body of a middle-aged man. A silver plate gave his name as Charles Coghlan, a name well-known on the island.

Only a few miles away was the village where he had been born and raised. Only a few miles away was the home where he had rested between his extensive travels. With appropriate ceremony and honor, he was buried near the church where he had been baptized.[12]

Across the trackless sea, Charles Coghlan had at last reached home to stay.

THE WATCHERS AND
THE AVENGERS

Doubtless all of you have heard of the apocryphal proposition that a million monkeys lashed to a million typewriters would eventually reproduce everything that Shakespeare wrote, down to the last comma. There is nothing theoretically impossible in this, but the time and certain other factors involved render it worthless other than as a mathematical game. Nevertheless, the chances of Charles Coghlan's coffin performing as it did would seem to call for an equal number of factors *and* a great span of "time"—of some kind. That it did so behave opens up still another horizon.

Are there forces at work that automatically or deliberately juggle with *time,* producing what we call coincidence? If so, what are these forces and what, if any, are the limits of their influence? In any event, incident, or coincidence there are so many separate unrelated but interlocking series of other events that we, with our limited grasp of reality, cannot predict anything with surety. Perhaps there is a law of coincidence. But is this all that is needed to account for what we mundanely call "coincidence"? Might there not be something quite else at work with what we call a more positive motive? Sometimes—no, rather, many times—it looks very much as if there were.

Coincidence, be it purely mechanical or not, would seem to be indifferent to our comparatively unimportant human interests and yet, from time to time, it seems not to be. It is as if some forces were at work deliberately for or against human interests. There are even cases in which inanimate objects, and notably ships, seem not only to have wills of their own but a specific purpose vis-à-vis human beings individually, in groups, or in mass. Take, for instance, the case of the U.S. submarine, the S-5.

This is the strange, almost unbelievable, story of the most amazing rescue in the history of the U.S. submarine service.

It began on an August morning in 1920 when two vessels left Boston harbor to proceed south down the American coast. The sun was rising in a clear sky, and a light fresh breeze heralded a perfect day for sailing.

The first vessel to leave the port was the World War I Liberty Ship *Alanthus,* skippered by Captain Edward Johnson. The captain stood on the bridge smoking his pipe in melancholy silence. He had grown to love the little wooden ship that he had mastered during the long war years. Now he was sailing to Norfolk. When he returned the *Alanthus* would be retired from service and later reduced to scrap. Already he had lost two deckhands and his radio operator.

We do not know why Captain Johnson decided to go beyond the usual coastwise shipping lane. Perhaps he had a premonition. Perhaps he only wanted to lengthen the last voyage of the *Alanthus.* He never explained.

The second vessel to leave port was the Navy's finest submarine at that time, the huge *S-5,* skippered by Commander Charles Cooke. Sailing smoothly and proudly, she passed the *Alanthus,* her flags flying. In order to avoid other traffic on her training cruise to Baltimore, she, too, went beyond the coastal shipping lane.

After running for most of the day on the surface, Commander Cooke ordered a routine test dive. Standing in the control room, he issued the various preliminary orders, then said: "Let her go!" But as soon as the dive began, he knew something was wrong and that it was entirely too steep. Excited shouts echoed through the vessel.

The air valve had been left open and sea water was rushing in from the ventilation duct.

"Torpedo room flooding, sir," said a voice over the inter-com. And here in this room at the forward end of the submarine, men slipped over grease-coated torpedoes as they tried to turn off the valve on the ceiling, only to retreat under the rush of the water. They abandoned the compartment and closed the bulk-head.

Now the weight of the water in the bow pulled the submarine into an almost perpendicular position as she continued sinking. With a jolt that shook the vessel, the *S-5* hit the sea bottom and rammed her bow into the muddy sea floor. The depth gauges read 165 feet.

"The question now," said Cooke, "is how deep are we buried in the mud?"

All ballast was jettisoned and air forced into the torpedo room, but the muddy trap that held the bow of the submarine in its jaws held fast.

Next they blew all tanks and ran the motors on reverse at top speed. The *S-5* trembled as the props roared and sparks from the overloaded circuits leaped from the control panel. With a sudden lurch, the submarine's stern swung into an even more vertical position, and a shower of equipment and tools plunged downward. Men clung to valve wheels and door handles. But the bow remained tight in the sea bottom.

Acid spilled from the batteries and flowed down into the sea water left after the torpedo room bulk-head had been closed. The result was deadly chlorine gas.

"Put on gas masks," Cooke ordered. "Seal off the battery room."

But the men in the battery room were trapped. They couldn't reach the hatchway which was now over their heads. Other crewmen clambered down and pulled them up through the opening with ropes and torn curtains. The hatch was closed.

The gas that had escaped poisoned the air. Coughing and gasping, their burning lungs laboring as they climbed upward, the crew finally reached the two upper or stern compartments where the air was close but still free from gas.

"We're in a hundred sixty-five feet of water and the sub is two hundred and thirty feet long," Cooke said, thinking aloud. "We don't know how deep the bow is on the bottom, but there's a good chance that our stern is above the surface."

Taking a hammer, the commander began climbing upward, tapping the walls. When he reached a point only twenty feet from the stern, his taps were still being answered by the dull thud of metal under water. Only the small tiller room remained. He entered and struck the wall, holding his breath. This time there was a higher pitched ring.

Cooke had one of the men bring him a drill and a wooden plug that could be quickly hammered into the hole in case water instead of air appeared. He turned the drill slowly against the steel and the bit finally broke through. No water appeared. The stern was above the water.

"We better cut a larger hole," Cooke said. "If the sub shifts position after we cut it and lets water in, we're goners. But that gas is going to get worse and we've got to have air."

It was night now, but the electrical system was still functioning.

A light was rigged up. An electric drill was passed up, and Cooke handed it to a sailor. "We'll take turns," he said.

The sailor turned the drill on, placed the bit against the stern wall and crumpled to the floor. The current was shorting through the wet casing.

"There's nothing we can do about the short," the commander explained. "It's rough, but the shocks won't kill us."

Taking turns, the men used the drill, holding it as long as pain would permit. But soon the batteries went dead, and they were forced to use hand drills. Hour after weary hour, the work went on. By daybreak they had a hole about six by five inches through the hull.

They took turns standing by the hole and waving an undershirt. As the sun rose, the submarine became a furnace, the temperature finally reaching 130 degrees. The sweat-drenched men stripped to their shorts, panting in the hot, stuffy chlorine-infected air.

"We're well off the shipping lanes," Cooke said, as he distributed emergency rations. "If a ship came near enough to see that shirt, it would be a miracle. Our only hope is to hang on until the Navy starts a search and we won't be overdue for several days."

Meanwhile the *Alanthus* on her final voyage had reached an area about fifty-five miles off the Delaware coast. Captain Johnson was on the bridge when the mate noticed something on the water several miles away.

"Looks like a buoy, sir," the mate said.

Captain Johnson shook his head. "No buoy would be this far out unless it broke loose. May be a menace to navigation, whatever it is. Guess we better take a look." He ordered the helmsman to head for the object.

The captain became more puzzled as the ship maneuvered close to the object. A white cloth was waving above the object. Then he caught sight of the hull as it descended through the first few feet of water. "I do believe it's a submarine," he told the mate.

A boat was launched and the captain with four seamen lowered themselves aboard. "We better put lines around that sub to keep her from sinking," Johnson shouted at the mate. "Might be live men in her. Drop us the cable from the forward windlass and we'll take it over."

They rowed over and fastened the cable around the sub's stern.

Then they returned and carried back a second cable from the aft windlass. With the stern secured, the captain moved the boat to the hole where the cloth was waving and peered down. He saw a white face staring back at him.

"Who are you?" Captain Johnson asked.

"I'm Commander Cooke. This is United States submarine *S-5*."

"Are your men alive?" asked Johnson.

Cooke's voice was weak: "All hands alive, but dying. Chlorine gas . . . need air . . . get help . . . radio the Navy."

Johnson couldn't bear to tell the commander that his ship had lost its radio with its operator. But what could he do? He could release the cables and head for port, but now the cables might be the only thing that would keep the sub from dropping below the surface and drowning the sailors. Since the submarine's bow was jammed in the ocean bottom, towing was out of the question. Even if the ship could pull the submarine free, the sub might break up if it was moved. The only action that remained was to stand by, give what assistance was available, and hope that another passing ship would come near enough to be signaled.

The captain returned to the ship and told the mate to run up distress signals. Two hose lines were carried from the ship to the sub. One line delivered fresh air, the other water. The high temperature in the *S-5* dropped a little.

Working from a float, Johnson and several seamen went to work with hand tools to enlarge the hole in the submarine's stern. But the steel was tough and the tools inadequate. They labored on for hours, but it was obvious that it would require days to make the hole large enough for a man's body to pass through.

Late in the afternoon a column of smoke announced the approach of a steamer. Johnson and his crew watched hopefully and the ship came close enough to observe the *Alanthus'* distress signals. The newcomer was the S.S. *General Goethals,* a liner from Panama.

Johnson rowed over to the liner and as soon as he had explained the situation, an S.O.S. was radioed to the Navy. It would be several hours, however, before the first Naval rescue ship could arrive at the scene. Meanwhile, the ship's doctor had been taken to the submarine where he talked with Commander Cooke. The doctor didn't think the men in the sub could last much longer.

"We've got to enlarge that hole," Captain Johnson insisted.

"Time is running out." William Grace, chief engineer on the liner, offered his assistance.

Equipment was transported from the *Goethals* to the submarine, and while Johnson manned the generators, Grace and several seamen worked to break loose the steel plates around the hole.

At midnight the engineer called to the men inside the sub, but there was no reply. He stopped the drills and shouted again. There was no answer.

"We'll have to work fast," Johnson commented. Grace nodded, and the drills again bit into the steel. At 1:20 A.M. a long pry bar was inserted under the plate that had been rimmed with drilled holes. Standing on the bobbing float, Grace and his assistants leaned on the bar. With a rasping groan, the plate came free.

Hot, stagnant air rose from the sub. Then came a shout from Commander Cooke, who had been revived by the fresh air. Then, one by one, the grimy, dazed men were lifted out of the submarine and into slings that raised them up to the deck of the *Alanthus*. At 2:45 the last man—Commander Cooke—emerged.

With the dawn came a fleet of destroyers, salvage ships, tugs, and the battleship U.S.S. *Ohio*. They surrounded the little wooden ship as high Navy officers stood on her deck.

Captain Johnson offered to tow the *S-5* in since he already had her secured with cables, but the job was turned over to the battleship. The *Ohio* pulled the sub loose from the ocean bottom and started away when suddenly the heavy cables snapped. The submarine rolled over, then vanished beneath the waves.

Now the crew of the *S-5* were lowered from the *Alanthus* to waiting Navy ships. Each man thanked the captain. Commander Cooke was the last man to go overside. He shook the captain's hand. The two seafarers looked into each other's eyes. There was no need for words.

Thirty-eight men who might have died were alive. The loss of the *S-5* remains the only submarine disaster in U.S. Naval history in which not a single life was lost.

It was all over now. As the *Alanthus* resumed her final voyage, every ship's whistle in the fleet gave her a salute. She sailed by proudly, her crew waving from the deck. In her final hours she had attained glory. Her name would be remembered in American naval records.[1]

On October 5, 1920, the Secretary of the Navy awarded Captain

Johnson a gold watch "in appreciation of valuable services rendered in the rescue of the crew of the U.S.S. *S-5*."

And when does chance or coincidence end and, perhaps, some subtle form of guidance begin? The following story is certainly a unique collection of coincidences in the annals of the sea; and with an astonishing climax. At the same time, it illustrates the many dangers and frequent loss of vessels that characterized the maritime world of over a century ago.

The schooner *Mermaid* sailed from Sydney, Australia, on an October morning in 1829 for Collier Bay on the west side of the continent. Captain Samuel Nolbrow was the skipper, and the ship carried a crew of eighteen and three passengers, a total of twenty-one persons.

On the fourth day out the wind died down and the vessel was becalmed. Captain Nolbrow observed that the barometer was falling and that a wall of black clouds was approaching. Worse, the *Mermaid* was now in the treacherous Torres Strait, separating Australia and New Guinea.

The storm struck shortly before midnight. Huge waves broke over the vessel's starboard deck as rain relentlessly fell and howling winds ripped through the rigging. Then the ship was driven toward a ridge of rocks.

Desperately, the captain and crew fought to swing the schooner from her course to disaster. But despite their frantic efforts, the *Mermaid* smashed into a coral reef that ripped her bottom. Waves lashed her hull and decks as churning waters poured into her hold.

"Abandon ship," the captain shouted above the scream of the wind.

Seamen and passengers dropped over the side and started swimming toward a large rock about two hundred feet away. The captain was the last man to leave the sinking schooner. When he arrived at the rock, he found that all twenty-one persons had made it to safety.

For three miserable days the survivors huddled on the rock, then the bark *Swiftsure* hove into view and took them aboard. The bark continued on her course off the New Guinea coast, but on the fifth day after the rescue she was caught in a powerful, uncharted current. Swept broadside into rocks along the shore, the *Swiftsure* began breaking up and, again, the order to abandon ship was given. And once again, all persons aboard were saved.

Later that same day the schooner *Governor Ready*, with a crew of thirty-two, appeared. After taking on the marooned crews of two other vessels, the schooner was somewhat crowded as she sailed away to the west. But even this situation was not to last for long.

About three hours later the schooner caught fire and the flames roared through the wooden vessel like a gale. All aboard climbed into longboats. They were many miles from land and off the regular shipping lanes. But along came the Australian Government cutter *Comet*, which had been blown off course by a storm!

The crew of the cutter did not welcome the crews and passengers of three lost vessels. It was not merely a matter of lost elbow room, but obviously a jinx was involved. All four crews shunned the company of the others. The members of the crew of the *Mermaid* regarded each other with suspicion—one of them must be a Jonah. And the crew of the *Comet* expected trouble.

The trouble came five days later in the form of a violent storm that snapped off the *Comet's* mast, ripped away her sails and carried off her rudder. When she began sinking, the cutter's crew launched the only longboat, while the other three crews kept afloat by clinging to bits of wreckage.

For eighteen hours they drifted in the cold sea fighting off sharks, then along came the packet *Jupiter* and again they were rescued. And when a check was made, it was found that for the fourth time throughout four shipwrecks *not a single life had been lost.*

Repetition is usually synonymous with monotony, yet we have one more round to go. Two days after the rescue the heavily populated *Jupiter* struck a reef and sank. But the passenger vessel *City of Leeds* was close at hand to take on every soul and transport all of them safely to Sydney.

Five ships had been lost under varying and dangerous circumstances, and the crew of the *Mermaid* had survived all five disasters. Yet not a single person had died or even been seriously hurt. Only the marine insurance companies were left unhappy.

This is remarkable enough, but our tale has a climax.

A passenger on the *City of Leeds* was an elderly Englishwoman named Sarah Richley who was critically ill. The ship's physician, Dr. Thomas Sparks, had given up hope for her recovery.

Mrs. Richley had told fellow passengers earlier that she was going to Australia in the hope of finding her son. He had run away and joined the Royal Navy fifteen years before and been sent to Australia, but she had never received any letters from him. Navy officials could only state he had served his term and left the service.

Delirious, she called constantly for her son, and the doctor decided to ease her dying moments. He would find a sailor who matched the age and general appearance of the lost boy and have him pretend to be Peter Richley.

The doctor went on deck, looked around and found his man—a thirty-year-old member of the *Mermaid*'s crew who had been born in England and had blue eyes and brown hair. The seaman agreed to help so the woman would die in peace.

Together, the doctor and sailor walked down the deck and paused outside the door to the woman's cabin.

"Now here's the way we'll do it," the doctor said. "The woman's name is Sarah Richley and she's from Yorkshire. You're to—" He stopped in mid-sentence and stared. The seaman's face had turned white and he had braced himself against the cabin wall.

"What's wrong with you?" the physician asked.

"My God, doctor," the seaman replied, as tears began running down his cheeks. "You see, sir, I *am* Peter Richley. Please take me in to my mother."

Happiness is the greatest of medicines. Mrs. Richley recovered. In fact her son built a house for her in Sydney where she lived for almost twenty years. Fate can be fantastic, and sometimes fate can be a friend.[2]

It happened during the wartime year of 1943. All through a gray day a convoy of ships had zigzagged across the cold North Atlantic to avoid prowling U-boats. Now night had come and with the darkness came a storm. Whipped by gusts of wind, rain swept over the decks of the pitching vessels.

On board the U.S.S. *Uruguay,* a troopship taking 5,000 soldiers to Europe, Sergeant Cecil Davis was seasick. He was lying on a bunk in the sick bay, miserably listening to the monotonous beat of the elements against the nearby hull.

Suddenly there was a thunderous crash. The lights went out. Davis could hear the shouts of excited men. Apparently the vessel had been torpedoed or bombed. As he lost consciousness he had the sensation of rising from his bunk into the air.

When the sergeant regained his senses and opened his eyes, he found himself lying on deck. It was still raining and his pajamas were soaked. A heavy board lay across his chest. He pushed the board aside and managed to get on his feet. He noticed blood on his pajama top.

A sailor appeared. "Where's the sick bay?" Davis asked.

"Come with me," the sailor replied.

Still dazed, Davis followed the sailor below decks and into a brightly lit infirmary. While cuts on the sergeant's face were being treated, a doctor glanced at his dog-tags. The doctor's eyes widened in surprise.

"Soldier," he questioned, "what are you doing on this ship?"

"What do you mean?" Davis answered. "I came aboard in the States with a lot of other GI's."

"No soldiers on this ship," the doctor said slowly. "This is the *Sallimonia,* a Navy tanker." Then he explained. . . .

An hour before the ships in the convoy had been ordered to proceed at full speed ahead. Their zigzag courses ceased. As the tanker swung about to sail due east, the steering gear temporarily jammed. The *Sallimonia*'s prow crashed into the *Uruguay,* and only the troopship's concrete ballast kept the tanker from slashing her in half.

The tanker backed off, leaving a hole in the *Uruguay*'s side and the bodies of thirteen dead men on her deck. Davis, at the instant of impact, had been thrown from his bunk. Then he had dropped through the ruptured floor of the sick bay onto the tanker's deck. Escaping death, he had changed ships while unconscious in mid-Atlantic.[8]

The fingers of fate can be nimble indeed.

Back in 1908 Theodore Roosevelt's "Great White Fleet" of sixteen U.S. Navy battlewagons was on the Manila-to-Tokyo leg of an around-the-world cruise when a typhoon struck the flotilla in the Philippine Sea.

Seaman James Wilkinson was on the U.S.S. *Minnesota* as she wallowed in the heavy seas. Behind his battleship was the U.S.S. *Vermont.*

Wilkinson was crossing the slippery deck hanging onto a life line when a giant wave engulfed the vessel to her superstructure and swept the sailor overboard. Wilkinson clawed his way to the surface, gulped air, then was buried again in a blue-green mountain of water. As the great wave raced on, he was flung over and over, sinking, then rising once more to the foamy crest.

Now, unexpectedly, he rose high and was hurled, half-stunned, along something smooth and hard. He heard the shouts of men, and felt hands gripping his arms and legs. The great wave that had carried him from the *Minnesota* had placed him unharmed on the deck of the *Vermont*.[4]

Sometimes the sea returns its victims to their own vessels.

In 1958 Chief Officer Francis Schremp of the American freighter S.S. *John Lykes* was washed overside by a fifty-foot wave while the ship was off Bermuda. Less than a minute later the crest of the next wave carried him toward the vessel. The ship yawed and the wave dropped him back on deck.[5]

Another huge wave near Aberdeen, Scotland, swept seaman John Craig from the trawler *Dorileen* on a November day in 1956. Minutes later when an equally large wave returned him to the boat, he found that his skipper, Captain John Watson, was out in a lifeboat looking for him.[6]

Waves, however, are seldom so accommodating; yet the fingers of a fantastic fate and the curious arm of coincidence may still save lost sailors from watery graves.

Per Svahlin, a twenty-year-old Swedish sailor, was assigned to duty as forward lookout aboard the *Horn Crusader* on the night of October 28, 1962. The freighter was plowing through fog twenty miles off the California coast near Santa Barbara.

Captain Alfred Johansen noticed that Svahlin was missing from his post at 8:55 P.M. but thought he had slipped away to get a smoke without permission. Fifteen minutes later the captain ordered a search for Svahlin, and at 9:30 he decided the seaman had fallen overboard. The ship turned back.

Captain Johansen said he had to return almost ten nautical miles to reach his position at 8:55 P.M. In the fog the stars could not be seen, and navigation was by compass and radar signals bounced off the land. When he reached the point where he had noticed that Svahlin was missing, on a pure whim *he altered course seven degrees to starboard.*

Seven minutes after changing course, the crew heard Svahlin calling for help from a position between twenty and thirty yards from the freighter. A boat was put overside and, by following the sounds of his cries, the oarsmen found their missing comrade.

"You have a feeling you can't explain when you're able to do something like this," the captain told UPI reporters. "You've given life to a man—a fellow human being."[7]

It was on Christmas Eve, 1955, when seaman Arne Nicolaysen began one of the most remarkable stories in the annals of human endurance and sea rescues. Aboard the S.S. *Hoegh Silver Spray* in the Gulf of Mexico, he was walking along the deck on his way to bed when he slipped in a pool of water, lost his balance, and fell into the sea. No one heard his cry for help. The lights of his ship faded away in the darkness.

Fortunately, Arne was an expert swimmer. He conserved his strength by treading water and made no effort to move from his location. He knew that the distances were far too great for swimming to land.

During the night several ships passed by, but the lookouts could not see him in the dark and his calls were unheard. At last daylight came. He saw several vessels, but they were too far away to see or hear him. He tried floating on his back, but the waves washed over his face.

Night came again and he was alone with the sea and the sky. He was tired now and he began to doubt if he would ever see the sun again. His consciousness faded into a dreamy state, and from the half-forgotten recesses of his memory lazily welled a kaleidoscope of confusing images. But subconsciously he continued his struggle to remain afloat.

Then came a vision. He seemed to see two of his shipmates walking toward him across the water. One was Vidar Ostegaard, the young cabin boy. The other was a sailor he knew only as "Bergen." They smiled at him.

"Where did you come from?" Arne asked.

They pointed toward the moon high in the sky. "From up there," Bergen replied. "Keep swimming into the moonbeams and you will be saved. Remember! Into the moonbeams!" And then the apparitions vanished.

Arne could see that the moon was casting a long beam over the water. Wearily, but with renewed hope, he swam into the beam toward the faraway moon. Frequently he rested, then struggled on. Hours passed.

In the distance Arne could see the lights of a ship. As it came nearer, he wondered if it was another vision. Still it came on and soon its great black prow loomed above him. With the last of his strength, he shouted: "Man overboard." He tried to whistle, but his swollen tongue filled his mouth.

Incredibly, miraculously, he heard the answering shout of a

lookout, the signal bells on the ship's telegraph. There were men running along the deck and a lighted life buoy was thrown into the water. He swam for it and worked it down to his armpits. Arne had been in the water for thirty hours. Now he was saved. Now he could rest.

The crew of the tanker *British Surveyor* launched a boat and hauled Arne aboard. He smiled and begged for a bucket of water, but he was given half a glass. They took him to a bunk and he fell asleep. Because of a vision in the lonely night of his peril, Arne Nicolaysen had followed the moonbeams to safety.[8]

The nature of hunches and intuition, premonitions, and prevision is still a mystery even to parapsychologists. Perhaps Professor Charles Richet, the French psychical researcher, was right when he wrote: "If we knew the totality of things in the present, we should know the totality of things to come. Our ignorance of the future is the result of our ignorance of the present."[9]

If time is an illusion of our limited senses, our little understood inner mental powers may occasionally place us beyond this barrier and give us a glimpse of the future. Forebodings of danger or disaster may arise from sources of information that can only be received subconsciously.

Captain Edmund Fanning of Stonington, Connecticut, was a noted mariner and explorer of his day. He determined routes for sealing expeditions and made almost a hundred voyages to China and the South Seas. In later years he was associated with Rear Admiral Charles Wilkes in exploring expeditions sponsored by the U.S. Government.

In 1798 he was exploring a little-known region of the Pacific Ocean when he discovered the island that bears his name. After leaving Fanning Island in his ship *Betsy*, he set sail for China. One night he retired as usual at 9 P.M., but an hour later awakened to find himself standing on the upper steps of the companionway. He was startled since he had never walked in his sleep before. Listening, he heard only the soft wind and splash of waves.

He continued up on deck, spoke briefly with the first mate, then returned to his berth. Less than half an hour later, he again awakened to find himself on the companionway steps. Once more he had a conversation with the mate and went back to his cabin.

Within a few minutes he awakened for the third time in the companionway, but this time he was fully clothed. In addition, he had a strong presentiment of danger. He made his way to the deck.

"I believe we are having a supernatural intervention," Captain Fanning told the mate. "Lay to for the night. Wake me up at dawn." The astonished mate followed orders. The captain retired and slept soundly.

At daybreak they came about and resumed their course, but an hour later they discovered breakers ahead. The helm was immediately put alee, the yards braced, and the sails trimmed. Captain Fanning and his crew now realized that, if their vessel had been running free in the night, they would quite likely have been shipwrecked.

The breakers were caused by a long stretch of coral reefs just below the surface. Two miles beyond the reefs was an island. Captain Mackay later visited this island, following Fanning's directions, and named it Palmyra's Island.[10]

A rescue riddle of quite a different type is dramatized by the story of Captain George L. Howland, master of the bark and whaleship *Canton*.

In June, 1887, the *Canton* left New Bedford, Massachusetts, for the whaling grounds of the South Atlantic. After several whales had been killed and rendered, the ship sailed north to the island of St. Helena to unload the barrels of sperm oil and take on water.

Soon after the *Canton* left the island early in September to return to the grounds, the ship assumed a course of her own in defiance of the helm and the wind. Time and again, Captain Howland pulled the vessel back on the determined course, but each time she swung away with a weird will to proceed in her own direction, her sails flapping in protest.

Captain Howland was a god-fearing man. With his eyes on the sky, he said: "This is a good ship and there's no reason she shouldn't respond to the wheel. It must be the hand of Providence. Let her steer the way she will. May God take us to where He wants us to go!"

During the next two days the Yankee captain spent most of his time standing silently at the rail, giving his orders gently. On the third day First Mate Antone Cruz noticed a number of dots on the surface ahead. When the *Canton* drew closer, the dots became small boats, scattered, loaded with gaunt human beings waving their hands and shouting hoarsely.

Captain Howland soon learned that he had rescued survivors of the British trader *Monarch*. The trader, with over two hundred cases of dynamite in her hold, had caught fire seven hundred miles off the Cape of Good Hope. The flames quickly spread beyond control and the vessel was abandoned. Suffering from thirst and hunger, the passengers and crew had drifted about one hundred and fifty miles.

"Thank God for your rescue," the captain told the survivors. "He was the skipper that brought us to you. Thank Him in humble prayer."

The survivors were taken to the Cape of Good Hope. Later the British Government awarded Captain Howland a solid silver teapot, and the Liverpool Shipwreck and Humane Society gave him a gold medal.

It was the only time during her long career that the *Canton* failed to be responsive to wheel and wind. She was a 227-tonner with an excellent record for seaworthiness. William H. Tripp, whaling museum curator, in a paper entitled "Brief History of the Bark *Canton*," says the ship was "blunt of bow and old-fashioned" (she was built in 1835 at Baltimore), but adds that she "was a *good sailor on the wind* and was always spoken of as a dry ship."

Captain Howland had been a seafarer since the age of sixteen and had sailed throughout the world. Records reveal he was an expert navigator of unblemished reputation. He died in 1923 at the age of seventy.[11]

Captain Elijah G. Baufman was a big, jovial man, his leathery skin tanned by many years of sun, wind, and storm. He was an expert mariner and a friend to all who knew him. He loved the sea and the poems of Robert W. Service.

For his ship, the S.S. *Humboldt*, the captain had a special and very deep love. She was his "little girl," a member of his family. He kept the small, trim, and sturdy steamer spotless and gleaming.

Built in 1897, the *Humboldt* began her career during the '98 gold rush to Alaska as a passenger and freight carrier out of Seattle. It is estimated that she brought gold valued at $100 million safely out of Alaska and went to the rescue of more than a thousand shipwrecked persons.

Captain Baufman was the only master she ever knew. For thirty-seven years he guided her through storm and sunshine, blizzards and fog. His affection for her, his pride in her accomplishments, were frequent topics of conversation along the Pacific Northwest waterfronts. He turned down offers to skipper large ocean liners to remain with his little ship.

But time is as relentless as the tides and in 1934 both the captain and his ship were heavy with years. Newer, faster vessels had succeeded the *Humboldt*. And the time had come for Captain Baufman to retire.

The captain seldom cried, but tears ran down his weather-worn cheeks when the *Humboldt* was taken south from Seattle to San Pedro, California. There she was placed with other old, forlorn vessels in the ship graveyard, eventually destined to be reduced to scrap. Captain Baufman, with his memories and still pining for the sea, moved to San Francisco.

Less than a year later, on August 8, 1935, just at "sunset and evening star," Captain Baufman closed his eyes for the last time and "crossed the bar."

That same night, four hundred miles south, the Coast Guard cutter *Tamaroa* was near the San Pedro harbor when the crew noticed an old steamer, outward bound, holding a true course for the channel. No smoke came from her funnel. Dark and silent, with only one red warning light glowing at her stern, she was headed for the open sea.

It was the *Humboldt*.

When no answer came to the guardsmen's challenge, the cutter swung ahead of the ship and launched a boat. But the boarding party found the ship deserted, the wheel in the pilothouse unmanned.

Whatever force it was that slipped the moorings loose from the *Humboldt* and guided her through the harbor, it was not strong enough to resist the towlines of the cutter. The ship was returned to the graveyard and her final destiny.[12]

It is quite possible that the late master of the *Humboldt* knew Captain Martin Olsen, one of Puget Sound's first purse seiners. With his fishing boat *Sea Lion*, Captain Olsen spent many successful years netting salmon, but at last the time came for him, too, to retire.

But Captain Olsen had grown to love his boat and he refused to sell it. He beached her on the Point Monroe sandspit near his home just across Puget Sound from Seattle. On sunny days the captain would sit on her deck, usually alone, and recall the days when she defied the elements and her decks were high with fish.

Ten years of quiet retirement passed for the man and his boat. And year after year the boat settled deeper into the sand.

The day came when Captain Olsen died, a quiet day without any storm or high tide. But, strangely, the *Sea Lion* floated off the spit and began floating around the bay.

On the third day the captain was buried in the old cemetery on Bainbridge Island. To their astonishment, the mourners found that the boat had drifted up on the island beach at a spot closest to the grave. After the funeral it drifted away, and a few days later it was found back on the sandspit where it had spent the previous ten years.[18]

Is there sometimes a strange, mystical rapport between a master and his ship? What enigmatic relationships may exist after long, beloved association between a man and an object?

Do ships have souls?

Two vessels may be built according to the same blueprints, yet each will have an individual quality and temperament differing from the other. Each will behave differently under the same conditions at sea. It requires several voyages before a new master knows his vessel, her tricks, and her mannerisms.

A ship is the product of creative thought by her designers and craftsmanship by her builders. Each man, from the drafting to the laying of the keel to pounding the last rivet, gives something of himself to this creation. Then the ship is christened with greater ceremony than that given a child.

Now she sets forth—something more than iron, steel, and wood. If she meets the challenge of the sea with mastery, her creators are proud. If she meets disaster, gloom will descend like a pall over the shipyard, for each worker has lost the gift of thought and hands he gave her. The Japanese always say prayers over the loss of a ship.

What is the secret of the psychometrist? Do we leave impressions of ourselves with all material objects we have owned or even touched? Are there "shadowy threads" between human minds and objects, as taught by the Polynesian *kahunas,* that know not the limitations of time and space? In the little-known but vast inner space of thought and consciousness and mental reservoirs, are inorganic things truly lifeless or do they bear tenuous auras of previous scenes and contacts?

Men are creators and it is said that thoughts are "things"—that thoughts can evoke an atmosphere that clings and exists independently around an object, a locality or a structure. A sensitive stranger may sense this atmosphere immediately. And this appears to be true also of some ships.

In a thick fog off the shores of northern France on March 19, 1884, two ships were moving slowly to a weird doom that would make their names remembered in the annals of the sea.

One was the *Frigorifique,* the first French vessel to carry refrigeration equipment. She was on her way to Rouen from Pasajes, Spain. Eight years before she had made her maiden voyage to Montevideo and she had enjoyed a prosperous career since.

The other was the English collier *Rumney* bound for La Rochelle from her home port of Cardiff.

On board the French ship Captain Raoul Lambert and the sailors on watch heard a siren wail, but they could not tell from which direction the sound had come. The captain ordered the engines stopped as he blew three sharp warning blasts.

No more sounds were heard, and the *Frigorifique* resumed her course at a speed of three knots, her bell tolling continuously.

Suddenly from out of the gray mist to starboard came a shrill wail and the throb of engines. The black hulk of a ship appeared. The steersman put the helm hard over to port to swing the vessel sideways, but nothing could prevent the inevitable.

There was a thundering crash. Reeling to port under the staggering blow, the *Frigorifique* came to a standstill and began to list heavily to starboard. Captain Lambert ordered a lifeboat overside and told the crew to abandon ship.

The entire crew of eleven men were taken aboard the undamaged *Rumney.* Meanwhile the French vessel had vanished in the fog.

The collier had steamed about two miles when its master, Captain John Turner, noticed a vague shape emerging out of the fog. It resembled a ship, but there were no sounds of a bell or siren. Seconds later the lookouts shouted: "Ship to starboard!"

From the mist came a vessel, its prow aimed directly at the collier, speeding silent and deadly, ready to kill. It was the *Frigorifique,* on an almost even keel with smoke pouring from her stack, seeking vengeance on the ship that had rammed her.

"Hard to starboard!" Turner bellowed.

The helmsman spun the wheel, swinging the English vessel to a course parallel to that of the attacker. Then the phantom, which should have been at the bottom of the sea, slipped by and vanished in the fog.

Captains Lambert and Turner discussed the mystery as the collier crept ahead. Could it have been a vessel that only resembled the French ship? Lambert, bewildered, shook his head. "I know my own ship," he said.

Less than a mile later, the lookouts shouted again. Incredulously, the two captains and the seamen watched the same vessel bearing down on them out of the mist. It was impossible! It must be a hallucination, a wild vision!

"Hard to starboard!" Captain Turner shouted again. "Reverse engines!"

As the *Rumney* slowly began to turn, the prow of the avenging vessel seemed to hurl itself at the collier. As the *Rumney* rocked, then reeled backward from the impact, the phantom again disappeared silently in the thick fog. Water poured into the collier's hold and engine room and she began to sink. Two boats, bearing members of two separate crews, pulled away and watched the *Rumney* upend her bow and slip beneath the surface.

The boats started for the nearest land—and in the same direction in which the phantom had vanished. Fifteen minutes later they had rowed out of the fog. Ahead of them was an empty sea and the distant blue of land. Behind them hung the hovering curtain of mist.

Then, out of the fog bank, came the *Frigorifique*. She was moving in wide circles, falling off her course as she swung around.

"Sure you didn't leave a man behind?" asked Captain Turner.

"Positive," Captain Lambert replied. "My men are all here. Let's see if we can board her. If she's not badly damaged, we might still make harbor."

The boats pursued the French ship, and after some difficulty the crews succeeded in pulling alongside. The two captains and several volunteers climbed aboard. They called, but there was no reply. The vessel was unmanned.

The water in the engine room had not reached the top of the boilers and it was evident that they had continued supplying pressure after the craft was abandoned. The ship's list had been partly corrected by water flowing among the bulkheads. But it was obvious that the final collision had doomed the *Frigorifique*. She was slowly sinking.

The answer to this mystery was in the wheelhouse. The wheel

had been left lashed hard over to starboard. Apparently the helmsman, finding it difficult to fight the wheel, had secured it and forgotten the act in the excitement of leaving the ship. Thus the vessel had continued on a wide spiral path that had brought her across the *Rumney*'s reduced-speed course at regular intervals.

Now came a warning rumble from the ship's bowels. For the second time that day Captain Lambert gave the order to abandon ship.

As the two boats were rowed away, the stricken vessel rolled over on her side. Her stern pitched skyward, then slowly she went under. Had the *Frigorifique* made a third circle just to be certain that she had been avenged and could now sink in peace?

This story of the crewless ship that avenged her own destruction is a classic tale of the seas.[14]

THE JINXED AND THE DAMNED

(5)

There are ships that are both jinxed and damned; and others that are apparently "haunted," or that themselves haunt. There are happy, gay ships, and others so impregnated with evil that they must be destroyed with fire. It should be made plain that these latter are not the same as the purely jinxed ships, which are simply vessels that are unlucky from the day they are launched and dogged by misfortune all their days. Such a ship was the *Scharnhorst*, a victim of her own special curse as well as the adverse fortunes of war.

A 26 thousand ton battle cruiser built by Germany just prior to World War II, the *Scharnhorst* should have had a long and notable career. She combined the most efficient features of a cruiser and a battleship. The most highly developed electronic equipment enabled her long-range guns to find their targets. Designed for speed, she could outrun the heavier British warships.

Yet, from the very beginning, the cruiser gave grim evidence that she was born under an evil star.

While still in her stocks, slightly over half completed, the *Scharnhorst* suddenly rolled over on her side. Sixty workmen were killed and over a hundred were injured. It required three months to raise her back into position.

A date was set for her launching. When the time came, Hitler himself led the parade of top Nazi officials to the ceremony. Unfortunately, however, the cruiser had launched herself the night before, destroying several barges when she hit the channel. The christening was an anticlimax.

The first use of the *Scharnhorst*'s fire-power was in the attack on Danzig. But while the ship bombarded the port, twelve of her gunners were suffocated in a turret when the air supply system broke down and nine others were killed when one of her big guns exploded.

Next came the assault on Oslo. Repeatedly struck by shells,

[62]

the cruiser was set on fire at several places on her decks and was finally towed to safety by the *Gneisenau.*

Creeping home for repairs, the *Scharnhorst* hid during the day and slipped along close to the coast at night to avoid detection by the British bombers. Finally she entered the mouth of the Elbe River one black night to proceed to her dock.

Directly in front of her was the S.S. *Bremen,* one of the world's largest ocean liners and the pride of the German pre-war passenger service. The lookout's alarm came too late, and there was a thundering collision. Damage to the cruiser was not extensive, but the *Bremen* settled in the river mud to become a sitting duck for Allied bombers.

After many months devoted to repairs, the *Scharnhorst* was again ready for action. She was sent down the Elbe, then northward off the coast of Norway to make hit-and-run attacks on convoys in the Arctic Sea. As she proceeded under cover of darkness to carry out her assignment, the cruiser passed a British patrol boat crippled by a disabled engine without seeing it.

The patrol boat radioed a warning and several British warships began searching for the cruiser. When they found her several shots were exchanged, then the speedy cruiser fled from her slower attackers into the black night.

Taking a chance, the British commander had a broadside fired at 16,000 yards. And sure enough, the jinxed cruiser was in the line of fire and was staggered by several direct hits. Flames shot up from her decks, providing a target for more shells. Then, fatally stricken, she sank into the icy water with most of her crew.

Two survivors in a rubber raft succeeded in reaching shore. Their bodies were found weeks later. They had been killed when their emergency oil heater exploded.[1]

Another hoodoo ship was the bark *Hinemoa,* a 2,000-ton vessel built in Scotland. On her first voyage in 1892 four apprentice seamen died of typhoid fever. Her first captain went insane, her second became a criminal, her third was removed from command as an alcoholic, her fourth was found dead in his cabin, and the fifth committed suicide.

On her sixth voyage she capsized, but was righted again. Two sailors were washed overboard on her seventh voyage. After a severe storm, she finally drifted ashore off Lorne Jetty in 1908, a total loss.

And why did all this happen to the *Hinemoa?* Sailors said it was because she carried a ballast load of gravel and rubble from an old London graveyard on her maiden trip to New Zealand to engage in the mutton trade.[2]

But it is not necessary to look into the past to find stories of a jinx striking vessels. Astonishing episodes of ill luck and even tragedy occur today.

For example, consider what happened within a ten day period in mid-July, 1962, to the German freighter *Carl Fritzen.*

While the vessel was docked at San Pedro, California, the captain hanged himself in his cabin. He was found by the steward who suffered a heart attack from the shock and had to be relieved from duty. Then the chief engineer died.

The two sudden deaths caused the chief mate to have a nervous breakdown and he was removed from duty. Next, the boatswain suffered a heart attack.

The ship's owners were notified and a new captain and chief engineer were flown from West Germany. With matters now somewhat under control, the ship sailed for Portland, Oregon, where it was scheduled to take on a cargo of grain.

When the vessel reached Astoria at the mouth of the Columbia River, the second officer became ill. The ship then proceeded for a hundred miles up the river to Portland.

The final shock came when the officers of the *Carl Fritzen* found they had arrived at the wrong port. The instructions had been in error. The vessel's 11,000-ton cargo of grain was actually on the docks at Seattle.[3]

Or consider what happened to the tugboat *Bratt* within a six-day period in March, 1956.

On March 19 the *Bratt* was towing a barge in Mobile Bay, Alabama, when the barge sank. On the following day the tugboat's skipper, Victor L. Johnson, died of a heart attack. Twenty-four hours after the skipper's death, a crewman named Leroy Landrey fell overboard and was drowned.

On March 22 the Coast Guard ordered the *Bratt* back into port for investigation after a search for Landrey's body was abandoned. But the tugboat sank on its way home, although all four men aboard were rescued.

After supervising the raising of the *Bratt,* Jessie Sires, a co-owner, drowned when the small boat he was in capsized. Charles Smith, the other co-owner, swam to safety.

A Coast Guard board of inquiry that conducted a hearing on March 26 could only conclude that sometimes disaster breeds more disaster.[4]

As immortalized in Samuel Taylor Coleridge's famous poem, "The Ancient Mariner," sailors for centuries have believed that to harm an albatross will jinx a vessel. The crews of at least two ships in recent years have learned the hard way to respect the age-old legend.

During the summer of 1951 John Slipp, a research assistant at the University of Washington, was aboard the U.S. Fish and Wildlife Service's exploratory vessel *John N. Cobb*. While the ship was off Cape Flattery, Slipp sighted a white albatross and asked permission to shoot it. Everybody aboard said no, but since the trophy was so rare Captain Sheldon Johnson finally granted the request.

Slipp brought the huge bird down after firing seven shots. And this, according to an Associated Press story, is what happened:

The net caught on the sea bottom and was ripped into pieces. Three times the net cables were fouled up, and the shaft of the main winch snapped. It took the crew almost six hours to reel in the cable.

Although the sea was calm, Slipp became violently seasick for the first time in his life. Ted Moellendorf, a scientific aid, fell down a hatch ladder and broke a rib.

Because of these disasters, the ship had to return to Seattle. It had no sooner docked than the cook quit.[5]

Far more tragic was the story of the British freighter *Calpean Star*.

During the early summer of 1959 the vessel transported a cargo of animals and birds to a German zoo. Among the creatures was an albatross. But just before the vessel reached Germany, one of the sailors fed the bird a sausage (one account says a pork pie), and it died. That jinxed the ship.

The *Calpean Star* was next assigned to serve as a transport with the Norwegian Antarctic whaling fleet. First, the ship's generators failed. Second, diesel oil seeped into the water supply. Third, the main engine compressor broke, and the vessel drifted helplessly for several days.

Arriving in Antarctic waters, the freighter's rudder was damaged and the ship was towed to Montevideo, Uruguay. As she was brought into the harbor, she swung out of control and ran aground. As she lay stranded an explosion wrecked her engine room. Later one of the crewmen accidentally drowned.

In June, 1960, with their ship a beached wreck, the crew decided to return to London by air. On the homeward flight, their plane's undercarriage was damaged when it landed at Rio de Janeiro. Only after they arrived safely in England did they consider the jinx at an end.[6]

The most famous of jinxed ships was the fabulous *Great Eastern,* mother of modern ocean liners and certainly one of the most amazing crafts ever conceived by man.

Technically half a century ahead of her time, she was launched January 31, 1858, from a muddy strand along the Thames in London. She was 693 feet long, 120 feet wide, and 58 feet high— five times the size of the largest vessel then in existence.

Everything about the 19,000-ton *Great Eastern* was revolutionary and some of her features have never been duplicated. Her skin was 30,000 curved steel plates secured by three million rivets. She had two hulls, three feet apart, and bulkheads that formed twelve watertight compartments.

This behemoth of the seas (for almost half a century it was to remain the biggest ship that had ever been launched) was designed to carry 4,000 passengers and 12,000 tons of coal. She had two power plants. The two huge paddle wheels that projected 15 feet from her sides were turned by engines of 3,411 h.p. The engines that operated her 24-foot propeller screw produced 4,886 h.p. In addition, she had six masts that carried 6,500 square yards of sail.

The *Great Eastern* was the final accomplishment of Isambard Kingdom Brunel, one of the greatest engineers of the nineteenth century. Known as the "Little Giant," he was a man of astonishing imagination and foresight who had the ability to bring his visions into reality despite obstacles.

Had Brunel's plan to use the ship in the Far Eastern-Australian trade been carried out (the voyages could have been made without refueling), the venture would probably have been financially successful. Instead the creation of this vessel was a tragic climax to a brilliant career.

Among the two thousand workmen who spent three years building the ship, the casualty rate was exceptionally low. Only four workers and one spectator were killed. But a riveter disappeared, and there was a suspicion that he had been accidentally sealed up in a hull compartment, his cries for help drowned in the noise of the hammers.

Originally called the *Leviathan,* the monster vessel was plagued by misfortune from the very beginning. The backers, who had formed a company, ran out of money when the cost of iron plate was increased. Brunel raised additional funds and worked without pay.

On the day announced for the launching, thousands of curious spectators lined both sides of the Thames. Since the Thames is not a very wide river, the plan was to launch the vessel sideways. As the ship began to move, Brunel suddenly realized that huge waves caused by her impact with the water might drown many of the spectators.

He ordered the movement of the vessel stopped, and postponed the launching. Now, however, the ship was jammed on the skids, and it required three months to get her into the river.

Construction and launching costs had totaled over $5 million, leaving the company deep in debt. The directors tried to sell her without success. The British Navy did not respond to suggestions that the vessel would make an excellent warship. Brunel had become ill after the launching ordeal and had taken a vacation. He returned to find the company bankrupt, but organized a new firm that purchased the ship for only $800,000.

The new owners named her the *Great Eastern,* and on September 6, 1859, Brunel, a suddenly aged man of only fifty-three, came to visit his creation. He collapsed on the deck, the victim of a stroke that left him paralyzed. He was carried away and died a week after the ship left the Thames.

According to Hendrik Willem van Loon in his book *Ships and How They Sailed the Seven Seas*[7] there was an explosion aboard the ship that killed quite a number of men the day before Brunel died. Fortunately, however, he never knew of any of her further misfortunes.

Ignoring Brunel's advice that the big boat would only be profitable on long voyages, the new directors decided to use her in trans-Atlantic crossings. Another fortune was spent in decorations and the finest of furnishings. Captain William Harrison was appointed her master.

Tugboats towed the behemoth to the Channel. Cut loose, she immediately proved she was the fastest vessel afloat. At the same time she proved almost immediately that she sailed under an evil star.

Like van Loon and other writers, we can only briefly outline the highlights of her career of disaster. For the full account and all the fascinating details, the reader is referred to *The Great Iron Ship,* by James Dugan.[8]

The first major mishap at sea occurred off Hastings when the forward of her five funnels exploded with a tremendous blast. Flames and ashes leaped up through the open hole in the saloon deck. Someone, never identified, had closed the escape cock on the funnel's steam jacket.

Five firemen in the forward stokehole were fatally burned and ten others injured. Another fireman, trying to escape, was killed by a paddle wheel. The grand saloon was wrecked.

Taken into port, the vessel was opened to sightseers as repairs were made. Then the ship sailed to Holyhead, Wales. Several weeks later, during a severe October storm, the *Great Eastern* was torn loose from her moorings and driven out to sea. For eighteen hours she rode out the storm while other nearby ships were destroyed, but the winds broke her skylights and water badly damaged the newly restored saloon.

Three months later Captain Harrison, the coxswain and the young son of the chief purser were drowned when a squall capsized their gig as they were going ashore. When news of this tragedy reached London, the directors resigned and the company was reorganized.

In May, 1860, the new directors announced that the "Wonder of the Seas" would sail to America. Beds for three hundred passengers were installed. But preparations for the voyage took longer than expected, and most of the passengers left and booked passage on more trustworthy liners.

When the mastodon finally sailed on June 17 she had only thirty-five paying passengers. She also carried a crew of 418, eight company officials, and 72,000 bottles of London Club sauce. But her troubles continued. The cheap coal used in her boilers damaged her funnels and forced the closing of the dining saloon.

Eleven days after sailing the *Great Eastern* entered New York harbor to receive an awe-inspiring welcome. Hundreds of vessels and boats loaded with thousands of spectators surrounded and followed her up the Hudson. Crowds lined the shores. A 14-gun salute was fired from Fort Hamilton. She arrived at her dock, only to have a side paddle badly damage the wharf.

It was, however, her one great day of triumph. Poets Henry W. Longfellow and Walt Whitman sang her praises. Newspapers filled glowing columns with her statistics. New brands of oysters, corn, hats, and beer bore her great name.

The last execution of a pirate in the United States was delayed when the marshal, the priest, and their assistants, along with the condemned man, took their boat upstream to see the giant visitor. Then they returned to Bedloe's Island where Albert Hicks, who had murdered and robbed his captain and two shipmates, was publicly hanged.

As a boy, I well remember the Currier and Ives lithograph of the *Great Eastern* made at this time. Time after time, in fascination, I stared at the monster sailing through dark seas, her huge side paddle churning giant waves, smoke and flame belching from her funnels.

On board, preparations for sightseers were made. But, as usual, all was not well. One sailor was killed when he fell into a side paddle; another drowned after he slipped off a ramp. Fights broke out among the crew. After two sailors were fatally hurt and thirteen others injured in brawls, six policemen were assigned to patrol the vessel.

On the sixth day sightseers were welcomed, but the admission price of one dollar was considered exorbitant. They began looting the ship by pocketing souvenirs. Two visitors were caught by the purser taking an oil painting from the grand saloon. When he tried to stop them, they smashed the painting over his head and left him lying unconscious on the deck.

Next a two-day excursion was announced and two hundred tickets at ten dollars each were sold. The cruise was a nautical nightmare.

The bar was open and many of the passengers brought their own liquor aboard. The great ship had hardly cleared port when members of several military bands playing on the decks and many of the guests became ill from a combination of intoxication and seasickness. Card and dice games were followed by numerous fights.

When mealtime came, no food appeared. A pipe had broken in the provision room and ruined all the food brought aboard for the passengers. When the hungry crowd became unruly, they were given salt pork, maggoty beef, dried fowl, and hard biscuits from the crew's storeroom. Hot tempers threatened to merge into riots.

Happy holiday spirits were not heightened when night came and the two thousand passengers learned there were only three hundred beds aboard. The unlucky 1,700 sprawled about the decks. Tempers flared again when some crewmen found a supply of mattresses and began demanding fifty cents apiece for their use.

As the night progressed, the wind changed and began blowing cinders down on the sleeping deck passengers from the funnels. This particular inconvenience was climaxed when it rained briefly toward morning, and the sleepers awakened to find themselves caked with grimy soot. Moreover, no breakfast awaited them. Even the last of the hardtack had been consumed the night before.

There was one hope. Early in the morning the *Great Eastern* was scheduled to stop at the popular seaside resort of Old Point Comfort. There the frustrated passengers could flee from the iron monster, get some decent food, and wash away their dirt in the surf.

Unfortunately, this hope was not to be immediately realized. During the night, for some reason never made clear, the ship had strayed far from her course and was a hundred miles out to sea.

The first reaction of anger was followed by alarm when rumors among the passengers alleged that the ship was out of control and might eventually end up in the arctic. Such grim speculations called for a drink, and that was one thing the *Great Eastern* had —plenty to drink—and on empty stomachs.

Once again those of the crew members who were still sober had to patrol the vast vessel taking care of the intoxicated guests and breaking up brawls. But by mid-afternoon land came into view and the ship finally reached the resort town. The discharging of the passengers could best be described as a rout.

Many of the passengers, thoroughly disillusioned and desiring a safe return to homes and loved ones, went back to New York by train. They were replaced by stowaways who emerged from hiding places grinning. Crewmen rounded up as many as they could find and charged them half a dollar for the ride back to New York.

Now the great ship evoked frowns instead of smiles. The newspapers bitterly condemned the ship's operators for their mismanagement. After the storm of criticism had died down, another excursion was announced. Only about a hundred brave passengers bought tickets.

The *Great Eastern* quietly, almost unnoticed, left New York with around ninety passengers and made the trip back to England in nine days and four hours—a new eastbound speed record.

During the following winter she continued her sad career. She collided with the frigate *Blenheim*. She fouled the hawser of a small boat and drowned two of its passengers. Her stern propeller tube had to be replaced.

In the spring she made her second voyage to New York. But the Civil War had started, and the city ignored the big ship. She was loaded with 5,000 tons of wheat—a record-breaking cargo—and sailed for Liverpool. Next, the British War Office chartered the vessel to transport 3,000 troop reinforcements to Canada, but the company's hope that the government would take over the monster white elephant was not to be realized.

Trans-Atlantic crossings continued, but as van Loon says, there was never enough freight to fill her hold and there never were enough passengers to make such a large ship pay. People preferred the smaller vessels that they could trust, while the *Great Eastern* was always having trouble—losing masts, smashing paddle wheels, or blowing boilers.

Dugan dramatically describes a hurricane that struck the ship in September, 1861, a storm that would probably have sunk any other vessel. Lead plates broke loose in the engine room and battered the inner bulkheads. All lifeboats were destroyed. Hundreds of gallons of fish oil added stench and slippery floors to the ordeal when two huge tanks were broken.

When the rudder began smashing against the screw, the captain ordered the engine stopped. Fierce winds ripped the sails to ribbons. The stricken mastodon drifted helpless with only the donkey engines laboring at the pumps. Huge waves shattered skylights and portholes. Many of the passengers suffered broken arms and legs.

When the idle stokers broke into the liquor storeroom and

refused to obey orders, the captain issued arms to a committee of male passengers assigned to patrol the ship and protect the women.

Hamilton E. Towle, an American engineer, used a chain cable as a lasso and finally succeeded in securing the rudder, thus permitting operation of the propeller. Repairs cost $300,000, and Towle won a salvage award of $10,000.

Disaster struck again the following year at New York when the ship hit a tower of rock twenty-four feet below the surface in Long Island sound. The tower is still called "Great Eastern Rock" on harbor charts.

Divers found a rip along her bottom eighty-three feet long and nine feet wide, but her inner hull was not damaged. Edward S. Renwick, a New York engineer, solved the repair problem by building a heavy wood caisson 102 feet long, curved to fit the ship's hull. Chained against the bottom, the caisson allowed water to be pumped out from between the hulls so that the outer hull could be patched.

One day, while the work was in progress, a frightened diver said he could hear the ghost hammering inside the hull. The mystery was solved when a heavy swivel was found to be striking the ship's side below the water. The job required four months and cost $350,000.

Early in 1864 Daniel Gooch, an English capitalist, bought the ship at auction for $125,000. He contacted Cyrus Field, the American financier whose company had already lost $2,500,000 in unsuccessful efforts to lay a trans-Atlantic cable, offering the ship free if she failed to lay a cable. If she succeeded, Field was to give Gooch $250,000 in cable stock. Field agreed.

In July, 1865, the *Great Eastern* left Ireland for Newfoundland, the black line of electrically charged cable unreeling into the sea. After the ship had passed the halfway point, the cable picked up the end of a loose wire and began snarling as it fell into the water. During efforts to recover it, the ship gave a lurch and the end of the cable—1,186 miles long—sank into the sea.

Efforts to recover the cable with grapnel lines back on Telegraph Ridge, a shallower area of sea three miles in depth, failed. The ship returned to England.

But all went well in 1866 when the *Great Eastern* again sailed with a cable. On July 27 the end of the line was attached to cables laid earlier from Newfoundland to the United States and Canada. The *Great Eastern* had at last justified her existence.

Now the great iron ship was chartered by a French company and again reconditioned for passenger traffic at a cost of $500,000. With accommodations for three thousand, she sailed from New York after her final visit with only 190 passengers. Within months the new company was bankrupt.

And now, once more, the great vessel was made a cable layer. Taken over by Julius Reuter, father of international press associations, the *Great Eastern* laid a 2,584 nautical mile cable between France and Canada. It laid three more trans-Atlantic cables, repaired four in mid-sea, and laid the British India cable across the Arabian Sea from Bombay to Aden.

When the cable ship *Faraday* was launched in 1874, the *Great Eastern* was brought back to England and anchored in Milford Haven. For years she lay there, neglected and massive and lonely, her hull rusting.

Partly blocking the port, she was considered a nuisance. It was proposed that she be used to raise wrecks, be a lodging house on the Thames, remove London's sewage, serve as a smallpox hospital or a coaling hulk at Gibraltar. None of these suggestions was accepted.

Finally, after a life of thirty-one years, she was sold for scrap. Her destruction began in May, 1889, and it required the invention of the wrecker's huge iron ball suspended from a derrick to knock her apart.

When the wreckers reached the compartments of the double hull, they found the skeletons of the long-missing riveter and his boy apprentice.

On a summer night in 1889, during the heyday of the notorious Barbary Coast, the Norwegian bark *Squando* was tied up at a San Francisco wharf. The captain and his wife got into a bitter argument with the mate. Finally the captain attacked the mate and succeeded in lashing him to the mast.

"I know how to stop the trouble on this ship," the captain's wife shouted. She picked up an axe, and furiously swinging it at the mate's neck, beheaded him.

Thereafter the vessel was jinxed, and haunted as well!

A new captain was placed in command. On his first voyage

he was killed in a mutiny and the crew scattered as soon as they reached port. Returned to her home port, another master was appointed. He died a month later. A third captain died at sea two weeks after he set sail.

After this no officer or sailor would board her. She was left tied up at Bathurst, New Brunswick, where the Norwegian consul hired two watchmen to look after her.

On their first night aboard the men were in the main cabin when a handspike flew through the air and struck a bulkhead. Later another spike embedded itself in the deck. They locked themselves in the cabin with every lantern they could find burning.

When they happened to glance through a porthole, they saw the phantom of a headless man pacing the deck. During the early morning hours a cold hand touched their faces, their bed-clothes were jerked away, and eerie voices ordered them to leave the ship and never return. They obeyed the order.

Similar experiences were reported by others who attempted to remain aboard overnight. The consul reported that the vessel was cursed.

According to Edward Rowe Snow (*Mysteries and Adventures Along the Atlantic Coast*), the *Squando*, abandoned by everyone, was allowed to rot at the wharf.

During the spring of 1940 the British tramp steamer *Stonepool* arrived in Boston from Cardiff, Wales, after a "haunted voyage." A seaman who had committed suicide on board earlier was blamed for the series of mishaps. One sailor told of seeing phantom eyes gleaming in the dark, another of being seized by invisible hands which threw him to the deck.

During the voyage two crew members became seriously ill. One, a fireman, was stricken with appendicitis, and with no ice aboard to relieve his pain, he suffered continual agony until the vessel reached port. The other, an engineer, was temporarily rendered blind and speechless from nervous prostration brought on by overwork in remedying engine room troubles.

The ship broke down fourteen times during the voyage. On one occasion, when danger lights had been hoisted, she was fired on twice by a German U-boat but managed to elude her attacker in heavy seas. During a storm one of the holds had to be flooded to keep her stern, with its propellers, under water.

In 1930 the death at Fishermen's Snug Harbor of John Winters, last of the crew of the Gloucester schooner *Charles Haskell*, recalled the story of the ship that was haunted by a ship.

The *Haskell*, during a blinding snowstorm in March, 1869, ran down a Salem schooner on the Newfoundland Banks. The schooner and her entire crew were lost. The following year, when the *Haskell* was off Eastern Point at the mouth of Gloucester Harbor, an eerie vessel sped down the wind alongside her.

Aboard the phantom schooner, sheathed in white from keel to topmast as if covered with foam, the misty figures of men could be seen climbing the rigging and ghostly shouts could be heard.

On the next voyage many of the crew of the *Haskell* refused to sail. A new crew was shipped, and they, too, returned with the tale of the spectral vessel that tormented them constantly, an uncanny cloud by day and a weird light by night. Two more voyages with new crews were undertaken, but the phantom vessel always appeared.

When men could no longer be signed up to sail on the ill-fated *Charles Haskell*, the schooner abandoned the sea and became a lowly sand freighter on the coast. The specter did not appear again.[9]

The *Utopia* was a passenger vessel. On a voyage from Genoa to New York, she collided with H.M.S. *Anson* in the Bay of Gibraltar and sank with great loss of life.

Later she was salvaged, reconditioned, and returned to the trans-Atlantic run. But whenever she passed the Bay of Gibraltar her crew and passengers heard wails and moans, the pitiable shrieks and cries of doomed souls. Her reputation as a haunted ship eventually doomed her, and she was sold for scrap long before her normal time.[10]

THE HAUNTS AND (6)
THE HORRORS

Just as there are haunted houses, whatever the term may mean, there are haunted ships. Like houses, moreover, there may be quite ordinary, even happy ships on which, from time to time, apparitions either benevolent or malign are alleged to appear. These may apparently work to prevent disaster, not just to predict it. But there are also ships that themselves appear to be haunted by other ships or by some absolutely terrifying "something" that affects them as well as the people aboard them.

There was—or is—a ghost aboard the historic U.S. Frigate *Constellation* at the national shrine of Fort McHenry, Baltimore. If the phantom is a figment of someone's imagination, it's an unusually photogenic figment. The ghost was photographed by Lieutenant Commander Allen Ross Brougham.

The story and a photograph appeared in the Baltimore *Sun* December 31, 1955, under the by-line of feature writer Patrick Catling. The article quotes the officer as follows:

> The first hint that something unusual might be going on was observed last September. Firemen said they heard strange noises and saw strange shapes aboard . . . the same phenomena were reported by the gangway watch of the nearby submarine *Pike*. . . .
>
> I regarded the whole affair with a certain amount of scepticism, but I told it to a friend who makes a hobby of psychic research. He did not seem surprised, but told me that the best time of year to observe such apparitions is at midnight between Christmas and the new year. We selected Thursday night and mounted a camera in place overlooking the quarterdeck. It happened at midnight, almost to the second.
>
> An instant before its appearance I believe I detected a faint whiff in the air, not unlike gun smoke . . . there was a sort of muffled scurrying sound . . . I was aware that he was motivated by a sense of great urgency.

Commander Brougham describes the phantom as "a blueish-white radiancy, partly translucent, wearing a definitely dated uniform, gold-striped trousers, cocked hat, heavy gold epaulets and a sword. It—or he—was—or seemed to be a captain."

The photograph shows a faint, but distinct, figure of a man in early naval uniform crossing the quarterdeck. The frigate had eight captains during her career, and it is assumed that the apparition represents one of these men.

In the folklore of the sea there are traditional ghosts and one of the most famed is "Ladylips," a phantom of the Pacific without a lower jaw. In the older generation of men and ships, over five hundred sailors aboard American and British vessels have witnessed his appearance.

Ladylips only appears during very severe storms, standing in places where it would be impossible for a living man to be. In addition to his missing jaw, he is distinguished by a corpse-white face and a dead fish odor.

For many years the legend of Ladylips was forgotten, although his name lived on. Then in 1928 a member of the crew of the tramp steamer *Waulea* found the log of the *Ville de Paris* on one of the Duke of Gloucester islands.

In 1782 the British defeated the French battle fleet off the island of Dominica. The *Ville de Paris* was a gunboat in the French fleet, and when the battle was over it was manned by a British crew to be taken to England. A terrific hurricane that struck soon after the battle, however, blew the vessel off her course.

Badly damaged by the storm, the vessel sailed with the prevailing winds to the vicinity of the Straits of Magellan. Food and water became scarce, and the crew finally launched a longboat and left the vessel in the sea slowly sinking. After they had rested on land for several days, they decided to enter the Pacific and travel north along the coast with the hope of either being rescued by a passing ship or reaching a port.

With improvised sails and a fresh supply of water and food, they began their voyage. Ladylips had been captain of the *Ville de Paris* and he remained in charge. Strong winds, however, blew the boat far from land to the west. At last their food gave out and they were starving.

Desperate, they began fishing for sharks with flannel as bait on the end of a boat hook. A large shark took the bait, then began lashing about, and the boat hook was jerked from the hands of the weakened men. The hook handle struck Ladylips on the chin, tearing away his jaw.

Ladylips, in agony and knowing that nothing could save him, drew his knife, slashed his wrists, and held them out to his men. Five of the men lived to reach a Pacific island, the name of which they did not know. Grimly, the log ends: "Sighting the island by the month of June, 1783, all the survivors of the longboat, excepting only the sailing master Ladylips who was eaten at sea, landed and hoisted English colors."

Percy B. Prior, who retired from the U.S. Navy in 1931 and settled in Australia, was responsible for collecting much data about Ladylips. His interest began when he personally saw the specter in 1929 while serving aboard the destroyer U.S.S. *Stoddart* during a storm off Puget Sound.[1]

Prior says that appearances of Ladylips have been recorded in the logs of other American warships, as well as those of British vessels including H.M.S. *Iron Duke, Ramilies,* the battleship *Queen Elizabeth I,* and the destroyer *Broke.*

The much more attractive "White Lady" is usually seen in the Atlantic. The story of one of her most famous appearances is told by Edward Rowe Snow in his *Mysteries and Adventures Along the Atlantic Coast.*

In the year 1863 Captain Richard Brown set sail from Cardiff, Wales, in the merchant vessel *Usk,* bound for Huacho, Peru. He had been delayed by bad weather, but the weather was fair as he approached Cape Horn.

One evening he was standing on the quarterdeck when among the shrouds a beautiful lady materialized, clad in flowing white veils. She came down and walked over to the astonished captain.

"Go back to the port from which you came," she said quietly, but firmly. "If you continue you will lose your ship and your life. It is so ordained."

The vision of the lady faded away, and shortly later the ship ran into a dense fog. Captain Brown considered the fog a warning.

When the captain ordered the course changed for the return to Cardiff, the mate bitterly protested. He was placed in irons. Word spread among the crew that a phantom had ordered the *Usk* home. A month and a half later the vessel reached Cardiff and the captain told the ship's owners what had happened.

The angered owners notified authorities and a hearing was held. It was pointed out that the vessel had been gone for months, and expenses for food, clothing, and wages were heavy. The cargo of coal and iron was still aboard. And all the captain could say was that he had been warned by a ghost.

The verdict was in favor of the owners. Captain Brown was declared unfit to command a ship and his papers were taken from him. Meanwhile, another captain was hired, but he found it difficult to assemble a crew. The story of the phantom had become well known along the waterfront.

At last the *Usk* again set sail for Peru. Several months later the owners received word from Coquimbo, Chile, that the *Usk* had been destroyed by fire at sea.

Certainly one of the strangest and most baffling of sea mysteries is the case of the phantom faces that followed the gasoline tanker S.S. *Watertown*. There is no doubt about the occurrence since the faces were photographed, yet to offer a reasonable theory to explain it, even in liberal psychic terms, is prohibited by the limitations of our knowledge.

The *Watertown* was owned by the Cities Service Company and a report on the case was published in *Service,* the firm's house organ, in February, 1934. Other accounts of this mystery will be found in *Forgotten Mysteries,* by R. DeWitt Miller;[2] *The Invisible World,* by Hereward Carrington;[3] *Pageant* magazine, March, 1945; and *Fate,* December, 1963.

Two seamen, James T. Courtney, known to his mates as "Sunny Jim," and Michael Meehan, were asphyxiated by gasoline fumes while the ship was bound for the Panama Canal from San Pedro, California. They were buried off the west Mexican coast at sunset on December 4, 1924, in water 1,400 feet deep.

Just before dusk on the following day the first mate observed the ghostly heads of the two men in the midst of the waves off the port rail and between the stanchions where their bodies had been slid into the sea. Their features could be clearly seen as they followed the vessel. Word of the apparitions quickly spread, and the heads were seen by practically every officer and seaman aboard by the time the tanker reached the canal.

The faces were seen daily, usually in late afternoon or early evening, about ten feet apart. They maintained a distance of about forty feet from the vessel, remaining in view for periods up to around ten seconds, then fading away only to reappear. Somewhat larger than physical heads, they appeared to float on the crest of the waves.

As soon as the tanker left the Pacific Ocean, the apparitions vanished. When the ship reached New Orleans, Captain Keith Tracy and Monroe Atkins, the engineer, submitted a report on the apparitions to the company's branch office. The late James S. Patton, an officer of the firm, was especially interested. He asked if any efforts had been made to photograph the heads. Captain Tracy explained that the first mate had suggested taking pictures, but it was found that no one aboard had a camera.

Before the *Watertown* left on her return voyage, the mate obtained a camera which was checked for defects, and Patton purchased a roll of film. And when the tanker was again in the Pacific, the heads reappeared.

Captain Tracy made six exposures, then locked the film in his cabin safe. On arrival again in New Orleans, Patton took the film to New York where it was developed by a commercial photographer. Five of the shots showed nothing unusual, but the sixth was astonishing.

The two faces are clearly in view off the port rail. Courtney's head is visible between the stanchions, and it is not as clear as that of the bald-headed Meehan, which is remarkably life-like. Patton had the negative and print examined by photographic experts of the Burns Detective Agency, and the report stated there was no evidence of fraud.

On the *Watertown*'s third voyage after the death of the seamen, the faces were observed only a few times. The vessel's crew was changed after Captain Tracy resigned to work for another company, and the first mate later drowned. Apparently the heads were never seen again after the third voyage.

For some years after this occurrence, a print of the picture was on display in the lobby of the Cities Service Company offices at 70 Pine Street, New York.

The theory that the faces or heads were simply optical effects seems eliminated by the following facts: They were seen for days at a time in the same general location amid the waves by a number of men, in groups as well as individually. Both heads were always visible at the same time and optical effects would

Hudson's Bay steamer *Baychimo*. Her ice-breaker's bow did not prevent her becoming "the ost of the Arctic Sea." *Wide World Photos*

A photograph of . . . ? Could the dead crewmen, Courtney and Meehan, of the *Watertown* have been actually filmed? *Lent by* Fate *magazine*

The mournful giant heads of Easter Island stare into infinity, the riddles of their creation and their strange home perennial mysteries. *Francis Lee Jaques, American Geographic Society*

n days of disaster. The *Carl Fritzen,* having knocked off her officers, arrives at the wrong port!
wrence Barber, Portland Oregonian

A truck and two groups of camels
illustrate a mirage, which may be the origin
of the Fata Morgana legend.

not consistently appear in pairs. In the photograph the heads are in the same positions the witnesses saw them.

Finally, the features of the faces corresponded to their actual appearance in life—and they appeared after their deaths to their shipmates. In all the weird annals of the seas, this case is unique.

But what strange laws in what strange realm limited the appearances of these apparitions to the water, and only in the ocean that had received their mortal remains?

The schooner *Nancy Hanks* was another famous haunted ship. A graceful three-master, 204 feet long, she roamed the world, but her home port was New York. Her career was one of violence and disaster, marked by storms, mutiny, and disappearances of crewmen.

The late Captain C. B. Foster, who was well known in Miami (Florida) shipping circles, assumed command of the vessel in the 1920's. Soon after he left New York for Durban, South Africa, the ship sprang a leak which was repaired with difficulty. Then the monstrous black cat with flaming eyes that haunted the vessel appeared, always a warning of trouble.

A severe storm damaged the schooner. Before the crew could rest up, the cat, trailed by four kittens, again appeared, and another gale battered the ship. Leaving Durban for West African ports, the devil-eyed cat cropped up, followed by a third storm.

A cargo of mahogany was shipped for Boston and the *Nancy Hanks* set sail, only to have the infernal cat loom up, bringing with it a squall and an outbreak of some African fever. With two weakened seamen, Captain Foster struggled on, but a sudden storm swept away the canvas which the enfeebled sailors could not reef. Finally the schooner managed to reach Boston.

Captain Foster resigned, and the ship was commissioned to carry coast-wise cargoes. One day she was found off Miami flying distress signals. The Coast Guard found that the captain had been washed overboard and a mutiny had followed in which another officer had been killed.

After the *Nancy Hanks* had been towed into Miami harbor, no crew could be hired to man her. For several years she lay at anchor, but she frequently threatened incoming vessels by swinging into their path, and once, during a storm, broke her moorings and was grounded on Fisher's Island. There she was left to rot.

THE HAUNTS AND THE HORRORS 81

During the winter of 1929–30 she was destroyed by fire, believed set by a superstitious seaman.[4]

But of all haunted vessels that have plagued earth's seamen, the Russian horror ship *Ivan Vassili* was the worst. Her almost unbelievable story is a grim warning that forces of inestimable evil beyond our ken may occasionally break through the barriers into our known world.

Built in 1897, the *Ivan Vassili* led a normal marine existence for five years. Then, early in 1903, as Russia was preparing for her ill-fated war with Japan, the steamer was sent from the Baltic to Vladivostok with a cargo of military supplies.

In the midst of the voyage this "force," known as *the thing,* struck. What it was, or is, no man can say. Its first effect was a sudden feeling that an invisible being was standing nearby. Then came a shock of terror, cold and paralyzing, that drained away all energy like some ghastly suction-pump. At times a faintly luminous, misty form, vaguely resembling a human being, could be observed.

But whatever it was, it was on board. Just before the ship reached Port Arthur, on a calm, clear night, a crewman standing on deck suddenly screamed. Fear is contagious, and panic followed. For twenty minutes the crew prayed and shouted and fought, running blindly about the vessel. Finally a sailor, Alec Govinski, jumped overboard into the sea to his death.

With this sacrifice of blood to the mysterious menace, the spell of horror was broken and the men fell on the decks in physical exhaustion. Three days later there was another outbreak of hysteria. On the following day the *Vassili* reached Vladivostok.

A dozen men attempted to desert, but they were recaptured. With her cargo safely ashore, the steamer sailed for Hongkong. It was a nightmare voyage. Two seamen committed suicide, one died of fright, and shortly before reaching port the captain, Sven Andrist, jumped overboard and drowned. After each death *the thing* seemed satisfied—for a few brief hours—then waves of horror would start anew.

At Hongkong the entire crew deserted with the exception of Christ Hanson, the second officer, and five Scandinavian hands. Hanson, a Swede, made himself captain and, with a crew of Chinese and Lascars, he set sail for Sydney. Again *the thing* struck with its tentacles of doom, and before the vessel could reach Australia, Captain Hanson had shot himself.

Once in the harbor at Sydney, the crew disappeared into the city. Only one man, Harry Nelson, dared to stay with the ship. A new skipper who didn't believe in ghosts was found, a skeleton crew was rounded up, and four months after her arrival the *Vassili* was outward bound for San Francisco. And again the terror-panic came—three times—and three men died, leaping overboard. And again a fear-crazed captain, tormented beyond endurance by a hellish, invisible "octopus" that fed on man's sanity, shot himself.

Harry Nelson managed to survive the horror. Persistent in his efforts to solve the mystery, he could learn little about it, however, except that the strange panic ended as soon as it had found a victim. Once a man died, *the thing* seemed to leave the ship.

Nelson succeeded in returning the cursed craft to her home port of Vladivostok where she remained. No sailor, no matter how much extra pay or bonus he was offered, would board her. For years she floated in the harbor, avoided, shunned, feared. Finally she was given the one treatment, the sure remedy, for all objects of evil that exist in this world. She was burned.[5]

But what was this horror from out of the nightmare realms of the endless unknown?

"There are sacraments of evil as well as of good about us, and we live and move to my belief in an unknown world," wrote Arthur Machen, "a place where there are caves and shadows and dwellers in twilight. . . . It is my belief that an awful lore is not yet dead."

FIERY PHANTOMS AND   (7)
NOISY SPECTERS

Unlike houses but more like people, ships can wander around to do some haunting on their own. Unlike human ghosts or apparitions which have often been described as somewhat ephemeral, they are almost always if not invariably described as appearing quite solid though often seen through fog or under other conditions of bad visibility. They are seen by day and by night, make noises, leave wakes, and even obey maritime conventions. One of their notable indulgences is burning up. This is not unique to ship ghosts, there being fiery chariots—aerial and earthbound—planes, coaches, and even trains and cars, but it does seem to be one of their specialities.

All these specters come out of the past: at least, this is what has been assumed because only a few very advanced-thinking ship designers have any idea what a ship of the future will look like. Yet, when one comes to review a large body of reports of things seen on, going into, or coming out of the sea, which are normally treated in quite a different context than this book, one begins to wonder. Of these, I give only one example; and one that appears to me to be on the borderline.

What was the eerie object observed by crewmen aboard the S.S. *Fort Salisbury* deep in the South Atlantic during the early morning hours before dawn on October 28, 1902?

The ship was sailing north over a calm sea under a starry sky when the lookout observed a huge, dark object several hundred feet off starboard. He called Second Officer A. H. Raymer, who hurried on deck and joined the lookout and the helmsman.

"It was a little frightening," Raymer said later. "We couldn't see too much detail in the darkness, but it was between five and six hundred feet in length. It had two lights, one at each end. A mechanism of some kind—or fins, maybe—was making a commotion in the water."

The officer reported that the object seemed to be slowly sinking. He didn't believe it was a vessel that had turned turtle.

The surface was not smooth, but "appeared to be *scaled*" (italics mine).

When the ship arrived at London, a check was made of shipping lists. No vessels were missing or overdue at the time in the South Atlantic. Whatever the object was, it apparently had no relation to the known maritime world.[1]

I would stress here the word *scaled*, in combination with the suggestion that the "commotion" might have been caused by fins instead of a mechanism. Further, at first, the presence of fore and aft lights might seem to indicate a construction, but there are many marine animals that carry lights of all manner of colors, though no animal is known of these colossal dimensions. Could this have been a ghost of a submarine of the future, or should it go into the sea-monster category, or perhaps even into that of Unidentified Flying Objects that have so often been reported as landing on the oceans, emerging from them, or skimming their surfaces. At least many UFO's have the fiery aspect in common with ghost-ships such as the following.

Inbound to Seattle on November 2, 1957, the Japanese freighter S.S. *Meitetsu Maru* sighted a fishing boat afire from bow to stern. The location was about thirty miles west of Vancouver Island.

The freighter stood by and a boat was rowed around the blazing craft. There was no sign of survivors. The wooden, white-hulled vessel was around seventy feet in length, and fishing boats of this size usually carry a crew of at least ten men.

Part of a registry number was visible: K-13-AC. The letter "K" indicated the craft was Canadian, but a later check revealed that all ships with a "K" registry were accounted for.

The U.S. Coast Guard and Canadian vessels launched a five day search that covered 13,000 square miles of sea. No charred debris was observed, and only two objects were found. One was a crude chopping block imbedded with fish scales; the other was a ruptured fuel tank measuring 18x24x40 inches. The tank had an odor of naphtha, which is frequently used on the galleys of foreign boats but seldom by Canadian or American vessels.

The crew of the freighter reported that an unidentified white light or object had been observed near the burning boat from afar, but as the freighter approached it moved away rapidly and disappeared.

A number of fishing boats were in the general area, but only one reported seeing a glow in the night. This could have been the vessel, the mysterious white object, or flares dropped by search planes.

Weather conditions throughout the search were excellent. "If anything had been there to find," said Coast Guard Captain Frederick G. Wild, "we'd have found it."

Since the burning boat was reported, there have been no reports of overdue vessels of that size, no claims for insurance, and no inquiries from the families of missing men.[2]

Was the blazing vessel, then, a ghost?

For ghost ships still sail the seas—caravels and galleons, clippers and steamers—endlessly roaming the earth's waters with phantom crews, suspended in time, caught in the web of eternity.

Their occasional appearance is sometimes regarded as a warning of trouble or a harbinger of disaster, but usually they are but shadows, emerging without apparent reason from the dim corridors of the past like mobile photographs at the scenes where they once existed in what we know as reality.

So vast is the available material on this subject that merely to outline it would require several volumes the size of this one. Ralph De S. Childs of the Cooper Union Department of Humanities, who made a study of phantom vessels for the American Folklore Society, says there are more than a dozen "well established" ships haunting the northeast coast of the United States alone (UP Dispatch, January 29, 1949). We will confine ourselves, therefore, to several classical examples and some more startling recent observations.

In the *Cruise of the Bacchante,* a work compiled from the journals of the late King George V of England (then Duke of York) and his brother Prince Albert Victor, is reported the sighting of a phantom ship. The brothers served as midshipmen on H.M.S. *Bacchante*'s round-the-world voyage between 1879 and 1882.

At 4 A.M. on July 11, 1881, while the vessel was sailing to Sydney from Melbourne, Australia, the late King's diary says an eerie red light was noticed. His account follows:

> In the midst of the red light, the masts, spars and sails of a brig two hundred yards distant stood out in strong relief as she came up on the port bow. The lookout in the forecastle reported her as close to the bow, while also the officer of the watch from the bridge clearly saw her. So did the quarterdeck midshipman, who was sent forward at once to

the forecastle; but on arriving, there was no vestige or sign of any material ship. The night was clear and the sea calm.

Thirteen persons altogether saw her. Two other ships of the squadron, the *Tourmaline* and the *Cleopatra*, who were sailing off our starboard bow, asked whether we had seen the strange red light.[3]

Probably America's most noted maritime apparition is the *Palatine*, observed for over two centuries from Block Island, twelve miles off the Rhode Island coast. Block Island has been the scene of well over a thousand shipwrecks.

The traditional legend is that the *Palatine* sailed from Holland for Philadelphia in 1752 crowded with immigrants. The crew mutinied and murdered the captain. When supplies of food and water ran low, the crew starved and plundered the passengers, charging them exorbitant prices for the necessities to maintain life.

Finally, when the ship began leaking, the crew took all the food and water on board into the small boats and left the vessel. Then the ship, either drifting helplessly or attracted by the false beacons of wreckers, ran into a cove on Block Island. The wreckers slaughtered the passengers, looted the vessel, and set her afire.

A crazed woman, who had refused to leave the ship, could be heard screaming as the blazing ship drifted out of the cove. So horrible was this crime that the Almighty doomed the phantom of the *Palatine*—like that of the storied *Flying Dutchman*—to roam the seas forever as a reminder that He had not forgotten the wickedness of the wreckers.

This tale, with slight variations, has been endlessly repeated in book and magazine accounts and is still retold by the press services in reporting the latest appearances of the "Palatine Light," as the apparition is now called. John Greenleaf Whittier immortalized the story in his grim poem "The Palatine."

Most of the approximately seven hundred inhabitants of Block Island today are descendants of a community of fishermen and farmers established there over three hundred years ago. Of Puritan stock, they are conservative, pious, and so sober that the Women's Christian Temperance Union honored them with a statue of Rebekah at the well. They have always resented the charge that their ancestors were criminal wreckers, insisting that the ship's survivors were given all the help and assistance possible.

Determined to reveal the truth, Miss Elizabeth Dickens, a

direct descendant of a founding family and the island's principal historian, launched (in 1925), a search of old records with the assistance of others interested. The results of this historical detective work were astonishing.

A Rhode Island official checking state records discovered that no ship named the *Palatine* had ever arrived at Block Island. The vessel involved was the *Princess Augusta,* shipwrecked on the island December 27, 1738. The misnomer stemmed from the fact that the passengers were Protestant Palatines, residents of the former German districts of the Upper and Lower Palatinates. Persecuted for their faith during the early eighteenth century, many of the Palatines had sought refuge in the New World where they hoped they could worship in peace.

Meanwhile, Howard M. Chapin, librarian of the Rhode Island Historical Society, located five corroborating reports in old Boston newspapers of what had actually happened; and Miss Mary Quinn, keeper of the Rhode Island State Archives, found three depositions sworn to by the ship's officers.

According to these records, the *Princess Augusta* sailed from Rotterdam in August, 1738, with 350 Palatine refugees and a crew of fourteen men. Her destination was Philadelphia. She was a 220-ton merchantman from Ramsgate, England, under the command of Captain George Long.

Death struck from the very beginning of the voyage. Drinking water had been poured into casks that had previously contained wine. A poison developed from the mold left in the casks and the polluted water felled three hundred people. Of this number, 114 died and their bodies were buried at sea. The dead included Captain Long and seven crew members.

With the first mate, Andrew Brook, in command, the vessel was blown north far from her course by gale winds. After three months at sea, fighting repeated storms, supplies of food and potable water dwindled. And, according to the documents, Brook and the crew were guilty of forcing passengers to give them money by threatening to withhold food and water.

A nor'wester pounded the vessel when she finally came in sight of land late in December. Battered by winds and waves, the mizzenmast had to be cut away, and the ship sprang a leak astern. Passing the eastern tip of Long Island, the vessel continued to a point off Rhode Island and laid to under topsails, flying distress signals. After no rescuers appeared, Brook decided to go south along the coast, still hoping to reach Philadelphia, but a heavy snowstorm came with the night.

Blown by strong winds, the *Augusta* struck a hummock on Sandy Point at the north end of Block Island early on the afternoon of December 27. Her bottom was damaged and water entered her hold.

Ordering the passengers to remain aboard, Brook rowed to shore in a small boat and found a group of the islanders awaiting him. Simon Ray, a lay preacher and leader of the island colony, insisted that Brook drop the ship's sheet anchor to keep the vessel from drifting away with the passengers' possessions. Brook, after some argument, complied.

When low tide came, the islanders helped the passengers ashore. Brook refused to permit the passengers to remove their belongings or to give them the food that remained, but he had his own sea chest carried to the beach. It seems likely that he had rifled the cabins and hoped the ship would sink before his thefts were discovered.

Two elderly women died on the beach. The other passengers, many with hands and feet frostbitten, were taken to cottages where they were treated, warmed, and fed.

On the following morning Brook and his crew at high tide cut the anchor cable and the vessel drifted away. A group of angered islanders got a boat, pursued the *Augusta,* boarded her, and succeeded in saving twenty chests that were given to the rightful owners.

One passenger refused to leave the ship. She was Mary Vanderline, a prosperous woman who owned several chests of gold and silver plate. Crazed by her sufferings, she insisted on staying in her cabin. Why she was not removed forcibly is not known.

The next day, December 29, the *Augusta* drifted to the western side of the island, crashed into a rock and sank. The records indicate there was no fire. Brook and his men were charged with heartless behavior by an island court of inquiry, but there was insufficient evidence for criminal prosecution. They fled to the mainland at the first opportunity and vanished from history.

About one hundred passengers had been rescued, and twenty of these soon died. Two others settled on the island, and the rest are believed to have eventually reached Philadelphia. The dead were buried atop a bluff and a memorial marker was placed on the site in 1947 by the Block Island Historical Society.

There are probably several reasons for the legend that unjustly accused the islanders. They are listed by John Kobler in his *Saturday Evening Post* article (June 11, 1960, issue) which tells the story of the preceding historical research. At the time Kobler was one of the magazine's editors.

The two survivors who remained on the island were both named Kattern (a corruption of "Katherine"). One was about six feet in height and was known as Long Kattern. The other, a small woman, was called Short Kattern.

A Negro slave known as New Port (named after the African village where he was born) had carried Long Kattern to shore from the *Augusta*. In gratitude, she became his wife and they had three children named Thomas, Mary, and Cradle Port.

Short Kattern lived the rest of her days quietly on Block Island, but Long Kattern became a sorceress and fortune teller, going into trances at the drop of a dollar. Her associates were a mentally deranged islander, Mark Dodge, and an unnamed opium addict. Naturally the other islanders frowned on her activities and her choice of companions.

"Toward the other islanders," writes John Kobler, "she evidently harbored resentment, for out of her eldritch fancies she spun the tale of wrecking, arson, and murder. This was later confirmed by Mark Dodge—who, in a fit of dementia, once burned down a windmill—and by the opium addict. And thus the affair passed beyond the confines of Block Island into New England lore."

Before the colony led by Simon Ray was established, there were criminal wreckers on the island as well as pirates, and the bad reputation of the island did not die quickly.[4]

But what about the "Palatine Light" that resembles a phantom blazing vessel and within which, some observers allege, are visible masts, ropes, and billowing sails?

The first observation was in Block Island Sound a year after the shipwreck. The witness was the captain of a trading vessel, the *Somerset*, and he wrote in his log: "I was so distressed by the sight that we followed the burning ship to her watery grave, but failed to find any survivors or flotsam."

The Rev. Samuel T. Livermore, an island pastor, in his book *A History of Block Island*, quotes a letter written in 1811 by Dr. Aaron C. Willey, an island resident:

The light actually is seen, sometimes one-half mile from shore, where it lights up the walls of a gentleman's rooms through the windows. . . .

The people here are so familiarized with the sight they never think of giving notice to those who do not happen to be present, or even mentioning it afterwards, unless they hear some particular enquiries have been made. It beams with various magnitudes. Sometimes it is small, resembling the light through a distant window, at others expanding to the highness of a ship with all her canvas spread. The blaze actually emits luminous rays. . . .

The cause of this 'roving brightness' is a curious subject for philosophical speculation. Some, perhaps, will suppose it depends upon a peculiar modification of electricity; others upon the inflammation of phlogogistous (sic) gas.*

The Reverend Mr. Livermore suggested that gas from petroleum deposits beneath the ocean floor was rising to the surface, and that this gas was occasionally ignited by lightning. He wrote his book in 1886, but only a few years ago a similar theory was expressed by Walter Johnson, a United States Government geologist.

Edward Rowe Snow (see his book *Great Storms and Famous Shipwrecks of the New England Coast*[5]) refers to the account of W. P. Sheffield, who wrote *An Historical Sketch of Block Island* in 1876. Sheffield listed a number of witnesses including ninety-two-year-old Benjamin S. Knowles who had seen the ghost ship seven times.

Through the years the story of the light refused to die. The phenomenon has been reported by too many reliable observers to be dismissed entirely as a figment of fancy.

In 1934 Edwin C. Hill, well known newsman and commentator, made a personal investigation. In his column *The Human Side of the News,* he wrote:

Hundreds have claimed to have seen the apparition, and the "Palatine Light" is a well known phenomenon along the New England coast. There is, apparently, some kind of light—strange, mysterious, inexplicable—which is seen far out at sea at certain times.

. . . there are people living this day on Block Island who will tell you, with their hand on the Book, that they have gazed seaward in the blackness of the night, startled by a bright radiance at sea, and have

---

* Quoted by John Kobler in his *Saturday Evening Post* article.

watched with straining eyes, while the *Palatine,* blazing from truck to keelson, swept along the horizon. . . .

A United Press dispatch of November 19, 1951, reported that during the preceding year harbor police had received more than a hundred calls from waterfront residents in the Boston vicinity reporting a mysterious glow at sea. Patrol boats, however, failed to find the light or any explanation.

Today the light is regarded as one of the island's assets. Summer tourists can find plenty of eyewitnesses of the light ready to oblige them with dramatic accounts, perhaps with tongue-in-cheek, perhaps with exaggeration.

But the legend and the light live on.

Time was a factor in the experience of Wing Commander G. E. Robinson, R.A.F., who is certainly not a superstitious sailor who believes in fantastic folklore.

He is a graduate of the Royal Air Force Staff College and the U.S. Air Force Command and Staff College. During World War II he served with the Royal Air Force in East Africa and the Middle East. Since the war he has been attached to the Logistics Staff, British Air Forces, Occupation Headquarters, Germany; later serving as Air Movements Staff Officer, Air Ministry, London, and as Commanding Officer, Royal Air Force Station, Llandow, Great Britain.

At the time Commander Robinson's experience was published in the sober *Proceedings* of the U.S. Naval Institute in 1958, he was Logistics Requirements Plans Officer, SACLANT Headquarters (N.A.T.O.).

In April, 1936, as a young officer in the British Merchant Marine, Robinson joined the crew of the S.S. *Khosrou,* a 375-foot vessel of British Indian Registry. During his first nine months aboard only two unusual events occurred: once the ship grounded on a sandbar which, according to charts, did not exist; and one fruitless night was spent searching for a ship which was firing distress rockets. The ship was never found, nor was one ever reported in distress.

The appearance of distress rockets at sea and observations of the fall of aircraft on land, with no later evidence of trouble or disaster, have occurred many times.

A week before Christmas the ship left Calcutta for Bombay. The weather was thick and overcast, with frequent rains. The only other vessel observed was the S.S. *Maimyo* which had left Calcutta at the same time.

Five days later the ship was off the Ceylon coast. Robinson went on watch at midnight as the skipper retired. At 2 A.M. the captain reappeared, shouting: "The ship's in danger! Take a sounding!" Robinson was puzzled since the chart indicated that the ship should have been in at least five hundred fathoms of water.

The reading, however, was only thirty fathoms. Course was immediately changed, and an hour later the radio operator handed the skipper a message reading: "S.S. *Maimyo* ran aground at 2 A.M. . . . heavy seas pounding ship."

"That was the time I came on the bridge, wasn't it?" the captain asked Robinson.

Robinson agreed.

"I had a nightmare that a ship had run ashore," the skipper explained. "Thinking it was our own, and still half asleep, I rushed to the bridge."

Dawn revealed the coast of Ceylon, numerous reefs where the ship had been during the night, and the wrecked *Maimyo* only a mile away. Was the skipper's dream a coincidence?

At Bombay the *Khosrou* was ordered back to Calcutta. The weather was still bad, and several days later the vessel was moving at five knots in blinding rain, sounding its siren every two minutes. Suddenly the blast of another siren was heard. Engines were stopped and the ship drifted.

Blast for blast, the sirens answered each other. Then the stranger appeared out of the gloom, off the port bow, the ghostly shape of a motor-ship of about 6,000 tons. She slid by only a cable length away, and Robinson and his companions could distinctly read her name—the *Tricoleur*. But no lookout or helmsman could be seen. Her decks appeared to be deserted.

Minutes later the rain stopped and visibility cleared. The coast of Ceylon was ahead. As navigator, Robinson turned to the chart to check bearings and his blood froze. He ran to the bridge, yelling, "Where's the *Tricoleur*?"

Robinson, the skipper, and the mate looked around. Visibility was seven miles and it was only ten minutes since the *Tricoleur* had passed. Considering respective speeds, the two vessels shouldn't have been more than three miles apart. Yet there wasn't a ship in sight.

Robinson took the skipper into the chartroom.

"Just behind our position," Robinson wrote, "about two miles back on our track, was a symbol denoting a wreck; we must have been right over that wreck when we saw the *Tricoleur*. Alongside the symbol was the notation—'M.S. *Tricoleur* with a cargo of chemicals exploded and sank at this point at 5 P.M. on January 5, 1931.'

"We looked at the calendar and at the clock in the chartroom. It was January 5, 1937, and the time was 5:15 P.M.—six years to the hour since the disaster that had sunk the *Tricoleur*. Had we seen a ghost ship, perpetually doomed to wander near its grave?"

The Associated Press, in reporting the disaster on January 6, 1931, stated that the *Tricoleur,* a 6,120-ton vessel, was the victim of a "mysterious explosion." Captain Arthur Wold, one passenger, and the radio operator were lost. Ten passengers and the rest of the crew were rescued by a French ship, the S.S. *Porthos.*

Many of these vessels from the void are famed for their repeated appearances.

There is the phantom ship of Northumberland Strait between Nova Scotia and Prince Edward Island. According to an AP dispatch of December 8, 1953, she was making almost nightly appearances, watched by hundreds of coast dwellers. "It has to be seen to be believed," the villagers said.

And there is the ghost ship of Chaleur Bay, New Brunswick, a three-master with its rigging engulfed in flame, her slender masts spouting fire. Reports of its appearance range from Dalhousie to the Perce Rock on Quebec's Gaspé coast.

Some of these ships are identified with long lost vessels and have names. The *St. Martins,* destroyed by fire, is seen blazing in the Bay of Fundy; the *Breeze,* whose captain allegedly kidnaped a girl, is observed off Nova Scotia; the *White Rover,* said to have foundered a century ago, is occasionally reported off the New Hampshire shore. On quiet moonlit nights the *Half Moon* is sometimes seen drifting along the Hudson, gleaming with an unearthly silver sheen. Most famed among the ghost vessels of the Cornish coast (England) is the *Goblin,* a black square-rigged specter that "sails" over land as well as sea.[6]

If you have time, money, and patience, you should be able to

see a spectral ship sailing to her fiery doom. The place to go is
Merigomish, a small fishing community in Nova Scotia. It is
situated on the north shore, south of Prince Edward Island where
the eastern end of Northumberland Strait joins the Gulf of St.
Lawrence.

Each year, if the weather permits, either before or directly
after the autumnal equinox, the weird vessel appears. Its coming
is a big event in the quiet lives of the coastal residents. After
the harvest the folks living nearest the water maintain a nightly
vigil at dusk. As the vessel is sighted, they phone their inland
friends and the news quickly spreads: "Here she comes!
Hurry!"

By horse and auto, carrying blankets, lanterns, and telescopes,
the Nova Scotians rush to the shore. They crowd the higher
observation points along the bank to watch the re-enactment
of an ancient tragedy. It is like seeing once again an old motion
picture that recorded an event of long ago.

The ship now in view is sailing northeast at about twenty
knots, a full-rigged three-master of around a hundred tons. If
there is moonlight, the spectators can see the shining copper
on her keel. If there is a light fog over the waters, she is out-
lined in phosphorescence. Eerie lights blink along her decks
and in the rigging.

Now, quite suddenly, the vessel lurches, as if striking treacherous shoals. A moment later flames appear and dim figures can
be seen jumping overboard. The fire explosively bursts from
bow to stern as great red tongues leap skyward from the sails.
Rigging—and then the masts—collapse, and, finally, a blackened
hulk, the specter plunges beneath the waves.

For three generations the mystery vessel has appeared and
died. Identity of the ship is not known, the most widely accepted
theory being that she was a pirate craft that was destroyed with
all hands in the strait's gale-tormented waters.[7]

What mysterious factor regulates the appearances of these
vessels from out of the past? Why should the ghost ship of Nova
Scotia appear almost every year, while the phantom ship of the
Goodwin Sands only comes into view every half century?

The Goodwin Sands, widely known as a ship graveyard, are
off the coast of Kent, England. Only one vessel is known to have
been deliberately wrecked on these shoals.

On February 13, 1748, the schooner *Lady Luvibund* set sail

for Oporto, Portugal, with a general cargo. It was far more than a routine voyage for Captain Simon Reed. It was his honeymoon, and in his decorated cabin he was celebrating the happy event with his bride and a group of friends.

On deck was John Rivers, the first mate, listening to the sounds of gaiety below with jealous hate. The captain had taken the girl he loved. But the captain didn't know this, and the frustrated mate had even been best man at the wedding. Now was the time for his vengeance.

He walked to the wheelhouse. "I'll take over for awhile," he told the helmsman. "You can go below."

When the helmsman had disappeared, the mate turned the wheel and swung the bow of the vessel toward the shore. Then he ran the ship into the bars and shoals at full speed. The captain, his bride and guests were trapped below. Every person aboard died as the *Lady Luvibund* broke into pieces.

At the inquiry, the mate's mother told of her son's love and his vow to have revenge even if it cost him his life. Witnesses that had been aboard off-shore fishing craft told of watching the schooner's deliberate plunge to disaster.

Fifty years later, on February 13, 1798, an angry Captain James Westlake, master of the coasting vessel *Edenbridge,* demanded that the authorities apprehend and punish the officers of a schooner that had almost collided with his vessel off the sands.

"The crew must have been drunk," Captain Westlake said. "We could hear sounds of loud voices and laughter like a party was going on. It required the united efforts of the helmsman and myself to avoid the schooner."

When the authorities questioned fishing crews in the vicinity, they were told that the schooner was a ghost that had smashed into the sands and broken up as they watched. They hurried to the scene, but there was no debris in the water and the sand bars were bare.

Again, on the same date in 1848, the crew of an American clipper and several Deal hovelers (small craftsmen) heard a feminine voice and sounds of gaiety from a schooner as it bore down on the fatal sands. After it ran aground and broke up, boats were launched and rowed to the spot. As usual, the searchers found no evidence of a wreck.

In 1898 and more recently in 1948, the ghostly appearance

and destruction of the *Lady Luvibund* was observed by watchers on the shore. Doubtless in 1998 spectators will be waiting on February 13, and the chances are good that they will not be disappointed.[8]

Why only certain events of the past may apparently be recalled from the "ethers" is, of course, not known, but almost all of the original occurrences on both land and sea were emotionally charged. On land there are tales of the re-enactment of battles, murders, and suicides. On sea there were sinkings, shipwrecks, and fires—love, hate, and always death.

And the matter of sounds heard from some spectral ships is an added mystery. Visual hallucinations (using the word in its broadest meaning) seemingly can induce auditory hallucinations. Only vibrations pass through our eyes and ears; we actually see and hear with our minds. Do these images have a built-in sound track that strikes responsive cells in the brains of observers? And is the flow of time radically different in other dimensions?

We are learning that all life responds to universal rhythms and is influenced by radiations from the far stellar mainland beyond our planet. Is it possible that man may also be affected at times by emanations from reservoirs of past sights, sounds, and emotions?

Whatever the explanation, phantom ships do exist. Robert de la Croix, in his *Mysteries of the Sea*, cites a number of historical observations. He also states that a study of the logs of merchantmen of European countries recorded during the years between 1831 and 1885 uncovered three hundred reports of apparitions. In reaching this total, the researchers eliminated all cases not reported by reliable mariners, and observations that occurred close to land, during heavy fogs, and under possibly questionable conditions.

That the appearance of phantom ships may sometimes be a warning is indicated by the experience of James Hampson, a former American west coast captain.

In July, 1934, Hampson was in the Strait of Georgia, British Columbia, on the first leg of the thousand mile "inside passage" from Seattle to Alaska. He was at the wheel of the forty-six-foot cruiser *Mary Ann* when he ran into heavy fog. To avoid reefs he proceeded on course at reduced speed, sounding his foghorn.

Hours later at mid-morning, having passed the Porlier Pass horn on shore, a rising wind began to raise the fog. Suddenly, without any warning, the bulk of a silent ship loomed up over the starboard bow. It was an old, weather-beaten sailing ship.

Captain Hampson spun the wheel to port, but it was too late. The prow of the *Mary Ann* passed through the vessel. But instead of a splintering crash, the cruiser simply turned sharply with the sailing ship abeam on her port side.

Bewildered, the captain looked at the ghost and he said cold chills raced down his spine. There was no one visible on the deck. Her gray sails were torn and faded, but bellying in the breeze. There was no rattling of blocks, no creaking of cordage, no sound of churning wake—"just silence; an odd, ghastly silence."

Before Hampson could try to read her name, she had vanished in the mist. He was so startled that he failed to resume his former course. A moment later the fog was dispersed by the sun. The sailing vessel had disappeared, but on the horizon was a boat towing a raft of logs.

"Then I suddenly perceived something that gave me another shock," Hampson reported. "A loose section of the tow-boat's raft lay deep in the water, directly on the course I had charted and from which I had been diverted by the timely intervention of the ghost ship."[9]

In November, 1942, the Navy destroyer U.S.S. *Kennison* was a hundred miles northwest of San Francisco, approaching the Golden Gate through dense fog. The radarman was watching his scope, waiting for the blips that would reveal the Farallon Islands.

Most of the crew were below, happily preparing for shore leave after months of dangerous duty. The vessel was proceeding cautiously through the mist, frequently sounding its foghorn.

Howard Brisbane was standing lookout on the galley deck. Jack Cornelius was on the fantail. A third sailor, the fire control man, was on watch atop the after gun deck.

Suddenly Brisbane heard a faint hissing noise to port that grew louder—the sound of bow wash. Then came a series of splashes. The sounds were tending aft.

Before Brisbane could report, the excited voice of Cornelius came over the phone: "Fire control, look aft! Fantail to bridge!"

"Bridge, aye."

The fire control man cut in. "I see something all right, Jack, but what is it?"

"It's a ship! An old-timer!"

Now the response came from the bridge: "Bridge to fantail. What's going on back there?"

"A ship almost hit our fantail," Cornelius reported. "Just missed us by a few yards. It was a two-masted sailing ship."

The Officer-of-the-Deck spoke from the bridge. "What course is it on?" he asked.

"A course of one-three-five relative. It's somewhere now on the starboard quarter."

There was a pause, then the OD's voice was again on the phone: "That's odd! Very strange! The radar scope is empty. Did you say that ship was a double-masted sail job?"

"Yes, sir."

"I'd say they're rather rare these days."

"Sir," Cornelius answered. "I got a good look at it. It left a wake and its rigging was creaking. But there was no one on deck and the helm was not manned!"

"What?"

"That's right, sir, no one at the wheel."

"You mean it was a ghost?"

"I don't know what it was, sir."

Both Cornelius and the fire control man saw the ship—and Brisbane heard it—but Cornelius was practically above its deck during the approximate twenty seconds it was in his view.

"It gave me the creeps," Cornelius explained later. "At first I was just scared at the near collision, then I looked and felt cold chills go down my spine. There she was sailing through the fog, unpainted and her deck and rigging dilapidated. She was under full but ragged sail."[10]

One of the most remarkable stories related about a "ghost ship" impinges upon still other fields with which we are not primarily concerned here, and would appear to have undertones that are definitely what are called psychic. If, on the other hand, so-called ghost ships are real entities as opposed to hallucinations, as they would appear to be since they are often seen repeatedly and by thousands of different persons and at all manner of distant points, this case may have nothing psychic (in the proper sense) about it. As, however, there was only one witness, although a man of very wide knowledge, one cannot assert that it falls into one category or the other.

Nevertheless, the noted British novelist who wrote *Beau Geste,*

Percival Christopher Wren, recounts an experience he underwent when he was a young man while "shrimping" on the beach one July morning at a seaside resort on England's east coast. His account originally appeared in *Prediction* magazine (England) and was retold in *Psychic Experiences of Famous People,* by Sylvan Muldoon (Chicago, 1947).

"It was as real as any ship I had ever seen," Wren wrote, ". . . normal and solid-seeming. . . . Its high bows formed their own figure-head, crudely dragon-shaped, and the stern was also high. The sturdy stump mast supported a long yard and a heavy sail, torn, stained and dirty, on which some device had been roughly limned in tar and red paint. Over each gunwale hung a row of shields, whether of wood or of hide, stretched over metal, I was not sure; for they were dirty, wet, and salt-encrusted.

"Seated on the thwarts of the ship were four lines of rowers, two men to each oar. Standing up in the stern and holding a tiller, or perhaps a long and heavy oar . . . was the helmsman. Other men . . . knelt in the bows, sat in the stern, and stood by the mast."

Wren says that what interested him especially was that he could hear the shouts of the sailors. He adds: "The consequent sounds were loud, clear, and precisely those that are heard when any big boat is thus handled."

The boat grounded gently and several members of the crew picked up a man who had been lying against the mast and threw him overboard. The man staggered to shore and collapsed on the beach. Then the boat sailed out to sea.

Wren said he looked at the man, who had weather-beaten skin, a white mustache and beard, and a rusty iron head-piece like a skull-cap, but unadorned by the wings one sees in Viking pictures.

"I sprang forward with outstretched hands to raise his head from the water," Wren continues. "He was not there! Quickly I looked to where the ship should be moving toward the horizon. The ship had disappeared as well!"

The author states that he was conscious, definitely not dreaming, and saw and heard what went on with his two bodily senses. "What I saw was real," he concludes.

What are ghost ships?

Obviously, in our three-dimensional world, they are images

and the men on their decks are but shadows. The actual vessels they may represent have disintegrated or lie deep in silt and slime on ocean bottoms. Their crews have long since passed to whatever bourne lies beyond the bar.

Not all reports of their spectral appearances are acceptable as phenomena beyond the borders of known science. Mere glows of light are especially suspicious. Gas from ruptures in the earth's crust, large schools of phosphorescent sea life, and reflective optical illusions are all possible explanations. Close to shore, in haze or fog, a buoy, promontory, or islet might be mistaken for a ship.

Doubtless mirages have been responsible for some of the more detailed accounts, but mirages cannot be the answer for visions of ancient craft that vanished from the seas centuries ago. And we can ignore such an undefined, unproved term as a "collective hallucination," which actually explains nothing including the myth of the Indian rope trick.

One of the greatest obstacles to the advance of knowledge is the rejection of phenomena because of the usual explanation given. Thus the ghosts of men and ships are popularly associated with the so-called supernatural—spirit realms where the souls of the departed endlessly relive former lives or events and the specters of vessels continue to sail on.

If our observation of Nature has taught us anything, it is that all beings, objects, and environments are in constant change. It has also taught us that the supernatural of today is the natural of tomorrow. Could a man who died a century ago be resurrected to see our instantaneous transmission of sound and sight over great distances as evidenced by radio and television, he would believe he was witnessing supernatural phenomena.

To paraphrase Sir Isaac Newton, man stands on a beach picking up shells of knowledge with the vast sea of the unknown lying before him. Part of that unknown concerns the nature of time and our concept of it, and in this realm may exist the explanations of many occurrences that still puzzle us. Time is relative. It may also be multi-dimensional.

Oriental philosophy conceives of "Akashic Records"—that in the "ethers" surrounding earth are embalmed all the scenes of the planet's history that occurred at any given point on the surface. Like the vibrations of sound that continue to circle the earth, gradually diminishing from their original volume but, theoretically, still existing, so it may be with the images of our perceptible existence. Scientists have speculated on the possibility that someday we might be able to recapture sounds—hear the historic words uttered by Christ, Confucius, and Caesar.

Is it possible that we might also be able to recapture scenes of the past—and is it possible that such scenes are occasionally observed spontaneously? Such visions would be warps in our space-time continuum and would explain many riddles. And while time is relative, in our earthly environment it is measured by celestial movements that may well induce cycles and rhythms to which these so-called "ethers" as well as life respond.

FLOATING MORGUES (8)

Ghost ships, whenever their names have been made out, would appear always to be the aftermath—according to the way we regard *Time*—of tragedy, either to ship, crew or both. I do not know of a case of a ship that ended her days peacefully or was given decent "burial" in a breaker's yard or a concrete dock, being reported as roving the seas of time. Then again, considering that ghost ships leave wakes, blow their sirens according to strict maritime rules, flap their canvas, and display lights, how are we to know that there are not those among the many that are not boarded which are tangible and solid. There are many ships that have literally appeared out of the past, have been boarded, and found to be perfectly solid so that logbooks and other items could be removed from them and preserved in museums. Almost all of these ships have subsequently disappeared again. Very few if any have been salvaged. How can we ever tell where to draw the line? If visual and audible items can appear out of the past, why not tangible ones? A good case in point is that of the *Marlborough*.

The British ship *Johnson,* while off the coast of Chile, sighted an abandoned sailing vessel. It was slowly drifting, its sails floating in the wind. As the craft was approached, it was noticed that its masts and sails were covered with some kind of green moss or mold.

A boarding party found the deck decayed to such an extent that it gave under their footsteps and the sailors proceeded to examine the vessel with caution. Beneath the helm was the skeleton of a man. Three more skeletons were found near a panel, ten were discovered in the crew's quarters, and six on the bridge.

Upon the faded prow of the vessel the words *Marlborough* could still be read, and below, in smaller letters, the word *Glasgow*.

Inquiry revealed that the *Marlborough* left Littleton, New Zealand, in January, 1890, with a cargo of wool and frozen mutton. She carried a crew of twenty-three men under command of Captain J. Hird, and several passengers including one woman.

She was last seen on her regular course in the Straits of Magellan. In April, 1890, an unsuccessful search had been made for the vessel.

Twenty-three years had passed before she was found, a ghost ship with a skeleton crew. And the fate that brought death to her crew and passengers will forever be a mystery.

In simple, matter-of-fact words, this story of tragedy and death was told on November 13, 1913, by the Wellington (New Zealand) *Evening Post,* and on November 26, 1913, by the official French news agency *Agence Havas.* A copy of the *Marlborough* report is reproduced by Robert Ripley in his *Believe It or Not Omnibus.*[1]

Ripley, in this same volume on page 188, tells of the discovery of the schooner *Jenny* south of Drake Straits on September 22, 1860, by the whaling schooner *Hope.* The *Jenny* had just been released from antarctic ice and the bodies of her crew had been preserved by the cold. The log revealed that the British vessel had left Lima late in 1822 and had been caught in the ice on January 17, 1823. The last entry in the log signed by the captain was as follows: "May 4, 1823. No food for 71 days. I am the only one left alive." Captain Brighton of the *Hope* deposited the log with the British Admiralty when he returned to England. This cruise of the dead had lasted thirty-seven years.

For long centuries mariners tried to find a shorter, deepwater route between the Atlantic and Pacific—from European ports to the riches of the Far East. It was called the Northwest Passage—a sea lane that would pass between the North American continent and the Arctic Ocean. It would eliminate the long, ever dangerous voyage 'round the Horn.

But ships vanished and men died. Always the Arctic, with its paralyzing cold, howling blizzards, and the polar ice pack, won. In its desolation and loneliness, the fabulous passage remained unconquered.

On the morning of August 11, 1775, the *Herald,* a Greenland whaleship, was becalmed near a vast sea of ice which included a number of towering bergs. Her position was 76° N latitude west of Greenland. To the west the sea was completely blocked off with icebergs. In other directions the cold, forbidding expanse of water stretched to blue and misty horizons.

For several hours the vessel drifted slowly with the current, her sails loose. Then, early in the afternoon, came a wind that quickly rose to gale force and was accompanied by snow squalls. The howling of the wind in the rigging was soon followed by a far more ominous sound—the crashing and grinding of icebergs that were being driven by the gale toward the ship.

By this time the snow was so heavy that it was impossible to see more than a few feet beyond the vessel. Only one safe course remained open—to make a run for it and hope to keep ahead of the ice monsters. Captain Warren, the master, ordered the sails set for a southeast tack.

All night long the *Herald* sailed through the darkness and swirling snowflakes. Three times she heeled over when she hit large lumps of ice. During the early morning hours the storm died down and with the dawn the weather cleared.

Looking to the west, Captain Warren could see several open channels in the ice that had been broken up by the gale. He changed tack to a southwest course and headed for the nearest of the channels about three miles distant.

Suddenly the lookout shouted "Ahoy! A ship! West ahead!"

Captain Warren turned and stared in astonishment. Ahead were the masts of a vessel above an intervening iceberg. As he watched the ship hove into view, passing the last of the ice along the channel and drifting into the open water.

From the beginning the crew of the *Herald* knew there was something strange about the vessel. A coating of ice covered her spars, sails, and rigging. The ice glistened in the sunlight, and she looked like a ghost as she approached the whaler.

"She'll pass us within a couple hundred yards," said the captain. "We'll hail her."

With his telescope, Captain Warren looked for some sign of life on her decks but there was none. As the stranger began passing, the captain and then the bo'sun hailed her. But no one appeared on her icy decks. There was no reply.

"Lower the longboat," Captain Warren ordered. "I'm going to investigate."

An uneasy murmur ran through the crew, but they obeyed. The longboat was launched and the captain picked eight men to accompany him. As the boat neared the vessel, the captain looked at her stern. The elements had almost erased her name but it could still be read—the *Octavius*.

By the time the boat was alongside, Captain Warren could see that his men were on the verge of panic.

"No need to fear her," he said. "She may have been left in the ice by some arctic expedition. Never heard her name before, but we might be making an important discovery."

Accompanied by four nervous seamen, the captain climbed up to the slippery ice-coated deck. There was still no sign of life. The only sounds were the soft whistles of the wind in the rigging and the creaking of her timbers as she rose and fell with the swells.

"Let's take a look below," said the captain. He led the way towards the forecastle, but the entrance was blocked with snow and ice. With the help of his men, he kicked the ice away and opened the door. A strong musty odor poured forth.

The captain entered, his men following. Then they stepped back in horror. In every bunk was a dead man, perfectly preserved by the arctic cold. Each was heavily bundled with blankets and clothing. Apparently they had fallen asleep, then the frigid chill had finally penetrated their coverings and thus they died.

Captain Warren counted the bodies. There were twenty-eight.

The five men turned away and proceeded aft to the captain's cabin. Again, as they opened the door, they were greeted by a dank, musty smell. And again they gazed upon a scene of horror.

The body of the captain was slumped in a chair, head bent forward. His hands were on the table, a pen lying beside the fingers of his right hand. A thin green mold covered his face, veiling his eyes, but otherwise the body was well preserved. On the table in front of the body was the ship's logbook.

Captain Warren picked up the logbook and handed it to one of the sailors, then he proceeded into an adjoining cabin.

Lying on a bunk was the body of a woman, covered with blankets. Unlike the captain, her flesh and features were unmarked and lifelike. Her head was resting on her elbow and it appeared as if she had been watching some activity when she died.

Following the line of her vision, Captain Warren saw the body of a man seated cross-legged on the floor and slouched over. In one hand he held a flint and in the other a piece of steel. In front of him was a heap of wood shavings. Apparently he had been attempting to start a fire when death had claimed him.

Beside the man was a heavy sailor's jacket. When the captain picked it up, he found the body of a small boy underneath.

When Captain Warren returned to his men on deck, they pleaded with him to leave the vessel immediately. "It's a ghost," one said, "there's a curse on it."

The captain argued that a careful, complete inspection should be made. He did succeed in checking the nearby galley where he found no provisions in evidence, but when he started to inspect the hold the men rebelled. They scrambled overside and threatened to pull away in the longboat. And so, seeing that the panicky sailors were desperate, he dropped down into the boat and the nine men returned to the *Herald*.

Captain Warren watched the derelict with its cargo of death drift out of sight. The *Octavius* was never seen again.

But there was the logbook. When the captain asked the sailor for it, he was given two musty covers holding only four pages. The sailor explained that in his haste to board the longboat, the book had started to slip from his grasp. Evidently rotted, the center pages of the book had fallen free from the binding and dropped into the sea.

Captain Warren retired to his cabin to examine what remained. The first three pages listed the names of the ship's company, which included the captain, his wife, his ten-year-old son, and twenty-nine crewmen. It also disclosed that the *Octavius* had left England bound east on the China trade on September 10, 1761. The third page bore the first voyage entries, dated September 18 and 19, which bespoke of fair weather, good headway and the sighting of the Canary Islands.

The remaining page was the final one and it had only one entry with the rest of the page blank. Dated November 11, 1762, it read: "We have now been enclosed in the ice seventeen days, and our approximate position is Longitude 160 W, Latitude 75 N. The fire went out yesterday, and our master has been trying to rekindle it again but without success. He has handed the steel and flint to the mate. The master's son died this morning and his wife says she no longer feels the terrible cold. The rest of us seem to have no relief from the agony."

No one will ever know who wrote this entry, but it was probably one of the sailors.

When Captain Warren checked the location given, he couldn't believe his eyes. He called in his officers and they agreed with him. On the day of the entry the *Octavius* had been frozen in the *Arctic Ocean at a point north of Point Barrow, Alaska*.

There was only one explanation: The captain of the *Octavius*, on his return trip, had decided to look for the elusive Northwest Passage instead of sailing all the way around South America. And like so many others before him, he had met disaster and death.

But his ship had sailed on. Year after year, it had crept eastward through the ice, defying the elements, until at last it had entered the North Atlantic. The *Octavius* was the first ship to negotiate the ice-bound passage. But its passengers were a captain and his crew who had been corpses for thirteen years.

Today, according to Captain Dod Orsborne, R.N.R. (*Prize Sea Stories* magazine, Summer, 1964), the logbook of the *Octavius* rests in the archives of the Registrar of Shipping in London.[2]

It was 130 years after the discovery of the *Octavius* that the late Roald Amundsen, the Norwegian explorer, succeeded in navigating the Northwest Passage during the years 1903–5 in his tiny sailing vessel, the *Gjoa* (pronounced Yoah). The ship may be seen today facing the ocean in San Francisco's Golden Gate Park. And in 1940–42 (the news over-shadowed by the events of World War II) a group of Royal Canadian Mounted Police sailed their motor sailer *St. Roch* from Vancouver, British Columbia, through the famed passage to Halifax, Nova Scotia.[3]

Early on the morning of November 6, 1881, the bark *Josepha* was in the mid South Atlantic. Her destination was Cape Horn, 2,200 miles to the southwest. To the east the nearest land was Cape Town, 2,300 miles away.

First Mate Johann Berg was on watch when the fo'c'sle-head lookout shouted: "Object—two points on the port bow—looks like a boat!"

Berg raised his binoculars to his eyes. It was a small boat, bobbing in the light sea. A man was sitting in the bow. There were figures of other men hunched over the thwarts.

The mate ordered the course changed to approach the boat, and then he called the captain.

"Wonder where it came from," the mate said. "We haven't passed a ship for weeks and we're way off the usual route to the cape."

"We'll soon know," the captain answered.

The ship came up on the stern of the tossing boat.

"Ahoy!" shouted the captain. But there was no response from the men in the boat.

Puzzled, the captain ordered a gig lowered with Berg in command. With four men at the oars, Berg steered the gig to the side of the strangely silent boat. At close range the grim reason for the silence of the crew became obvious.

The man in the bow was clothed in the remnants of an officer's uniform, but underneath the garments were the bare bones of a skeleton. What had once been a group of oarsmen lay across the thwarts, their rag-clad bones and skulls bleached white by the sun.

The mysterious craft with its phantom crew was hauled aboard the *Josepha*. The officer's uniform rapidly disintegrated, and it was impossible, through any remaining insignia, to determine nationality, or whether it had belonged to a naval or merchant officer.

A search of the boat failed to reveal any papers or other objects that would have identified the bodies. The boat, a twenty-two-foot British clinker-built, was also anonymous. The elements had destroyed the paint and any name the boat might have borne.

When the *Josepha* made port and reported her discovery to shipping authorities, a deeper mystery became apparent. A world-wide search of marine records failed to reveal any trace of a lost vessel or men in this part of the Atlantic that would explain the origin of the boat.

Who were these unknown sailors who became a skeleton crew in a boat drifting aimlessly on a voyage to nowhere so far from the regular shipping lanes?[4] In this case the cause of the death of the human beings would seem to be satisfactorily explained—starvation, lack of water, and exposure. However, the cause or causes are not always clear by any means, and sometimes they are totally unexplained or quite inexplicable.

During the summer of 1880 the Portuguese brig *Santa Maria* was found drifting in the Indian Ocean with all hands dead. The vessel was well stocked with food and water and was in good condition. There were no marks of violence on the bodies.[5]

The most obvious explanation of cases like these is that the crew was stricken by a plague. In the days of sailing vessels, especially, outbreaks of typhoid and tropical fevers, small pox, cholera, and similar diseases could wipe out a crew if all members were susceptible and the ships were far enough from land.

Fourteen years after the *Santa Maria* was found, the German steamer *Pickhuben,* in September, 1894, came upon another vessel in the same general area of the Indian Ocean. It was the British brig *Abbey S. Hart,* under full sail but drifting in the slight wind. The Germans spoke—that is, signaled and hailed—the brig, but there was no response.

A boarding party found the decks deserted. Going below they discovered three seamen dead in their bunks. A fourth, apparently the captain, was alive but helpless. With glassy eyes he stared at the Germans, mumbling incoherently. Obviously, he was either delirious or mad.

The sailors carried him to their boat and took him back to the steamer. He died an hour later without uttering a single sensible word.

When the *Abbey S. Hart* was towed to port, it was learned she had sailed about a week previously from Tandjoeng Priok, Java, with a cargo of sugar. It was assumed that a fever had struck down the crew.[6]

It was definitely fever that felled the crew of the British barkentine *Guiding Star* on a voyage from India to Tasmania. A bad storm struck her, and with men too ill to handle the sails, they were soon blown away. A Dutch steamer finally sighted her, rescued the three surviving members of the crew, and left the ship adrift.

Years later an old mariner, once master of the *Guiding Star,* saw a strangely familiar ship at anchor in Batavia. She was painted black, with new houses on her deck and a Javanese crew on board. But there was no mistaking the sturdy lines of the *Guiding Star.*[7]

Disease is not by any means the only cause other than freezing, or other exposure, and/or lack of food and water. And this leads us into the uncanny; as eerie an example as any that can be found in the annals of maritime history occurred on a morning in early February, 1948, when the S.S. *Ourang Medan,* a Dutch freighter, was steaming through the Straits of Malacca between Sumatra and the Malay Peninsula, bound for Jakarta, Indonesia. The sun was warm above a calm sea.

Suddenly Dutch and British marine radio listening posts picked up S.O.S. calls from the vessel, followed by the ship's location. Other vessels in the general area were notified and rescue ships set out from shore.

The distress calls were repeated. Then, after a short silence, came a final message: "All officers including captain dead, lying in chartroom and on bridge . . . probably whole crew dead." Now came a series of indecipherable dots and dashes, then, quite clearly, the words, "I die."

Radio directional equipment established the ship's position as slightly different from that given by the radio operator. With this advantage, rescue ships located the *Ourang Medan* within a few hours. The steamer seemed to be in good condition, but drifting with the current and leaving behind her a thin ribbon of smoke from her funnel. Repeated hails brought no response.

Boarding parties found a ship of the dead. The captain lay dead on the bridge. In the wheelhouse, chartroom, and along the deck were the silent bodies of the other officers and the crew. In the radio shack the body of the operator was slumped in a chair, his lifeless hand still resting on the transmitting key.

"Their frozen faces were upturned to the sun," stated a report in the *Proceedings of the Merchant Marine Council,* "the mouths were gaping open and the eyes staring." The doom that had struck the vessel had been complete. On the deck was the ship's dog, lifeless, its lips drawn back and teeth bared.

The bodies were examined, but there were no signs of wounds or injuries, no evidence of violence. No weapons were in view, and there appeared to be no damage to the vessel.

The rescuers held a conference on deck and decided to tow the freighter with its eerie cargo to the nearest port. Suddenly smoke and flames belched out of the hold and spread rapidly. The boarding parties, unable to fight the fire, hastily left the ship and returned to their own vessels.

Minutes later the boilers of the *Ourang Medan* exploded, and trailing flame she rolled over on her side, then sank beneath the waves.[8]

In view of the ship's destruction, we may consider carbon monoxide or other toxic fumes from a smoldering fire or a leak in the boiler system as the cause of the deaths. This can easily occur in closed spaces, but it would be most unusual for a poisonous gas to asphyxiate men on an open deck even in the absence of a breeze.

THE WANDERERS AND THE HOMERS

(9)

There are ships that apparently have strange abilities.

Back in the early 1920's the *Governor Parr,* a disabled British schooner, endangered North Atlantic shipping for months by her erratic behavior after she was abandoned by her crew during a gale. Superstitious sailors credited her with the power to induce storms.[1]

Twice steamers left Nova Scotia to tow her ashore and salvage her cargo of Canadian lumber, but each time after the crews had boarded her a sudden storm forced them to abandon the attempt.

Months later she appeared off the Azores. And again efforts at salvage met with the same defeat. Her final fate remains a mystery.

The S.S. *Baychimo,* famed "ghost of the Arctic Sea," has been the only derelict in history to repeatedly defy the crushing ice packs year after year and escape destruction or even severe damage.

A 1,300-ton steel-clad twin-screw steamer owned by Hudson's Bay Company, she joined the far northern fleet in 1921 after the schooner *Lady Kindersley* was destroyed in the Polar Pack. Based at Vancouver, British Columbia, she visited the posts around Beaufort Sea and McClintock Channel for nine seasons. No other vessel had made the dangerous passage for more than two successive years.

On October 1, 1931, the *Baychimo* was caught in the ice during a howling blizzard off Wainwright, Alaska, with a million dollars worth of bundled furs in her hold. With the vessel in danger of being crushed, Captain Cornwall and his crew of sixteen men established a camp on safer ice near shore and within sight of the ship. They planned to wait until the spring thaw if the vessel survived the winter.

A storm on the night of November 2 caused a rise in temperature. When it abated three days later, it was found that the *Baychimo* had snapped her moorings and disappeared. The sailors broke camp and moved to Point Barrow, fifty miles away.

An Eskimo hunter reported finding the vessel about forty-five miles southwest of her former position. The crew and a party of Eskimos traveled over the ice with dog teams and after fifteen days of difficult work succeeded in removing most of her cargo. But on their last trek they discovered that the ship had again vanished.

She was observed five months later in ice near Herschel Island. A group of prospectors boarded her in the summer of 1932. They said she was in perfect condition.

In 1933, when she was passing Point Barrow, thirty Eskimos set out in small boats and boarded her. They were trapped aboard by a sudden blizzard and for ten days drifted helplessly, believing that the derelict had brought the storm. Three of their group died before they reached shore on a raft of ice.

Year after year she was sighted by whalers, trading vessels, and Eskimos. In 1934 the crew of the schooner *Trader* boarded her. Paul Brock, writing in *Fate* (April, 1958) tells of their observations: broken bales of fur and cargo boxes, samples of mineral ore, books, a silent rusty typewriter in the pilothouse, charts of the seas scattered on the floor.

Captain Hugh Polson and his crew are believed to have been the last boarding party in November, 1939. They were prevented by the weather from towing her into port. As the *National Geographic Society Bulletin* states, "she always eludes capture."

As far as I can determine, the *Baychimo* was last sighted by Eskimos in March, 1956, in the Beaufort Sea, moving north and still apparently seaworthy, riding the sea as if an expert mariner was at her helm. Her story has no parallel. No other derelict in modern times has been known to survive the ice for more than two years. The *Baychimo* has been around, crewless, for twenty-five years!

There are those who feel or even assert that examples such as these demonstrate a further extension of a deliberate "will" on the part of the ships as would appear to have been the cases of the *Humboldt* and the *Sea Lion*, recounted in Chapter 4. The more pragmatic view is, of course, that it is merely a combination of coincidence and "good luck" as far as the vessel is concerned. But we enter still another area of mystery when we come to what I call the Drifters and more especially the Homers—the latter being those ships that sail back to their home ports under their own power, be it mechanical, sail, or none at all. And this in turn leads us to the perhaps more simple problem of abandoned ships. For these there are, or at least could be, quite simple and logical explanations. But now to the matter of drifters and mere derelicts.

It was on February 7, 1953, that the M.S. *Holchu* was found adrift between the Andaman and Nicobar Islands by the British freighter *Ranee*.

The crew of the freighter had hailed the motorship. There was no reply and a boarding party was sent to investigate. No one was aboard. Her crew had disappeared.

The vessel was in excellent condition. A meal had been prepared in her galley and was ready to be served. She was well supplied with food, fuel, and water. Her radio was in working order. There were no signs of trouble or violence.

The only damage was a broken mast, but this would not have affected her operation since she was a motorship and her engines were in good condition.

The freighter towed the derelict to Colombo, Ceylon, where harbor officials carefully examined the ship. They could find no clues as to why the *Holchu* was abandoned and the fate of her crew is unknown.[2]

Other than the well-known menaces to shipping—storm, fire, collision, tidal wave, or hidden reef—what could cause a crew to leave a sound ship for the questionable safety and doubtful destiny of a lifeboat? And why, in some cases of deserted ships, were the lifeboats still suspended from their davits? There may be as many reasons as there are occurrences, but certainly these reasons are enigmatic. There have been a number of fictional theories of what really happened aboard these ships, but all have called into play the utmost limits of the writers' imaginations.

Uncommon as these desertions are, they have been occurring for a long time. Lieutenant Commander Gould (*The Stargazer Talks*), tells of the Dutch schooner *Hermania* found back in 1849, drifting and deserted, by a fishing vessel about ten miles southeast of the Eddystone. She was dismasted, but was still quite sound.

Valuables were found on board, and clothing indicating that the captain's wife and child had been on board with him. Her only boat was lying in its chocks, undamaged. Nothing was ever heard of the crew.[3]

A classic riddle is the bark *James B. Chester,* a large sailing ship discovered by the *Marathon* of Newcastle on February 28, 1855, some six hundred miles SW of the Azores.

"She was yawing back and forth," the captain reported later, "and appeared to be sailing with no one at the wheel." The boarding party, commanded by Chief Mate Thomas, searched the *Chester* from bow to stern. Apparently the vessel had been hurriedly abandoned. Chairs and tables amidships were overturned, drawers had been pulled out and the contents dumped, and clothing and personal possessions were scattered in disarray. However, there were no signs of bloodshed, weapons, or a struggle.

The cargo of wool and provisions was intact. There was plenty of food and water aboard. Although the ship's papers and compass were missing, every boat was still hanging in the davits. It was suggested later that a spare life boat may have been carried on the deck, but the ship's owners denied this.

A skeleton crew was assigned to sail the ship to Liverpool where hundreds of spectators came to the Albert Docks to see her. Speculation on the fate of her crew ranged from piracy to a giant octopus.

Evidently the crew had fled the ship in panic, as Edward R. Snow says in his *Mysteries and Adventures Along the Atlantic Coast.* But what caused the terror that would force seasoned sailors from a sound ship in mid-sea hundreds of miles from land? Are there occasional menaces at sea more mysterious than the mysteries they create?[4]

Then there was the schooner *Zebrina* that left Falmouth for St. Brieux, France, in October, 1917, and was found two days later drifting aimlessly and abandoned. Everything aboard was shipshape and her sails were set. The weather had been good for the relatively short voyage.

Her crew had evidently been in the midst of a meal when something happened that caused the desertion, but there was not a clue on board as to this cause.[5]

Again, there was the French cutter *Belle Isle.* She was found near the Gulf of Lyon by the Portuguese lugger *Islandia,* an International Red Cross charter vessel, in July, 1941. Her sails were set. Captain Amadio Mathias said there was no evidence of violence or a disturbance, everything seemed in good condition, but there was no one aboard.[6]

These are examples of many cases. The circumstances are

usually the same; only the names of the ships and the locations are different.

There are, however, some abandonments with unusual features that deserve our attention.

In the year 1881 the British ship *Ellen Austin* encountered an unidentified abandoned schooner in mid-Atlantic. Our story repeats: the derelict was seaworthy, everything was in order, nothing was missing, and no signs of a struggle were visible.

The captain of the British vessel decided to claim salvage and placed a small prize crew aboard. Both vessels then set sail for St. John's, Newfoundland, but the ships parted company in foggy weather.

Two days later the fog cleared and the captain of the *Ellen Austin* sighted the derelict. To his astonishment, she was pursuing an erratic course. He ordered the helmsman to approach the derelict. When there was no response to signals, a boarding party was sent over.

Once more the derelict was deserted. Like their predecessors, the prize crew had vanished. Every foot of the strange ship was searched, but there was no clue to what had happened to the sailors.

To a man, the frightened remaining sailors refused to join another prize crew. The *Ellen Austin* sailed away, leaving the derelict riding the swells. Slowly it dropped below the horizon never to be seen again.[7]

The sea was rough and the sky was sullen on a day in 1850 when fishermen and residents at Easton's Beach, near Newport, Rhode Island, observed a large sailing vessel heading for the channel reefs and disaster. The men close to the shore ran to the water's edge, shouting and waving their arms, waiting for the splintering crash.

And then, under strange guidance, the vessel swung around, maneuvered past the reefs and through the narrow channel and headed straight for shore, the wind filling her sails. As the ship hit the beach, a large wave lifted her bow and grounded her gently in the sand, undamaged.

The fishermen swarmed aboard to congratulate the captain for his seamanship. But there was no one except a mongrel dog sitting quietly on deck to greet them.

Coffee was boiling away on the stove in the ship's galley.

Breakfast had been laid out on the table for the crew. The odor of tobacco smoke was still strong in the crew's quarters.

The ship was the *Seabird,* under command of Captain John Durham (some accounts give the last name as Huxham) , and due to arrive that same day in her home port of Newport. She was returning from a voyage to Honduras with a cargo of hardwoods, pitch-pine, coffee, and dye-woods.

Captain Durham, a rugged New Englander, was known to many of the fishermen. The last entry in the log noted the sighting of Brenton Reef several miles offshore. The crew of a fishing boat reported that they had exchanged signals with the *Seabird* at sea about two hours before she was beached.

It is possible that the crew, frightened by the breakers on the reefs, had abandoned the ship and drowned. It is not clear in any of the accounts that the lifeboat was missing. But no bodies were ever washed up along the coast in the weeks following the abandonment.

The cargo was unloaded and transported to Newport by wagons. Attempts were made to refloat the vessel, but it had fallen deeper into the sand.

Several months later a storm struck the coast at night, hurling mountainous waves over the beach. In the morning the beach residents expected to find the ship pounded into pieces, her remains littering the shore. But the ship was gone and the beach was bare. The *Seabird* had returned to the sea and vanished.[8]

Another case of a crew vanishing just offshore under even more mysterious circumstances occurred thirty-three years later on the Pacific coast. For the facts we are indebted to the extensive research undertaken by Mr. Walker A. Tompkins.

The schooner *J. C. Cousins* was an eighty-seven-foot two-master originally built as a luxury vessel in San Francisco. Her hull was copper-plated. Her superstructure was paneled in mahogany and teak and bore hand-carved intricate designs.

In 1881 she was placed in pilot service at the mouth of the Columbia River at Astoria, Oregon. It was a time of intense, bitter competition and price wars among the pilot services that operated through the treacherous river entrance, known as a graveyard of ships.

It was bright and sunny on the morning of October 6, 1883, when Captain Alonzo Zeiber left Astoria in the *Cousins,* accompanied by two seamen and a cook. He was under orders from the ship's owners to proceed through the waterway, await the arrival of a French barkentine from the Far East the following day, then guide the newcomer to port.

At noon the ship dropped anchor in mid-river off Fort Stevens to await the ebb tide that would carry her over the sandbars to the open sea. During the afternoon she was in view of the crew of the tug *Mary Taylor* lying off Ilwaco, Washington, and of lookouts on Cape Disappointment.

At 5 P.M. the *Cousins* raised anchor and rode the tide out beyond the river mouth. During the starlit night that followed she was under observation by U.S. Coast Guardsmen at Canby Lighthouse.

When dawn came on October 7 the sky was clear, the wind light with a moderate ground-swell running. The guardsmen, who kept watch on all harbor traffic, noticed that the ship was moving out to sea to meet the barkentine.

Suddenly, for no apparent reason, the *Cousins* swung around and headed straight inshore toward the sandy bank of Clatsop Spit, her sails set to the wind.

Coast Guardsmen and other witnesses watched with bewilderment, growing concern, and then amazement. As she approached the outer breakers above the shoals, she gave no sign of heaving to or dropping anchor. Her voyage to doom continued as spectators stood helpless.

With a crash the vessel struck the sandbar of Clatsop Spit. Her masts lurched violently as combers lashed her stern. Telescopes were trained on the beached ship, but there were no distress signals, no efforts to lower a boat, no figures dropping over the side to swim ashore.

Surfboats were launched by the guardsmen. As they approached, there was no answer to their hails. They climbed aboard. The ship was deserted. Everything was shipshape. Lifeboats were in their davits. But there was no one on board. Not a soul.

The stove in the galley was warm. Potatoes had boiled dry in a pot. In the cabin an untouched meal was on the table. The crew's quarters were in order. The last entry in the log had been made in mid-river at sunrise. In Captain Zeiber's handwriting, it gave only the time and location, adding: "All's well."

Now the search turned to the sea—for swimming men, for bodies, for anything that might have come from the ship. But nothing was found.

Captain Zeiber was known to have had good relations with his men and the members of his crew had good reputations. Insurance inspectors found the hull undamaged, and the rudder and helm in excellent operating condition. They could find nothing to account for the ship's sudden return to shore. A watch was kept along the shoreline for some distance for weeks, but no bodies appeared.

One theory, unsupported by any evidence, was that the captain had been bribed by competitive pilot services—that he had murdered his crew, weighted the bodies and dropped them overboard during the night, then grounded the vessel to make his escape. Seamen argued that the *Cousins* could not have sailed so steadily shoreward without someone at the wheel.

But the ship was under telescopic observation from the Coast Guard station during its fatal run. There were other witnesses as she approached the sandbar. They did not see anyone leap from the vessel and it would have been impossible for a boat to have escaped their observation. All lifeboats were on board. If the captain had been a plotter, he could have devised a better plan than one that endangered his life by jumping off the ship.

The *Cousins* could not be tugged off the sandbar. Salvaging firms removed her equipment and fittings. By the following spring the remains of the vessel had been broken up by waves, storms, and tides.

There was lengthy litigation in the barratry courts. The insurance company could not see paying a loss on a ship that apparently had been deliberately wrecked. Finally the ship's owners were paid $4,000, about a tenth of the ship's value.

For several years afterward there were occasional rumors that Captain Zeiber had been seen in far ports—Singapore, Madagascar, the Straits of Magellan. These reports were investigated and all proved false.

Certain it is that Captain Zeiber and his crewmen never again appeared along the Astoria waterfront. What actually happened aboard the *J. C. Cousins* will never be known.[9]

The disappearance of the crew of the five-masted schooner *Carroll A. Deering* off the Carolina coast in 1921 is in a class by itself.

It involved not only suggestions of mutiny and even piracy, but hints of international complications. And it was followed by the unprecedented vanishing of a dozen vessels off the Atlantic coast that to this day remains unexplained.*

Seven federal agencies participated in the investigation: the Coast Guard, Navy, and the Justice, Treasury, State, Navigation, and Commerce Departments. In the end one government official said: "We might just as well have searched a painted ship on a painted ocean for sight of the vanished crew."[10]

In the gray light of dawn on January 31, 1921, watchmen at the Cape Hatteras (North Carolina) Coast Guard Station observed a large schooner rammed against Diamond Shoals along the Outer Banks. She was under full sail, her prow deep in the sand, straining against the land.

A Coast Guard crew, under the direction of Commanding Officer B. B. Miller, launched a surfboat. But the sea was running strong, with waves breaking over the schooner, and the boat could only come within a quarter of a mile of the ship to make observations.

There were no distress signals or signs of life aboard. Lines hanging down the hull at the stern and empty davits revealed that the lifeboats had been lowered and were gone.

Giant breakers continued during the day to comb the shoals and lash the grounded vessel. A chill wind whistled through her rigging and beat her sails, driving her bow deeper and deeper into the sand. A Coast Guard cutter arrived from Wilmington, North Carolina, but it was still unsafe to board the wreck the following day. It was not until the morning of February 4, after the arrival of the wrecking steamer *Rescue,* that the seas calmed and the vessel could be boarded.

The ship was then identified as the *Carroll A. Deering,* of Bath, Maine, a $200,000 schooner of 2,114 tons.

The only living things aboard were two gray cats found mewing in the galley. (Pet lovers will be pleased to know that they were adopted by L. K. Smith, steward on the *Rescue.*)

All sails except the outer jib were set, although two of the topsails had been blown into ribbons. No effort had been made to save the vessel by lowering or trimming sail. Two large sea anchors were missing along with one chain. A small stream anchor had been attached to the remaining chain as a replacement.

---

* See also Chapter 13.

Both lifeboats were gone. Food was still in the galley. Pots on the stove containing soup, meat, and coffee indicated a meal was being prepared when the ship was abandoned.

Steering equipment had been ruined. The steering wheel was broken, and the rudder stock was shoved up through the deck. The binnacle had been smashed, apparently with a sledge hammer lying nearby. Two red lights had been placed in the rigging— a signal that the vessel is abandoned, wrecked or out of control.

Water below deck plus the waves that had swept over her would have destroyed any evidence of bloodshed. There were no signs of a collision with another vessel. The rope ladder and gangway were still stowed and lashed in place.

Missing were the ship's papers, logbook, chronometer, luggage, and clothing from the forecastle, and the ship's clock from the dining room.

Conditions in the master's cabin later became important when evidence came to light that the captain was not in command prior to the abandonment.

The bed was unmade and drawers were pulled open. In a side closet were three pairs of rubber boots indicating other men had been using the cabin. The cabin's spare room, usually vacant, looked as if someone had been sleeping in it. All this was odd, but odder still was the fact that the captain's large trunk, canvas sea bag, and grip were missing. If he had abandoned the ship, he would hardly have taken the heavy trunk and bag in a lifeboat.

It was a puzzle why the experienced sailors on board would have left the safety of the vessel at all for the risks of small open boats that were almost certain to be swamped in heavy seas. What had happened to cause this apparent foolhardy abandonment?

The *Deering* was launched on April 4, 1919, at the Gardiner G. Deering Shipyards, Bath, Maine, and was named after Deering's son.

Her last voyage began in August, 1920, from Norfolk, Virginia, with Captain William M. Merritt in command. The captain's son, S. E. Merritt, was first mate. The cargo of coal was destined for Rio de Janeiro.

Captain Merritt became ill at Delaware Breakwater and the vessel put in at Lewes, Delaware. The ship's owners sent Captain Willis B. Wormell, of Portland, Maine, to replace Merritt. Since Merritt's son was returning to Maine with his father, the new master hired Mr. Charles McLellan as first mate.

The *Deering* sailed from the breakwater on or about September 9.

Captain Wormell at the time was sixty-six years of age, a veteran ship master who had recently retired. He was known to be a deeply religious man, well-known and well-liked in shipping circles.

While the cargo was being discharged in Rio, Captain Wormell met an old friend who was in port with another vessel. He was Captain George Goodwin. They had a talk together.

"My first mate is worthless, incompetent," Captain Wormell told his friend. "I've been having difficulties with my crew. If anything should happen, though, I have an engineer I fully trust. He's Herbert Bates, from Islesboro, Maine."

"Yes, I know Bates," Captain Goodwin replied. "He's a good reliable man. I certainly hope the situation improves before you get back to the states where you can line up a new crew."

At the same time the captain wrote a letter to his brother-in-law that indicated he was concerned about the future: "I sometimes feel the thread of life is slender. And soon with me the labor will be wrought. . . . The time is short."[11]

The *Deering* left Rio on December 2 for Barbados. There Captain Wormell, according to John Harden (*The Devil's Tramping Ground*), complained to his ship's agents at Bridgetown about "the unruliness of his crew and mentioned his own ill health." He was instructed to proceed back to Norfolk without cargo.

Before the ship could sail, McLellan, the mate, was arrested by local police and lodged in jail, apparently for drunkenness and disorderly conduct. However, the captain arranged for his release so he could leave on the schooner.

Captain J. W. Bunker, of Calais, Maine, stated later that he met Captain Wormell at Bridgetown and that the captain told him he was having a difficult time getting his crew sober enough to leave port.

John Harden writes that "cafe loungers at Barbados were reported to have overheard a heated argument in which the mate of the *Deering* threatened to 'get the old man' before the vessel reached Norfolk, referring presumably to Captain Wormell."

The ship left Barbados on January 9 for Norfolk, clearing a port for the last time. Early on the afternoon of January 23, 1921, she passed the Cape Fear (North Carolina) lightship. The lightship officers and crew did not notice anything unusual about the schooner as she sailed by.

Then a storm arose, a northeasterly gale that by the night of January 27 produced gigantic seas along the Carolina coast and winds clocked at seventy-five miles per hour. It calmed down on the 29th, and at 4 P.M. on that day the *Deering* approached the Cape Lookout lightship off Diamond Shoals. The distance between the Cape Fear and Cape Lookout lightships is about eighty-five miles, and the vessel was six days in sailing that distance.

"She was a beautiful ship," Captain Thomas Jacobson of the lightship said later. "She rode the water like a giant swan with all sails set except the flying jib. James Steel, my engineer, hurried away to get his camera and take a picture. Yet I felt there was something wrong.

"For one thing, the crew was assembled on the quarterdeck, an odd place to gather. The captain would hardly have permitted his men to assemble there. It indicated lack of discipline."

One of the men on the schooner hailed the lightship, shouting through a megaphone: "We've lost both anchors while riding out the storm off Frying Pan (Cape Fear) Lightship. We want to have it reported ashore."

Captain Jacobson testified that the shouting man was redheaded, spoke with a foreign accent, and did not look or act like a ship's officer. The speaker certainly was not Captain Wormell, who ordinarily would have performed this task and identified himself. Nor does he appear to have been the first mate, according to the description. Edward Snow says he was possibly the Boatswain Johan Frederickson, a Finlander. However, Captain Merritt, who met McLellan in Delaware before returning to Maine and thus knew all of the crew, said he didn't remember any red-headed man in the group.

Captain Jacobson said he couldn't relay the *Deering*'s message ashore because his radio was out of commission.

An hour or so after the *Deering* left, an unidentified craft passed the lightship sailing in the same direction as the schooner.

This mysterious vessel, according to Harden, refused to stop when Captain Jacobson flagged an international code signal meaning "Have important message." The captain then blew his No. 12 chime whistle which could be heard for five miles, but the vessel still refused to stop. The captain said he wanted to notify the vessel that the *Deering* had lost her anchors and to relay the report to shore.

In one account (*Fate*, August-September, 1951) it is stated that the strange ship had a tarpaulin lowered to conceal its name, but I have been unable to confirm this. It might have been a rum-runner, although they usually kept out of sight of lightships.

The *Deering* was abandoned sometime between 4 P.M. on January 29 and dawn on January 31 when she was found beached on the shoals. The food being prepared aboard indicated an evening meal, so the schooner was probably deserted on the evening of either January 29 or 30. It was a period of moderate to heavy seas, but there were no storms.

But the crew left a chart on the schooner. It revealed that Captain Wormell had marked the course in pencil until January 23 when the ship was off Cape Fear. Then his writing ended, and another person began tracing the course about a week before the vessel was found abandoned. A second coastwise chart was missing. Is it possible that some crew member attempting to destroy evidence took or destroyed one chart, but inadvertently left the other?

All the evidence points to the fact that Captain Wormell was not in command when the ship passed the Cape Lookout lightship. Discipline was lax. A crewman transmitted the message about the lost anchors. Another person had been marking the chart. Added to this evidence are the conditions found in the master's cabin when the schooner was grounded.

Was the captain ill below decks? Was he dead? If so, did he lose his life accidently during the gale, did he die of natural causes, or was he murdered?

It is very significant that whatever had happened to the captain was not reported to the lightship. The loss of a skipper is far more important to a vessel than the loss of anchors.

Had there been a mutiny during the six days the *Deering* was riding out the gale? Why didn't the mate give the message about the lost anchors? Were the men gathered on the quarterdeck because a gun was trained on them to keep them silent?

Soon after the crew of the *Deering* vanished, the S.S. *Hewitt,* owned by the Union Sulphur Company of New York, was reported overdue. The steamer was known to have been in a position near the schooner on January 30 from her radio reports. It is possible that the crew of the schooner abandoned their vessel for some unknown reason and were picked up by the *Hewitt.*

Harden cites a report that a few days after the *Deering* went aground, "there was a great flash of fire off the New Jersey coast and high billows of smoke hung in the air." He suggests that the *Hewitt* exploded at sea and that both crews, then aboard, were lost.

The ominous fact, however, is that during the weeks and months that followed the *Deering* disaster ship after ship began disappearing without trace off the Atlantic coast. The disappearances at first were attributed to the known hazards of the sea, then their frequency within a relatively limited period of time aroused suspicions.

In June the mystery was in newspaper headlines. The New York *Times* on June 21, 1921, announced that "five departments of the Washington Government were investigating . . . difficult to think of piracy . . . seemed to be no other explanation." On the following day the *Times* reported "More ships added to mystery list . . . almost simultaneous disappearances without a trace regarded as significant." On June 24 the *Times* listed a dozen vessels (see *The Books of Charles Fort*).

The list included some small vessels, but larger ships mysteriously missing included the *Hewitt,* the *Entine Florina,* the *Svartskag,* and the *Lorringa.*

At the same time the American representative of the Washington *Post* reported that he knew of several vessels entering the port of Vladivostok with their names obliterated and with Russian crews.

At this time the United States did not recognize the Soviet Union and relations between the two countries were highly strained. It was openly suggested that Russian pirates may have been responsible for the disappearances.

It seems incredible, however, that the Russians would seize vessels literally off the American doorstep and take a chance transporting them the thousands of miles to Vladivostock. They could far more easily and safely seize ships closer to their own home ports.

It should also be remembered that this occurred during Prohibition when rum-runners were active off the coast. A number of these smugglers picked up their cargoes in Barbados and brought them ashore in the Carolinas.

Edward Snow introduces the possibility that a group of these men, possibly in league with the mate, seized the schooner. There may have been resistance by other crew members that led to the schooner running aground. The rum-runners would not have dared to remain aboard and risk capture by the Coast Guard. The other crewmen may have been lost when their boats were swamped.

Meanwhile, on April 26, a Mr. Christopher Columbus Gray reported that he had found a bottle with a message inside while he was walking along the beach near Buxton, North Carolina, a village near Cape Hatteras. The paper was soggy and in an oddly shaped bottle. The message, written in ink apparently with a fountain pen, was as follows:

"Deering captured by oil burning boat. Something like chaser taking off everything, handcuffing crew. Crew hiding all over ship. No chance to make escape. Finder please notify headquarters of Deering."

The handwriting was distinctive. Captain Wormell's wife and daughter, Lula, first obtained the signatures of the crew from the employment records and the signature of the first mate from the hotel register at Lewes, Delaware. Only the signature of Herbert Bates, the engineer trusted by the captain, resembled the handwriting on the message.

Mrs. Wormell then secured several letters written by Bates to his mother in Maine. She submitted the letters and message to the three most highly qualified handwriting experts she could locate and all three agreed that the writing was identical. She also pointed out that Bates, probably alone in the engine room while everyone else was on deck, would be the one crew member having an opportunity to write the message.

In Washington, D.C., it was determined that the fine-lined, lavender-striped paper on which the message was written was made in Norway and sold in large quantities in South America. The peculiarly shaped bottle was of a type produced in Buenos Aires.

Herbert Hoover, then Secretary of Commerce and concerned about the disappearance of other vessels off the coast, agreed to launch the governmental investigation after a conference with

Mrs. Wormell and her daughter, Senator Hale of Maine, Captain Merritt and others.

In September Mr. Lawrence Richey, assistant to Mr. Hoover, announced that the Departments of Commerce and Justice had proven "beyond a doubt" that Christopher Columbus Gray had written the message he claimed he had found. However, there were some persons, including several relatives of Captain Wormell, who suggested that pressure had been brought on Gray and he had admitted guilt merely to avoid further questioning.

The government failed to explain how, if the bottle message was a hoax, Gray could have so incredibly duplicated Bates' handwriting that three experts were deceived. This is one of the many minor mysteries involved in the greater mystery.

To compound the confusion, the London *Daily Mail* on June 22 had reported the discovery of another bottle message. This one was allegedly written by Captain Wormell and stated that he had been taken prisoner by his crew and placed aboard another vessel.

In all the accounts of this mystery that I have read, no reference is made to this discovery of a second bottle message. We can be sure that it was branded a hoax.

Meanwhile, the government had notified port officials and shipping circles throughout the world to be on the lookout for any living member of the *Deering*'s crew. Two men were held for questioning at Vera Cruz, Mexico, when they signed aboard a ship. They were released when it was found that the similarity of their Danish names to two *Deering* crew members had caused the mistake.

But what actually happened? Is twentieth-century piracy the answer?

The schooner had no cargo and pirates would hardly have bothered to capture a vessel for the personal possessions of the crew. The government investigation produced no evidence of piracy. The nation was moving into the exciting decade of the 1920's—the era of bathtub gin and speakeasies, the Charleston and the Lindy Hop. The story of a strange, lonely ship was soon forgotten.

What about rum-runners?

We can be certain that Captain Wormell, a religious, law-abiding man, was not carrying contraband. Rum-runners would have no reason to go aboard the schooner. The ship itself was too large, too slow, and too likely to attract attention to be used for smuggling.

The possibility that Captain Wormell's murder had been planned at Barbados by a crew member and that he made arrangements with rum-runners to be picked up at sea is unlikely since such action almost certainly would be carried out soon after leaving port. Captain Wormell marked the chart until January 23—fourteen days after leaving Bridgetown.

Is mutiny the answer?

Engineer Bates and probably other crew members would have remained loyal to the captain. If there was a mutiny, it likely was a limited one.

Edward Rowe Snow says we can be fairly certain of three facts: that Captain Wormell was having trouble with some of his crew, that he was not in charge of the vessel when it passed Cape Lookout lightship, and that someone else had taken over command.

Snow then goes on to suggest that the crew may have been frightened by the storm that carried away the anchors, that they decided to abandon the ship, and that during a period of calm they fixed two red lights in the rigging, ransacked the ship (even taking the captain's trunk and sea bag), and left in the boats. The overloaded boats were probably swamped, or the men may have been picked up by the *Hewitt* or another vessel that disappeared about that time.

I would add these suggestions:

During the storm there was a bitter argument between the captain and a crew member who had been drinking heavily since leaving Barbados. The captain was slain.

Now there was a killer aboard, and he was a desperate man. If the schooner reached port, he faced arrest, trial, and possibly the death penalty. Loyal crew members might seek to seize and confine him.

He had a gun and if there were other firearms on board he threw them into the sea. At gunpoint he was master of the ship. He and either accomplices or hostages occupied the captain's cabin. But the ship had lost its anchors and would have to be towed into port. Perhaps Engineer Bates persuaded him to send the message to the lightship, and since he had not completed his plans, he agreed.

But when the message was sent, he warned the crewman with the megaphone to say nothing about the captain under pain of death. The other crew members were ordered to stand together on the quarterdeck where they could be watched while he stood out of sight, his gun ready.

After the schooner left the lightship, probably late the next day, he made his decision. There must be no evidence. The captain may have left some written record of trouble aboard. He threw the trunk and sea bag and grip overboard. He checked the drawers in the cabin. He destroyed the coastal chart, but in his haste overlooked the sea chart.

Now he ordered both boats lowered, and with his weapon forced the rest of the crew into one boat. As the crew was about to cast off, he began firing. There must be no surviving witnesses. He may have aimed at the men or at the boat bottom. But he made certain that holes were shot in the bottom and that the men had nothing with which to bail the water out.

Now he and possibly an accomplice or two were alone on the *Deering*. The red lights had been placed in the rigging earlier. Now he threw overboard the crew's luggage and clothing to make the abandonment seem a voluntary action. He also got rid of the ship's papers and logbook.

With a sledge hammer he damaged the steering equipment, then smashed the binnacle to remove the compass. Taking the compass and chronometer, he slid down the line to the other boat and cut the rope. Now he set a course west for the mainland and escape.

But that night the heavy seas came that beached the *Deering*. His boat was swamped or was overturned by a large wave. In the night, probably alone, he died with his burden of guilt.

Is this what happened? We shall never know, but this theory does consider all the circumstances that are so puzzling. We can be certain that the mystery of the *Deering* has no simple explanation.

The *Carroll A. Deering*, once so trim and sturdy but fatally stricken after less than two years of existence, could not be removed from the shoals. She was stripped of her sails, furnishings, fittings, and equipment. Then she was left to the winds and the waves.

She became the roost for several thousand sea gulls. The birds became a nuisance. Their shrill cries during the nights disturbed the summer residents on a nearby beach and they complained to the Coast Guard.

As arrangements were being completed to blow up the wreckage with dynamite, a severe storm struck the coast one night. Huge breakers and howling winds battered the derelict. Under the impact of the elements, the timbers of the schooner began to loosen as she creaked and groaned in her last great struggle, alone and deserted, in the darkness.

Calm came with the morning light. The homeless sea gulls, forlornly crying, circled the shoals. But all that remained were broken timbers scattered along the beach. The *Carroll A. Deering* was no more.

Up in Maine the Deering family still have the bell and riding lights that were aboard the schooner. Sometimes they look at these relics, they touch them, and they wonder. And in upper New York state the descendants of Captain Wormell still have the chart that was left on board. They, too, occasionally look at it and remember.

Long years have passed since the *Carroll A. Deering* sailed billowing and crewless to her doom—but the mystery remains.

No account of sea mysteries would be complete without the story of the *Mary Celeste,* symbolic now for almost a century of all derelicts and vessels found strangely deserted. Despite the passage of years, interest in the enigma she presented remains undiminished. Year after year, the tale is retold in newspaper features, magazines, and books.

Unfortunately, most of these stories are inaccurate. A mystery of this type inspires imaginations, and, bit by bit, a cocoon of myth is created that later writers accept as true. To discover the actual facts, one must turn to those few writers who base their accounts on the testimony given before the Vice-Admiralty Court at Gibraltar in 1873.

There is probably no maritime museum in the western world that does not have a model of this ship. So vast is the literature on her riddle, that the marine library at the Atlantic Mutual Insurance Company in New York has an entire room on the subject. The mystery remains as fascinating today as when it happened.

Christened the *Amazon,* the ship was built at Spencers Island, Nova Scotia, in 1861. She was a brigantine that after some later alterations was 282.28 tons and 103 feet in length.

During her first eleven years of existence, she had her misfortunes. Her first captain died a few days after she was registered. On her first voyage down the coast to Maine she ran into a fishing weir, damaging her hull. Later, on a European trip, she struck a brig in the Straits of Dover, sending the brig to the bottom.

When, in 1867, she grounded on Cape Breton Island, she was considered a total wreck and was left to the salvagers. She was sold, however, to a man named Alexander McBean who pulled her off the island bay and reconditioned her. It was McBean who renamed the ship the *Mary Celeste* in 1869, but eventually, apparently because of heavy debt, McBean was forced to sell the ship to a John Beatty.

James H. Winchester, founder of a shipping firm that still bears his name in New York, acquired the vessel from Beatty. He found that her timbers had suffered dry rot, and he rebuilt the bottom with a copper lining and placed the ship in excellent condition.

Late in the year 1872 the *Celeste* was tied up at a pier on the East River, New York, taking on a cargo of 1,700 casks of commercial alcohol (unpalatable as a beverage, incidentally).

Captain Benjamin Spooner Briggs, of Marion, Massachusetts, was master of the vessel and he had also purchased a part ownership of the ship of eight twenty-fourths. Captain Briggs, aged thirty-seven years, was an experienced seaman, robust and temperate, of New England Puritan stock. Practically all the books later found on the brigantine were of a religious nature, and members of his family said, weather permitting, he read a chapter in the Bible daily.

At a nearby pier was the British brigantine *Dei Gratia* taking on a cargo of petroleum, with Captain David Reed Morehouse in command. The two captains were old acquaintances and they had dinner together the night before the *Celeste* sailed.

In those days it was not unusual for the captain's wife to sail with him. Mrs. Briggs, the former Sarah Elizabeth Cobb, was a distant cousin of her husband. They took with them a daughter, two-year-old Sophia Matilda, leaving their older son, Arthur, with relatives so he could attend school.

Others on board were Albert G. Richardson, twenty-eight, the first mate, member of a seafaring family of Stockton Springs, Maine; Andrew Gilling, twenty-five, second mate, a native of Denmark; and Edward W. Head, twenty-three, the steward-cook, of New York.

The seamen, all Germans, were Volkert, twenty-nine, and Boz Lorenzen, twenty-five, brothers; Arien Martens (or Harbens), thirty-five, and Gottlieb Goodschaad (or Goodschall), twenty-three. In letters to relatives, both the captain and his wife said the crew gave the impression of reliability.

The vessel left her dock on November 5 for Genoa, Italy, but anchored off Staten Island because of severe head winds. Two days later the winds died down and the *Celeste* proceeded out to sea to keep her date with destiny. And for at least eighteen days she held her course across the North Atlantic.

Meanwhile, on November 15, the *Dei Gratia* left New York

for Gibraltar on a similar course. She carried eight men, including her captain.

Early in the afternoon of December 5, approximately halfway between the Azores and the coast of Portugal, the crew of the *Dei Gratia* sighted a brigantine. Under short canvas, only two sails were set on the starboard tack—the jib and the foretopmast staysail. Her lower foretopsails were hanging by the corners, and the foresail and upper foretopsail were missing. Moving at less than two knots an hour, she was yawing erratically.

"She's in trouble all right, captain," said First Mate Oliver Deveau, "but I don't see any distress signal."

Captain Morehouse raised his telescope to his eye. "No one at the wheel," he answered. "Can't see anybody on deck. Guess we better take a look at her."

The *Dei Gratia* was not an easy ship to handle. Moreover, the weather had been heavy, with frequent squalls, and the sea after the storm was running high. It required almost two hours to maneuver the ship near the mystery vessel.

"It's the *Mary Celeste*," said Captain Morehouse in surprise when he could read her name. "Wonder what's wrong with Briggs."

Mate Deveau, accompanied by Seamen John Wright and John Johnson, rowed over in a boat. Johnson remained in the boat alongside while Deveau and Wright climbed aboard.

Deveau's first act was to sound the pumps to be certain the vessel was not in danger of sinking. There was only forty-two inches of water in the hold. At the same time he noticed that the box had been drawn on one of the pumps to permit the sounding rod to go down. The rod was lying beside the pump.

Deveau and Wright quickly searched the vessel. To their bewilderment, they found no one aboard, living or dead.

The logbook was on a desk in the mate's cabin. The last entry was dated November 24 and it gave the ship's position about one hundred miles southwest of San Miguel Island in the Azores. There was also a chart above the mate's bed tracing the route of the vessel up to November 24.

The last entry on the log slate, found in the captain's cabin, revealed that on November 25 at 8 A.M. the ship had passed Santa Maria (St. Mary's) Island in the Azores about six miles to the northeast. It had been eleven days since this final entry had been made.

THE CLASSIC DRIFTER   133

According to Deveau's testimony before the Vice-Admiralty Court, he made the following discoveries:

There were no boats aboard. A spar had been lashed across the stern davits to hold them steady. However, two fenders on the main hatch indicated that a yawl had been kept there, and both gangways on the top gallant rails had been removed, apparently to launch the yawl.

Both the fore hatch and the lazarette hatch were open. Some writers have said that the forward hatch cover was upside down, a position no sailor would leave it in. This would indicate an explosion. There is, however, no mention in the court records of its being in this position.

The ship's wheel was not damaged, and had not been lashed. Heavy waves, apparently, had knocked the binnacle out of place and shattered the glass over the compass. The main staysail had been hauled down and was lying on the forward house. Winds had blown away the running rigging, but the standing rigging was in fair condition. The forward house was filled with water up to the coaming.

All six windows in the deck cabins were tightly battened up with canvas and planks, but the skylight was wide open. Rain and heavy seas had soaked bedding, clothing, and floors, and ruined the ship's clock. In the captain's cabin, the beds were unmade and on one bunk was the impression of a child's body.

The rack that prevents dishes from sliding off onto the floor was on the dinner table, but contrary to many accounts, there was no food on the table. In the galley pots and pans were stowed away and there was no evidence that a meal was being prepared. However, there were six months' provisions in the storeroom and plenty of drinking water.[1]

"There seemed to be everything left behind in the cabins as if left in a great hurry," Mate Deveau testified, "but everything in its place."

The captain had left his greatcoat and boots. In the forecastle the crew had left their personal possessions, clothing, oilskins, boots, and even their pipes and tobacco. Deveau later told the court: "A sailor would generally take such things, especially his pipe, if not in great haste."

The only articles that seemed to be missing in addition to the yawl were the chronometer, sextant, and the ship's papers including the register.

Mate Deveau and his companions returned to the *Dei Gratia* and made their report to Captain Morehouse. This report included the fact that the *Celeste* had a valuable cargo, and Deveau proposed taking her in to claim salvage. This would leave the *Dei Gratia* short-handed, but since the distance to Gibraltar was only about 650 miles, the captain agreed.

Late on the same afternoon Deveau and two seamen, Augustus Anderson and Charles Lund, returned to the derelict, taking their ship's small boat, a barometer, sextant, compass, watch, and some food prepared by the steward. It required two days to get the ship ready. The three men repaired the sails and found a spare trysail to replace the missing foresail.

The water was pumped out of the hold. It was determined later that the vessel's hold only took in about one inch of water every twenty-four hours, so most of the water found there by the mate when he first boarded the ship had come down through her open hatches and through her cabin.

The two ships set sail and remained in sight of each other until they reached the Straits of Gibraltar and ran into a storm. The *Celeste* arrived at Gibraltar on December 13, 1872, one day after the *Dei Gratia* had anchored in the port.

Within two hours after the *Mary Celeste* dropped anchor, the brigantine had been "arrested" or "attached" by T. J. Vecchio, marshal of the Vice-Admiralty Court. Salvors, by their services, acquire a lien on recovered property, and the attachment places the property in court custody. At the hearings the owners and underwriters of the ships and cargoes appear to defend their interests in the rescued property.

The court's hearing began on December 18 with Sir James Cochrane as the presiding judge. Mr. Frederick Solly Flood, the Queen's Proctor, described as "rather a fussy little man" by Lieutenant Commander Rupert Gould,[2] could think of no reason why a seaworthy vessel with a cargo valued in excess of $30,000 should be abandoned in mid-sea. He suspected foul play and the inquiry opened in an atmosphere of suspicion.

Mr. Flood, on December 23 and again on January 7, had two thorough examinations made of the *Celeste*. The examiners included a diver, the local surveyor of shipping, the court's marshal, four captains of the Royal Navy, and a colonel of the Royal Engineers. Looking especially for evidence of foul play, he thought he had found it.

THE CLASSIC DRIFTER   135

One writer in recent years, Mr. Harold T. Wilkins of England, has also pointed a finger of suspicion at the *Dei Gratia*'s crew. In his books *New Light on the Mary Celeste* and *Strange Mysteries of Time and Space*,³ he has emphasized the discoveries of Mr. Flood.

I was in correspondence with Mr. Wilkins before his death and once we collaborated in writing a magazine article. Since he secured a complete transcript of the Vice-Admiralty Court proceedings from which he quotes extensively, his books are valuable as basic source material. But as much as I admire his ability at research and collecting data, I cannot agree with his conclusions.

First, Mr. Flood found grooves, which he described as cuts made with a sharp instrument, on each side of her bows, several feet back from the prow and a foot or two above the waterline. Although no explanation was offered for the damage, Mr. John Austin, surveyor of shipping, testified the grooves were "very recent and not due to weather."

At the request of U.S. Consul Horatio J. Sprague, who represented the flag in the case, an examination was made of the damage by Captain R. W. Schufeldt of the U.S.S. *Plymouth*. The captain said the damage was nothing more than "splinters made in the bending of the planks which were afterward forced off by the action of the sea without hurting the ship."

Next, Mr. Flood told the court of finding a deep cut, made apparently with an axe, on the starboard top-gallant rail. Mate Deveau testified that he had not noticed the cut until the rail was brought into court, that he had found an old axe on board, and that he could "form no opinion about the cause of the axe cut on the rail."

Obviously, a cut on the rail apparently made sometime in the past to cut a rope overside was not especially suspicious, but near the cut on the rail, and also at a spot on the deck, Mr. Flood said the examiners had found brown stains that might have been blood.

Even more sensational was Mr. Flood's announcement that a sheathed sword with several tiny brown stains had been found under Captain Briggs' berth.

Let us turn now to the court testimony:

Solly Flood: "Have you any opinion to offer the court as to the origin of the bloodstains on the deck?"

Oliver Deveau: "I noticed no marks or traces of blood on

deck. I cannot say whether there were any or not. We never washed or scraped the decks of the *Mary Celeste*. We had not men enough for that. The sea washed over the decks."

Solly Flood: "Salt water contains chloric acid which dissolves the particles of blood."

Oliver Deveau: "If there are some parts of the deck or rail scraped, I did not notice them, and they were not done while we were on board."

Solly Flood: "Did you pick up a sword aboard the *Mary Celeste*?"

Oliver Deveau: "I saw the sword on board the vessel. I found that sword under the captain's berth. I took it from there, and looked at it by drawing it from its sheath. There was nothing remarkable on it, and I don't think there is anything remarkable about it now. It seems rusty. I think I put it back where I found it or somewhere near. . . ."

Solly Flood: "The sword has been cleaned with lemon, which has covered it with citrate of iron, which has destroyed the marks of the supposed blood, which therefore is not blood at all as at first supposed, but another substance put there to disguise the original marks of the blood which were once there."

We have here an example of Mr. Flood's "very vivid imagination," as Consul Sprague later termed it. Why, if the sword had been used in foul play, it was not simply tossed overboard is not explained. Captain Briggs' relatives reported later that the sword was a souvenir of an Italian battle that he had been given by a friend.

Mr. Flood's request to have the stains on the sword, rail, and deck analyzed by Dr. J. Patron of Gibraltar was granted by the court, the cost to be deducted from the *Dei Gratia*'s salvage award. There are, however, two curious facts about this request.

First, Sir James Cochrane, the judge, censured Deveau for "doing away with the vessel which had rendered necessary the analysis of the supposed bloodstain." The record does not reveal what this "vessel" was or what it contained, but apparently it was a container of red liquid that Deveau said might have been responsible for the stains on the deck and/or rail.

Second, the doctor's report on his analysis was sealed and kept secret without any explanation. Sir James Cochrane and Mr. Flood not only refused to give a copy to U.S. Consul Sprague, but withheld the information from the British Governor of Gibraltar. It was not until 1887, fourteen years after the hearing, that the U.S. Consul was able to secure a copy and forward it to the Department of State at Washington.

We can only conclude that the reason for this action was that the analysis, based though it was on the crude methods of 1873, was negative, acting to disprove Flood's suspicions.

Dr. Patron's report states that he removed with a chisel several "red brown spots about a millimetre thick and half-an-inch in diameter" from the deck and another small spot on the top-gallant rail. He also took the sword.

After describing in detail the various tests he made, he writes: "From the preceding negative experiments, I feel myself authorized to conclude that according to our present scientific knowledge, there is no blood either in the stains observed on the deck of the *Mary Celeste*, or on those found on the blade of the sword that I have examined."

Another argument offered by Mr. Flood was the mystery of how the *Celeste* could have held to her course for ten days with the wheel loose, on a starboard tack, with the wind blowing from the north all that time. The distance from the last entry on the deck slate log to the position where she was found by the *Dei Gratia* was slightly over five hundred land miles.

Solly Flood, in his report to the British Board of Trade, said the "obvious inference is that the *Mary Celeste* was not abandoned till some days after the last entry in her log."

We do not know, of course, just when the brigantine lost some of her sails. It could have been a relatively short time before her discovery.

More important, we do not know just when the vessel was abandoned. Many small merchant ships did not make daily entries in the log, and only the more important observations were recorded. Gould points out that the *Celeste* had been at sea eighteen days before sighting the Azores, but there were only seven entries in her log, all told!

Deveau, in the midst of the hearing, left on a voyage to Italy for which he was severely criticized by the judge. Meanwhile, Captain Morehouse had testified that he did not go on board the *Celeste* until it arrived at Gibraltar. This statement was in conflict with the log kept by Deveau.

When Deveau returned, he was again questioned by the court and made this explanation:

"I kept the log of the *Mary Celeste* after I got on board, that is to say, I wrote it by memory after we got in to Gibraltar. I did not write it down at the time, but the captain of the *Dei Gratia* having come on board and said he wished I had done so, I said I thought I still could do it from memory, with the help of my chart on what was the ship's course and the latitude and longitude, and from that I entered the log up as it now appears.

"The entry made on Friday, 6 December, 1872, is not correct. I see there it is stated that the captain of the *Dei Gratia* came on board, that day, of the *Mary Celeste*. That is not so. The entry 'Captain Morehouse came on board with a letter of instructions' is not correct. In point of fact, Captain Morehouse did not come on board. He had stated that he should come on board, but he sent the letter of instructions in a boat by two men without himself coming. I cannot explain otherwise how I made this error."

Solly Flood: "Has Captain Morehouse already seen this entry and previously spoken to you about it?"

Oliver Deveau: "No, he has not seen the entry or spoken to me about it. My attention is now called for the first time to the error by you. I cannot say positively whether the letter of instruction was brought to me on that day or the day before. It was on the first or on the second day."

Wilkins considers this matter grounds for perjury. Certainly it was carelessness, neglect, even dereliction of duty on the mate's part, but whether Captain Morehouse came on board or not, I see no reason to suspect criminal activity.

Other reasons listed by Wilkins for suspicion are:

That Mate Deveau used the log slate and may have rubbed out a final entry on the side he used.

That the bill of lading, manifest, and ship's register were missing. These may well have been taken by Captain Briggs, however, when he left the vessel.

That Captain Morehouse was known under the alias "Boyce." He was called "Boyce" by James H. Winchester, principal owner of the *Celeste,* and by Captain Parsons, former president of the New York Maritime Exchange Office, who met the captain several years after the hearing while in Havana, Cuba.

Captain Morehouse may have had a personal reason that had nothing to do with illegal activities for using an alias.

Finally, Mr. Wilkins publishes a letter he received from the sister of Albert G. Richardson, first mate of the *Celeste,* which states that she and her brother, the late Captain Lyman Richardson, had always suspected that the crew of the *Dei Gratia* might have been responsible for the mystery. But suspicions are not evidence.

Edward Rowe Snow (*Mysteries and Adventures Along the Atlantic Coast*) states that he has spent much time interviewing the son of Captain Morehouse.

"Harry S. Morehouse is now a well-known resident of Boston," Snow writes, "and I was careful to take sufficient time to interview him on all known facts of the case. His replies always rang true, and I cannot believe that his father would falsify any statement he made under oath. I am convinced that Captain Morehouse told the truth when he said he discovered the *Mary Celeste* abandoned at sea."

Lieutenant Commander Gould voices a similar opinion: "The theory that Morehouse and his men deliberately murdered the crew of the *Mary Celeste* for the sake of the salvage is simply insane. Even if they'd been a crowd of Chicago gangsters, instead of being just ordinary, decent-minded British seamen, they'd surely have had the wits to see they were simply putting their heads in a noose—that they couldn't possibly hope to keep their crime hushed up for ever. It would probably be blurted out, at the inevitable inquiry or later, by the first one of them who lost his nerve or wanted to blackmail the others."

I believe we must conclude that any case against the captain and crew of the *Dei Gratia* is extremely weak, and is based on several puzzling factors that could be explained if we had all the facts.

In March, 1873, the court, while expressing no opinion as to why the brigantine had been abandoned, awarded £1,700 (about $8,500) to the *Dei Gratia* for services rendered—this amount being approximately one-fifth of the sworn value of the ship and her cargo.

The *Mary Celeste* was returned to her owners. Captain George W. Blatchford, who had been sent from America to take over the vessel, sailed to Genoa where he unloaded her cargo. Then he returned to the United States.

Why was the *Mary Celeste* abandoned?
Circumstances aboard indicate the same cause that has cost so

much human life on land—panic! As to what inspired this panic, there are three theories.

The first was considered probable by Captain Morehouse and Captain James Briggs, a brother of the missing master. The vessel may have been becalmed on that November 25. When the ship began drifting toward the precipitous rocks of Santa Maria Island, the crew quickly took to the boat to await the outcome. Then a sudden breeze carried the ship away from them and their boat was swamped.

The fact that the brigantine held roughly to her course for ten more days, however, seems to imply that she was abandoned on a later date.

The second theory is held by a majority of writers who have carefully studied the mystery, including Edward Rowe Snow and J. G. Lockhart.[4] It was first suggested by James Winchester, principal owner of the *Celeste*, when he arrived at Gibraltar during the court hearing.

The cargo was crude alcohol—1,700 barrels. According to Winchester, Captain Briggs had never carried such a cargo before and was unfamiliar with its vagaries. We know from court testimony that at least one barrel was damaged (Snow says nine barrels).

Buffeted by gales and heavy seas in cold December temperatures since leaving New York, the cargo, even though well stowed, was severely shaken up. Upon reaching the Azores, warmer weather would cause the barrels to leak and sweat, creating vapor. Enough force from the built-up pressure may have been generated to blow the forward hatch cover off. On the other hand, Captain Briggs may have ordered the two hatch covers opened to permit the fumes to escape.

What appeared to be smoke would have poured forth, possibly followed by ominous sounds. Was the cargo about to explode? The captain's first responsibility was to his wife, child, and crew, not the safety of the cargo. The sea was relatively calm. He ordered abandonment of the vessel simply as a precaution.

As the seamen released the yawl from its lashings over the main hatch, Mate Richardson would have secured the chronometer and ship's papers. A section of the deck railing was removed, and the yawl was lowered into the sea. In their haste the men forgot their boots, oilskins, and pipes.

THE CLASSIC DRIFTER

Now the main peak halyard, three hundred feet long, was made ready for towing and attached to the small boat's painter. At the end of such a long towline the yawl would ride safely as they waited to see if the ship would blow up.

Then, as they waited, the wind freshened. Captain Briggs may have decided to return to the *Celeste*. As the men began pulling on the line, a stiff breeze filled the sails and the main peak halyard snapped. Desperately, they rowed in an effort to catch up with the vessel, but the brigantine was blown far beyond their reach.

How long they drifted, cold and helpless, no one will ever know. The seas grew heavier in the growing wind as the yawl, loaded with ten persons, rose and fell. Finally a heavy wave capsized the boat, and thus they died.

Snow believes the abandonment took place on the morning of November 25 since the beds in the cabins had not been made up. He says the weather report from the Ponta Delgada Station in the Azores reveals that a storm raged the night of November 24, but by morning it had subsided. By afternoon a cold front moved in, accompanied by a bad gale that would have swamped the yawl.

All this, however, could have happened on a later date.

Although there are objections to this theory, they do not eliminate it altogether. Both Gould and Wilkins believe that any explosion violent enough to send the crew overboard would have left evidence in signs of fire or damage. However, a minor explosion that would blow off a hatch cover would not necessarily do other damage in a tightly stowed hold. Moreover, fumes that resembled smoke might be sufficient to frighten seamen unfamiliar with alcoholic effects.

The third theory was first expressed by Mate Oliver Deveau and is supported by Gould.

At the Gibraltar court sessions Sir James Cochrane asked Deveau if he had any idea why the *Celeste* was abandoned.

"My idea is that the crew got alarmed," Deveau replied, "and, by the sounding rod being found lying alongside the pumps, that they had sounded the pumps and found perhaps a quantity of water in the pumps at the moment, and thinking she would go down, abandoned her."

Gould tells us that the ship had been through heavy weather and was still carrying only a small amount of sail set. However, the sea must have gone down to some extent since the hatches had been opened to inspect the cargo.

"Some of the water between decks may have found its way into the holds," he writes,* "and given the impression that the ship was leaking badly. So the pump-plunger was drawn and the well sounded by some excitable hand who misread the depth and, leaving the plunger where it lay, spread the alarm that the ship was on the point of going down under their feet. And panic followed."

As to the belief that Captain Briggs would have investigated and stopped the panic, Gould suggests that he was no longer there to do so. He may have died of a heart attack or other sudden illness, or he may have been swept overboard—with others—during the storm.

Without an experienced, responsible officer to stop them, the crew could have given way to panic and quickly launched the yawl, with or without a towline. And the vessel, still under sail, would have forged ahead, leaving the crew behind in the boat, perhaps without food or water, to starve or drown.

Such an occurrence would not be unique.

In 1919 the schooner *Marion G. Douglas* was abandoned by her crew off the Newfoundland Banks under the erroneous impression that she was sinking. If the men had stopped to think, they would have realized that the vessel's cargo of timber made its possibility of sinking extremely remote. It was a case of sheer panic.

The *Marion G. Douglas,* under sail but a derelict, then sailed herself across the Atlantic and was later found off the Scilly Isles, south of Ireland, where another vessel towed her into port for salvage.

Again, in 1770, Captain Cook's ship *Endeavour* was off the Australian coast when the carpenter was sent to sound the well. He misread the depth, spread an alarm, and for some time the crew believed that the ship would sink in a matter of minutes.[5] Calm was restored by the experienced captain.

We can disregard the fantastic "explanations" for the *Mary Celeste*'s abandonment of past decades—the giant squid or octopus, the plagues, the volcanic gases. And we can forget the blood-and-thunder yarns of bogus "survivors" with their tales of mutiny, piracy, and homicidal maniacs.

One of the three simple and rational solutions to the mystery

---

* *The Stargazer Talks,* p. 29.

must be the correct one. They fit the circumstances without the necessity of imaginative flights.

In the years that followed, the *Mary Celeste* had several owners. Most of the time she was in American coastal service, but she made at least one voyage to South America, where she lost part of her deck cargo of lumber and her rigging in a storm.

Late in 1884, twelve years after she achieved immortality off the Azores in the annals of the sea, the *Celeste* was over twenty-three years old. Her bottom was barnacled and she leaked badly in heavy weather. Her hull was scarred and her woodwork needed paint.

On December 16 she left Boston with a crew of seven for Port-au-Prince, Haiti, under the command of Captain Gilman C. Parker, sixty-one, of Winthrop, Massachusetts. The cargo was listed and insured as the finest quality of shoes, butter, and ale, but some of the boxes and bottles were empty and the items that existed were the cheapest of inferior products.

On January 3, 1885, the vessel entered Haiti's Gulf of Gonave, a bay which has Port-au-Prince at its eastern apex. Two channels in the bay are divided by Gonave Island. Captain Parker chose the southern channel in the middle of which is a coral reef called Rochelois Bank surrounded by deep, safe water.

As the ship approached the reef, Captain Parker ordered the helmsman, a youth named Ernest Berthold, to hold the course straight ahead. Berthold objected and spun the wheel. He was too late! With a crash the *Celeste* smashed into the reef. Splinters from her bottom floated to the surface. The time was shortly after noon.

As water began entering the hold, Captain Parker set the crew to work bringing the cargo on deck. Late in the afternoon he ordered the mast cut away. That night the crew slept on the grounded vessel.

On the following day the crew rowed ashore. The captain sold the cargo valued at $30,000 by the shippers for $500 and paid off his men. After the cargo had been removed, kerosene was poured over the ship and she was burned.

Thus died the ill-starred *Mary Celeste*.

Back in Boston an insurance agent became suspicious. Two investigators, Kingman N. Putnam and Henry M. Rogers, uncovered convincing evidence that Captain Parker, in collusion with others, had sailed with a fraudulent cargo and deliberately wrecked the ship.

The captain and three other defendants were tried for barratry in the federal court at Boston. Conviction on the charge carried the death penalty. The aged and penitent Parker aroused the jury's pity. They asked the judge if they could acquit Parker and find the others guilty. The judge said this could not be done.

The case ended in a hung jury and the defendants were released. Within days one of the defendants went insane. A member of one of the shipping firms involved committed suicide. All of the firms that participated in the fraudulent cargo were bankrupt within six months after the trial.[6]

Most accounts state that Captain Parker died three months after his release. But Edward Rowe Snow tells us he lived for seven more years, dying in 1891. In disgrace, his last job was crossing-tender on the Narrow Gauge Railroad at Winthrop Beach Station. He paid in humiliation for his crime.

Today the blackened ribs of the *Mary Celeste* lie beneath the waves off Rochelois Bank. Few persons know the location of her lonely grave in the tropic waters of a Caribbean bay far from her Nova Scotian birthplace.

Yet she is the most famous of mystery ships. Since that gray, bleak day in the misty Atlantic back in 1872 when she was found forlorn and deserted, her story is the classic example of mystery at sea.

THE MOST FAMOUS DERELICT

The story of the twin-screw motorship *Joyita* is more than the tale of a ship that met a strange fate. It is also the story of the passengers who mysteriously vanished from its decks. In the enigmatic climax of its maritime career, the *Joyita* has become the *Mary Celeste* of the Pacific.

There was Captain Thomas H. "Dusty" Miller, the skipper. A good-natured, middle-aged Welshman, he had a dark complexion, a long but narrow mustache, and a short beard that extended from ear to ear.

Dusty Miller was an experienced seaman. He was also a colorful character who frequently wore a lava-lava (male sarong) at sea. But when he set sail on his last voyage, he was a desperate man, plagued by troubles.

The mate was "Chuck" Simpson, an American Indian who had come out to the islands in 1954 and married a Samoan girl. Known locally as "Captain Jah," Simpson, in his mid-thirties, was a powerful man with a barrel chest. Some of his friends said he was making his last voyage before settling down with his wife on a Pacific island.

Most prominent among the passengers was R. D. Pearless, twenty-nine, the recently appointed district governor of the Tokelau Islands, fresh from New Zealand. He was a tall, slim man, with fair hair, serious and concerned about his responsibilities.

Next, there was Dr. Parsons, forty-one, a burly, heavy-set, handsome Irishman. Wounded during World War II, he walked with a limp. His friends blamed permanent head injuries for the fact that he could become violent and even dangerous under the influence of alcohol.

Sailing with the doctor was J. Hodgkinson, nicknamed "Herb," a medical dispenser at Apia Hospital. He was a quiet, pleasant man of about fifty, married and the father of three children.

Another passenger was G. K. Williams, a gray-haired man of

sixty-one, a retired manager for the Yorkshire Insurance Company of New Zealand. He and his companion, J. Wallwork, represented E. A. Coxon and Co., Ltd., who had chartered the *Joyita*. Williams was carrying £1,000 in Samoan bank notes to be used in buying copra.

The crew included two Gilbertese islanders, Tokoka, the bosun, and Tanini, the engineer, who were devoted to Miller.

The rest of the passengers were natives of the islands. Altogether, the vessel carried twenty-five persons, including two children.

The *Joyita* was a beautiful ship, diesel-powered, with an overall length of sixty-nine feet and a beam of seventeen feet. She was seventy tons gross and forty-seven tons net weight.

At 5 A.M. on the third of October, 1955, the *Joyita* left Apia, Western Samoa, for the port of Fakaofo in the Tokelau Islands, 270 miles to the north. The voyage would require about forty hours.

Certainly no early morning observer at the docks would have felt any apprehension as he watched the *Joyita*, white and trim, sailing north in excellent weather over the blue waters in the growing light of dawn. In terms of inter-island traffic, the trip would be a short one.

Later investigation, however, would reveal that if ever a vessel set sail destined for trouble, it was the *Joyita*. No one aboard her would ever be seen again. And whatever happened to her crew and passengers, according to computation of the diesel fuel consumption, occurred soon after she left port.

When the vessel failed to arrive at Fakaofo, a search was launched. Planes of the Royal New Zealand Air Force took off from Laucala Bay, Fiji, and eventually covered an estimated 130,000 square miles of the sea, but no trace of the ship was found. Apparently the *Joyita*, like so many ships since man first took to the sea, had simply vanished.

Then, early on the morning of November 10—the thirty-seventh day after the vessel left Apia, the British colony ship *Tuvalu* sighted a derelict wallowing lifelessly in the swells some 450 miles west-southwest of Apia. Captain Gerald Douglas ordered the course changed for a closer look.

The derelict was half water-logged, listing at about fifty-five degrees to port with her port rail under water. As it rose from the troughs to the crests in the light sea, the name of the ship painted in bold, black letters on its side could be clearly read.

Captain Douglas sent a "landing party" to the *Joyita*. There was no one aboard, although there was a possibility of bodies in the flooded compartments. The port side superstructure, which included the funnel, had been washed or blown away, and the logbook was missing.[1]

A canvas awning aft of the bridge had been lashed over a broken stanchion after the accident that had carried away a part of the superstructure. Since the purpose of the awning could only be for catching rainwater or protection from the sun, it was evident that at least one person had remained aboard the damaged ship.

Captain Douglas radioed his discovery to Suva in the Fiji Islands. The Colonial Secretary had the Fijian tender *Degei* tow the derelict ninety miles to the harbor at Vanua Levu where the water was pumped out. Captain Robert James of the tender reported that no bodies or holes in the hull were found, and as far as construction of the vessel was concerned, it was seaworthy.

Next, the *Joyita* was towed to Suva where it was hauled up on a slip completely out of the water. Marine and salvage experts made an intensive examination of the craft. Other investigators began checking into the background of Captain Miller, the passengers, and the ship in preparation for an official inquiry.

Meanwhile, the discovery of the *Joyita,* silent and deserted, became world-wide news. A massive search for possible survivors was started and continued for weeks, but it was fruitless.

In the bars at Suva and Apia, speculation about the fate of the passengers soon launched wild rumors. One involved the Japanese, who are unpopular in Fiji. The presence of Japanese fishing fleets in the waters around the islands is resented.

On November 19 the Fiji *Times and Herald,* described by *Life* magazine as "a small but vigorous South Seas newspaper" (December 12, 1955), came out with a headline: ALL ABOARD JOYITA MURDERED.

Referring to an unidentified but "irreproachable source in Suva," the story said it was assumed that the *Joyita* had passed through a Japanese fishing fleet known to have been operating along the ship's course to the Tokelaus, that the passengers had seen "something the Japanese did not want them to see," and that the resentful Japanese boarded the *Joyita* and either murdered or took prisoner the passengers and crew.

The British Colonial Office, which usually ignores newspaper comment, reacted immediately to this imaginative newspaper story. Within a few hours after publication, the Fijian Colonial Secretary A. F. H. Stoddart issued a statement of denial:

"I say most emphatically that the report is not true. It is not the view of the government of Fiji nor is it a view held in responsible official circles."[2]

The secretary added that no official opinion on the disaster would be possible until a full and technical examination of the ship had been completed, but "all the evidence so far obtained . . . supports the suggestion that the cause of the disaster was natural causes—that is to say, that she was overwhelmed as a result of some freak weather at a time when perhaps her engines had stopped."

Two days later marine inspectors, after a preliminary study, said the disappearance of passengers and crew "could be explained in only one way—a seaquake."[3]

Earlier in 1955 a Tongan vessel not far from the Fijis had been struck by a sudden, violent undersea eruption that had thrown her crew and passengers overboard. Port authorities confirmed that the area had a record for volcanic eruptions and that islands in the vicinity had been known to "pop up and down."

A check with other vessels in the area throughout the time of the *Joyita*'s disappearance, however, failed to produce any evidence of an eruption or seaquake. Freak waves are certainly not unknown on the Pacific, but it is unlikely that all persons aboard would be on the deck at the same time.

There was no evidence of a fire, explosion, or collision. Loss of the port superstructure was apparently due to the pounding of waves after the ship heeled over. Seamen said waterspouts would not have damaged the ship sufficiently to scare everybody overboard.

There were other theories and rumors—mutiny, piracy, deliberate scuttling, but all fail to explain all the facts, as we shall see.

The disappearance of the M.S. *Arakarimoa* resulted in another harvest of rumors. With eight passengers and a crew of fifteen, the sixty-foot vessel left Tarawa for port in Maiana in the Gilbert Islands on the evening of December 28, 1955. The cargo was seven hundred empty copra sacks.

According to the New Zealand *Herald* (February 7, 1956), the

Arakarimoa left Tarawa with her sister ship, *Aratoba,* and both ships were in sight of each other until midnight when the *Arakarimoa* put on speed and went out of sight. The *Aratoba* arrived at Tebikerai anchorage on December 29 at 5:30 A.M.

The missing vessel was in excellent condition and her engines had been "extensively overhauled" in Tarawa. Maximum current drift was about three knots and the direction WNW and WSW.

Captain A. B. Macadie of the survey ship *Tunaru* is quoted by the New Zealand *Herald*: "In 36 hours—between the time of the first alarm and the Royal Colony ship *Nareau*'s search—the *Arakarimoa* could have drifted no more than 100 miles." The *Nareau* began its search on December 30 and covered 1,700 square miles.[4]

The rumor this time was pirating submarines. On February 3, 1956, the crew of the M.S. *Komaiwai* reported sighting a submarine near Kandavu in Fijian waters. A Royal New Zealand Air Force Sunderland made an unsuccessful search. Several days later passengers aboard the *Tuivalavala* between Kandavu and Benqa Islands said they saw a dark object about a mile away that resembled a submarine. It disappeared suddenly.

On February 10, the New Zealand *Herald,* referring to the *Komaiwai* report, said the Chief of the Naval Staff, Rear Admiral J. E. H. McBeath, had expressed his opinion that the object "was a whale sleeping on the surface." He added: "Our reports said it came within twelve yards of a lighted ship. No self-respecting sub captain would take his ship that close unless something had gone wrong."

But on February 14 a fisherman said he observed a strange vessel lying inshore near Pawarenga on the west coast of Northland, New Zealand. It was lying motionless, appearing about forty feet long with no mast or funnel, and with a sweeping bow and stern. A Navy spokesman said the report did not "fit in with what we felt would be the actions of a submarine." He suggested the object was probably a trawler.

Earlier, however, in this general area of the Hauraki Gulf and the Coromandel Peninsula, strange events had occurred.

On the stormy night of February 3 five "rockets" were observed south of Leigh at Kawau, apparently from a craft in trouble in the Haurika Gulf. They were fired at two minute intervals.

The New Zealand *Herald* (February 6) reported: "Rockets

Seen off Kawau Are Mystery." The account said no ships were missing and other vessels in the area had not seen any ships in distress.

Seven days later, on February 10, a violent explosion coming from the sea shook Leigh. Cause of the blast is not known.

Finally, on February 16, the Fijian government made a tentative identification of the mystery craft lurking near Fiji from sketches drawn by a native skipper who spotted the craft when it surfaced. It was a long range Russian submarine.[5]

Meanwhile, the investigation of the *Joyita* mystery was continuing.

Since most accounts of the *Joyita* give conflicting details, I am relying on the report of Robin Maugham, the writer and novelist, as published in *Argosy* in June, 1962. Maugham went to Fiji to make a personal investigation. He read all the official reports. He interviewed the men involved in the investigation. He uncovered new information.

Maugham was so fascinated by the mystery that he purchased the *Joyita*.

"I now own the *Joyita*," he writes. ". . . I'm glad I own her, because I honestly believe that I'm the only person who has found a solution to the mystery of what happened to the twenty-five people on board the *Joyita,* so I have a kind of proprietorial feeling towards her."

To understand a person, a place, or a ship, one should know something about his or its history and background.

The *Joyita* was built in 1931 by the Wilmington Boat Works in Los Angeles. Its construction was solid—the hull made of two-inch cedar planking on oak frames. . . . Its lines were trim and graceful.

Her first owner was Roland West, a former movie director and husband of the film actress, Jewel Carmen. Since Joyita means "Little Jewel," the vessel was probably named for Miss Carmen.

West was a business partner with actress Thelma Todd, whose strange death in December, 1935, is a classic Hollywood mystery.

Some writers state that the ship was once owned by Mary Pickford,[6] but her name does not appear in Maugham's list of owners.

In those days the *Joyita* was a happy ship, sailing along the California coast, her passengers the famed personalities of stage and screen.

In 1936 she was sold to Milton E. Bacon who retained owner-ship until World War II. Then, during the war, the U.S. Navy used the vessel as a patrol ship.

After the war the Navy sold the vessel to the firm of Louis Brothers in Honolulu and she was converted into a fishing boat with refrigerated holds. The new owners also installed two new 225-hp Gray marine diesel engines.

Finally, in September, 1952, the *Joyita* was purchased by Dr. Ellen Katherine Luomala, an American citizen and lecturer in anthropology at the University of Hawaii, Honolulu. A few weeks later she chartered the ship to her friend Dusty Miller. Thus the vessel was registered in Honolulu and flew the United States flag, although Miller was a British subject.

Until April, 1954, Miller conducted fishing operations out of Hawaii under the name of Phoenix Island Fisheries, at first with moderate success and later at a loss. He then went to Pago Pago in American Samoa, but his bad luck continued.

The refrigeration equipment wasn't working properly and some of his fish went bad. He got deeply in debt and was unable to pay his harbor fees. The American authorities brought pressure to bear on him, and they finally seized some of his ship's papers, presumably as a lien to assure future payment and to prevent Dusty from selling a ship he didn't own.

In March, 1955, he left American (Eastern) Samoa for Apia in Western Samoa, which is under New Zealand trusteeship. There he met R. D. Pearless, who only recently had been ap-pointed district officer of the Tokelau Islands. Pearless accom-panied Miller on a one-month combined fishing trip and tour of inspection of the islands. They arrived back at Apia on May first.

Pearless, as stated in the Commission of Inquiry report, "was particularly anxious to establish better and more regular com-munications between Western Samoa and the islands under his care."[7]

The *Joyita* was the answer to the problems of both men. Miller was almost destitute. Discouraged over the failure of his fishing ventures, he welcomed an opportunity to sail his ship and still make a living. Pearless hoped to have the vessel chartered by the Western Samoan government on an annual basis for the trans-port of supplies to the Tokelaus. But the government refused to grant the charter because Miller was unable to produce certain of the ship's papers still being held by the American authorities in Pago Pago. And, meanwhile, Miller had no resources to undertake additional fishing voyages.

For five months, from May through September, the *Joyita* lay at anchor in Apia harbor. It was a period of bitter frustration for Dusty Miller. He lived alone on the ship, his crew having scattered when there was no money to pay them. Once he admitted to a friend that for several days he had nothing to eat, and once had only a small loaf of bread for three days. Miller was too proud to go to the club when he had no money to buy drinks. That he managed to exist at all can be attributed to the kindness of friends and several odd jobs he managed to find.

Yet Dusty always had a smile on his face and a joke to tell. His friends, interviewed by Maugham, agreed that he was honest and always paid his debts when he had the money. But months of waiting and lack of proper food had exhausted him by the time October approached. At the official inquiry, a friend described him as "pretty well run down . . . he was a worried man."

Adding to Miller's worries was a problem back home.

During World War II he had sailed the South Pacific. Then he had returned to Wales, married, and attempted to live the life of a landsman. But after several years he had answered the call of the sea.

Now, back in Cardiff, his wife, Beatrice Matilda Miller, had charged him with desertion. Divorce proceedings were scheduled to be held early in October.

Miller was proud of the *Joyita*. When the vessel had been converted into a refrigerated fishing boat in Honolulu, 640 cubic feet of cork had been placed in her hold. It is important to remember that Miller knew, and often boasted, that his ship was practically unsinkable.

By the end of September the situation in the Tokelau Islands was becoming very serious. The islanders badly needed medical supplies as well as basic foodstuffs—flour, rice and sugar. Also, there were seventy tons of copra in the islands waiting for export.

Pearless was desperate. If the government would not charter the *Joyita,* he would look elsewhere. He was finally able to arrange a charter with E. A. Coxon and Company, Ltd., a Samoan copra trading firm.

It was the opportunity Dusty Miller had been waiting for. With some difficulty he succeeded in rounding up a crew. Chuck Simpson agreed to sign up as his mate since a ship of American registry must have an officer who is an American citizen. Tokoka and Tanini, the Gilbert islanders in his former crew, returned. The last man in the crew was found only four days before sailing.

After five months of idleness, the vessel was not in good condition. Miller and his crew worked long hours to get the ship ready with all equipment operating. The primary difficulty was with the engines, and especially the clutch to the port engine.

Miller told Mr. Von Reiche, the charterer, that he had experienced trouble with the clutch previously, but that it could be easily repaired and he would fix it during the trip. Since the *Joyita* was found with her port engine clutch partly disconnected, it seems evident that the vessel went to sea with only one engine in operation.

On previous voyages the *Joyita* had failed to maintain contact with Apia Radio. The Superintendent of Radio notified Miller that he should work Apia Radio at 10 A.M. and 4 P.M. daily, and he asked Miller to test his transmitter before leaving.

Miller ignored the request. After the ship had sailed, however, Mr. Von Reiche notified the station that Miller had agreed to work the *Joyita* at the times suggested, and that the vessel's call letters were WNIM. Apia Radio called and listened at the assigned times thereafter, but there was never a reply.

In addition to Pearless, two other New Zealand government representatives were to sail. They were Dr. Parsons, a physician, and J. Hodgkinson, dispenser at Apia Hospital. They were to accompany the medical supplies and check on health conditions in the Tokelaus.

At the inquiry Mr. T. R. Smith, Acting High Commissioner, explained that he had approved the sailing of the vessel as a "mercy trip" to get badly needed medical supplies to the islands.

Under terms of the registration, the *Joyita* was not authorized to carry passengers. Earlier Miller had overcome this restriction by listing Pearless as supercargo.

The *Joyita* attempted to set sail on Sunday morning, October second. Commander Peter Plowman, Member for Marine in the government, was watching from his home which overlooks the harbor. He saw a burst of black smoke, then the vessel drifted rapidly toward a reef until an anchor was thrown out.

"After I'd seen that performance," Plowman told Maugham, "I rang the acting high commissioner to ask him if he didn't think we ought to take off our officers who were on board. But we decided to leave it until Monday morning, and by then she was gone. . . . He (Dusty) knew we'd have stopped him if he'd stayed in harbor on Monday morning."

Meanwhile the European passengers left the ship and went to the club to wait until the engine was repaired and have a few drinks. They expected to sail by evening.

At 5 A.M. the following morning when the *Joyita* did sail, Captain Miller and his crew were exhausted from long hours of hard, dirty labor, and the passengers were irritable and short-tempered.

Thus the *Joyita* began her fateful voyage—without a properly equipped lifeboat, with a defective radio transmitter, with only one engine that could be trusted, and illegally carrying passengers. Moreover, Captain Miller was a tired and desperate skipper, hoping to make good on the charter and have one last chance at success.

Dusty was a good seaman, but he badly needed the money from the charter. Quite likely it was his knowledge that the ship was unsinkable that gave him the courage to set sail and take a chance.

The Commission of Inquiry met in Apia on February 3, 1956. The testimony revealed some additional facts.

Whatever happened probably occurred on the night of October 3, the day she sailed. Light switches, including the masthead navigation light, were turned on. The clocks, which operated on the ship's generators, had stopped at 10:53. Fuel consumption and the fact that barnacles were growing above the waterline were evidence the ship had been out of commission and listing for weeks.

Salt-encrusted radio equipment found after the vessel was pumped out was tuned to 2,182 kilocycles, the emergency frequency for small ships. However, the break in the aerial lead above the transmitter would have prevented the signal from being heard more than two miles away.

The deck cargo, consisting of 2,000 feet of lumber and a number of empty oil drums, was missing. Some of this material might have been used to make an extra raft; the rest of it may have been jettisoned. If not, it should have fallen into the sea when the ship listed. In either case, the material should have floated on the surface.

"Deck cargo, timber, and empty drums from the *Joyita* should have left a path like a trail of blazing lights across the Pacific," said a member of the Western Samoa Legislative Assembly. "But not one item of cargo has been found." [8]

What happened to the lumber and drums?

More mysterious is the disappearance of the cargo from the holds. Seven cases of aluminum stripping (used for rat guards on cocoanut trees) were missing from the midship hold. And seventy bags of foodstuffs—flour, sugar and rice—their weight ranging from 56 to 150 pounds—had disappeared from the after hold.

Was all of this cargo jettisoned, or was the vessel looted?

There was other food on board and the main refrigerators contained meat that was in a very obvious state of decomposition when the ship was found.

The three Carley floats, lifebelts, the logbook, sextant, and compasses were missing.

It may have been optimism on Miller's part, but 2,640 gallons of diesel fuel were on board, enough to give the ship a range of about 3,000 miles. The vessel also carried food supplies and water for a much longer voyage than 270 miles.

Captain E. L. James, assistant harbormaster, reported that after the vessel had been pumped out, he had heard the sound of water coming into the engine room. Investigation revealed that the water was pouring in through a broken one-inch pipe on the port bilge well below the floor plates. It was badly corroded, and a section of the pipe had fallen away.

The captain explained that a galvanized pipe had been threaded into a brass T-piece in the salt water cooling system for the engine. The heat of tropical water sets up an electrolytic action when a ferrous metal is joined to a non-ferrous metal.

This discovery explained the cause of the flooding. It explained why the ship had become waterlogged making it a difficult object to be seen by search planes.

Since the pipe leak was nine inches below the engine room floor and the noise of the diesel drowned out the sound of the entering water, the location of the leak was apparently never found by the crew.

Four mattresses had been found in the engine room. Apparently the crew planned to use them to block the leak when it was located or to prevent the spray thrown by the flywheel from short-circuiting the electrical equipment.

The two bilge pumps were inefficient, probably because cotton waste and rubbish had accumulated in the suction pipes. A motor had been lashed to a beam across the engines in a desperate attempt to pump the water out.

After hearing twenty-eight witnesses, the commission announced its verdict[9] that the "cause of the casualty was flooding of the vessel, due primarily to the corrosion and breaking of the one-inch galvanized pipe which formed part of the cooling system of the port auxiliary engine."

Since the *Joyita* did not have watertight bulkheads, the water flooded the entire ship, stopping the engines and generator. The ship became unmanageable and fell broadside to the seas.

Robin Maugham, however, discovered one important bit of evidence that was never given to the Commission of Inquiry. He heard about it from Commander Peter Plowman who had been scheduled to testify but was later told his testimony would not be needed because the evidence he could give had been covered by earlier witnesses. Maugham bases his theory of what happened on this key evidence.

Plowman said that as Member for Marine, he had been sent to look over the *Joyita* at Suva. In the midst of rubbish in the scuppers, he found a doctor's stethoscope, a scalpel, some needles and catgut, and four lengths of bloodstained bandages.

Obviously, someone had been injured. And it must have been Captain Miller. Every one of Miller's friends, and even the judge who presided at the Commission of Inquiry, agreed that Miller would never have left his unsinkable *Joyita* for a float in a shark-infested sea. And if he had been in charge, he would not have permitted the passengers to leave the ship.

Plowman also said no attempt had been made to get out sea anchors, though a very effective one could have been made from the lumber lying on the deck.

Finally, there was the fact that the awning aft of the bridge had been secured after the damage to the port side superstructure. This superstructure had been added when the ship was converted to a fishing vessel, and its construction was not as sturdy as the rest of the ship.

It seems apparent that the superstructure was damaged soon after the ship began listing, probably by a heavy wave.

What, then, happened aboard the *Joyita*?

This is what Robin Maugham believes occurred:

THE MOST FAMOUS DERELICT 157

Soon after the *Joyita* left Apia, the port engine (if it had been operating at all) stopped. That night the ship ran into heavy seas and the strain broke the corroded pipe below the engine room floor. Sea water poured into the ship. The pumps were inadequate due to the blocked suction pipes. An auxiliary pump was lashed to a beam, but before it could be connected the water was over it. Meanwhile, the mattresses had been dragged down into the engine room, but the leak beneath the floor could not be located.

The starboard engine stopped when the water reached a height of eighteen inches. Meanwhile, the radio transmitter had been tuned to the distress frequency, but its signals failed to carry due to the break in the aerial lead.

Now the ship was plunged into darkness, became unmanageable and fell broadside. At this point—or shortly later—a freak wave tore away the port-side superstructure, adding to the flooding.

At some time prior to or during these events Dusty Miller was hurt. He was nervous, tired, and in poor health. There may have been an argument. He may have lost his balance. He probably fell or was thrown from the bridge to the deck, suffering severe head injuries.

Either Dr. Parsons or Mr. Hodgkinson gave him first aid as evidenced by the medical materials and bandages found by Commander Plowman. He was probably unconscious.

Frightened and in panic, the passengers may have jettisoned part of the cargo to lighten the vessel. It is extremely unlikely that all of it was thrown overboard under the circumstances.

Not knowing that the *Joyita* was almost unsinkable, they then made fast the Carley floats and tossed them into the sea. By this time the ship would be listing heavily and waves would be breaking over the decks. They may have seen a reef to the south and thought land was near. They cut the ropes to the floats and drifted away, only to have the rafts capsize in the rough sea.

But someone stayed aboard with Miller. Maugham thinks it may have been Tanini, the Gilbertese islander who was so devoted to Dusty.

The money being carried by Mr. G. K. Williams to buy copra—£950 in bank notes and £50 in silver—had been in a strong box in Miller's cabin. Williams might have ignored the heavy silver and stuffed the bank notes in his clothing, yet he knew the Bank of

Samoa would replace the notes, as they did later. It is unlikely that he took the money with him on the float.

Simpson, however, may have taken the compasses, chronometer, and logbook.

The storm passed. On the following day Tanini put up the awning, tying the ropes with sailor's knots over the broken stanchion to protect Miller from the hot sun.

Sometime during the next few days—or even weeks—the drifting hulk was sighted by another vessel. They hailed her. There was no reply. They launched a boat and boarded the *Joyita*.

Miller was dead. Tanini may have attacked the men and in doing so lost his balance and fallen into the sea. The newcomers were now alone. They had not come as pirates, but they could not resist temptation. Quickly they looted the ship after dropping Miller's body overboard.

"And their ship sailed to other shores," writes Maugham, "leaving the *Joyita* alone on the calm sea, waterlogged, with a list to port, and with not one soul on board, drifting slowly toward the setting sun."

Robin Maugham's explanation is clever, covers known facts and may well be approximately correct. Yet there will always be unanswered questions.

Chuck Simpson certainly knew the ship was cork-lined. He had survived three shipwrecks during World War II. Why didn't he remain on board? And if he did, what happened to him? Were the looters far more dangerous men than simple islanders who took advantage of an opportunity?

The ship was placed on the auction block in July, 1956,[10] and sold to David Simpson, a Fiji planter, for $5,400. On January 7, 1957, tagged as a "hoodoo" ship, she struck a horseshoe reef and was abandoned. Later she floated off the reef under her own power and was finally taken to the beach of Levuka on the island of Ovalau.[11]

Early in 1961 Dusty Miller was declared officially dead by Judge Temple Morris in a court at Cardiff, Wales, where Mrs. Miller's long-postponed divorce case was held. She was granted a divorce on grounds of desertion and presumption of death.

Judge Morris said that Captain Miller had sailed in an unseaworthy ship and had deceived people to get it to sea. "Had he reached his destination he might eventually have become a millionaire," the judge added. "But he never got there. Instead he became a corpse."

Robin Maugham announced his determination to see that the *Joyita* once more would know the sea. The Fijians believe the ship is haunted by the ghosts of the twenty-five missing persons. If so, the phantoms can be exorcized. The *Joyita* was a happy ship when she cruised along the California coast before the war, Maugham says, and she can be a happy ship again.

With the case of the *Joyita,* we might almost say that we have reached bottom—the lowest rung on the ladder of mystery—and re-entered the world of reality. There are, as I have said, several ways in which this tragedy could be lifted from the class of mystery but there remain, once again, undertones of the bizarre to say the least. In this case the question "how" *could* be answered; but again, the question "why" remains. And, *why* indeed should the *Mary Celeste* and the *Joyita* have become the classics of the deserted-ship sea mysteries of the Atlantic and the Pacific respectively? Why not any of the scores of others reported and fully documented, some of which were briefly mentioned in Chapter 9?

This book might be called facetiously "The In and Out of Sea Things," and so far we have dealt mostly with the in-coming—messages in bottles, mariners returned to safety, ghosts, spectral ships, floating morgues, and abandoned ships. Now, taking the miraculously returned *Joyita,* with her vanishing crew and passengers, as our nadir, we must turn to the grimmer side of our story and the side that brings on the creepy shivers and the feelings of utter hopelessness. Almost everything so far has appeared over the Invisible Horizon; the following have *disappeared* over it. So far, there is not one single thing that science, religion, the mystics, or anybody else has been able to offer by way of suggestion as to what happened: where these people and other things went; or what we might possibly be able to do about finding them. As to how to get them back, nobody, it appears, has even so much as considered it, though there is a more than strange series of letters from a person unknown—real, unreal, or merely imaginative—that purports to tell us plainly and directly just how to do this. This may be entirely fatuous but, once anything has been said, however insane it may sound, it should be taken into consideration, for we are dealing here with matters that nobody knows anything about and almost everybody denies even exist.

Yet, since dozens of modern aircraft with their crews and passengers have now vanished unaccountably in one limited area alone, it is high time that we at least tried out anything and tested everything that is suggested as a possible way of solving this ghastly riddle. Had not scientists tested "crazy" ideas throughout the ages we would still be sleeping behind lean-tos and chasing wild horses or digging for roots. Our cosmos is a great deal more complicated than we realize even now, and, if inexplicable things occur, we should do all we can to fathom them; and if some "nut" comes along with a suggestion as to what to do about them, we ought to find the time at least to listen to him on the off-chance that he may have stumbled across something that is worth-while. Such a procedure takes time, personnel, and money but, if your family had disappeared without trace in midair less than fifty miles from a large airport, would you not wish for everything possible to be done to find out why, and how to get them back? But we will come to this aspect of the matter later. For now, let me give a few examples of this terrifying matter of disappearances.

I will start off with one of the weirdest cases in history and mostly because it did not take place under, on, or above the sea but beside it, on an island, albeit a minute one that might just as well have been a ship. In fact it is no more than a geologically anchored lightship.

Wherever British sailors gather, in the forecastles of ships or in far ports, and the talk turns to mysteries of the sea, there is one tale that will likely be told. It is the weird story of lonely men on a rocky promontory, of three lighthouse keepers who met a strange fate, and the puzzling logbook they left behind.

West of the Outer Hebrides off the Scottish coast lie the Seven Hunter islands, better known today as the Flannan Isles. To the east is the nearest land, the island of Lewis, largest of the Hebrides, twenty miles away. And to the west the North Atlantic stretches unbroken to North American shores.

The desolate Seven Hunters are the rocky tips of mountains projecting above the water. Uninhabited and bearing little vegetation, they stand bleak and forlorn beneath gray northern skies. The largest, only five hundred feet across at the longest point, is Eilean Mor.

Close to the sea lanes to Scotland and Scandinavian ports and the scene of frequent winter storms, the rocks were a menace to shipping. For hundreds of years they marked the final resting place of numerous ships. And on tranquil days when fishermen

162   *O-U-T—OUT!*

managed to land on Eilean Mor to search for the eggs of sea birds, they would find the bleached bones of shipwrecked sailors who had reached the drab rock only to die of hunger and thirst.

In the seventeenth century, after a life of service and devotion, kindly St. Flannan, then Bishop of Killaloe, decided to end his days alone, away from human contact. He came to Eilean Mor and built a small chapel out of the rough stone. From time to time his followers brought him enough food to live on.

Here on his desert of stone, surrounded on all sides by the majesty of the mighty Atlantic, he communed with God in the peace and solitude he had sought. After his death a legend grew that on his island one could find eternal peace. Dedicated to the God of Land and Sea, it was hallowed ground.

But to mariners the Seven Hunters symbolized only danger and death, and in 1899 the British government built a lighthouse on Eilean Mor. It was erected atop a rocky promontory over two hundred feet above the sea. The light of 140,000 candlepower would be visible for at least twenty-five miles on clear nights.

Since landing on Eilean Mor was frequently dangerous, east and west docks were built, and either could be used depending on the wind and the tide. Almost perpendicular steps were hewn out of the rock above each dock leading up the side of the promontory to the top.

Late in December the work was completed, and the lighthouse towered into the winter sky only a few feet from the crumbling ruins of St. Flannan's chapel. As the Northern Lighthouse Board supply vessel, the *Hesperus,* arrived with the four retired seamen who were to care for the light, a white blanket of snow covered the island and the raw winds of a northern winter howled dismally around the structure and over the chapel ruins.

Joseph Moore, a bluff Scottish ex-mariner who escaped the strange fate of his companions, later, before a board of inquiry, told of his first day on the bleak rock.

We were left alone when the ship returned to Scotland, and that night we lighted the big lamp and shot the first rays of light. It was a grand sight. We all felt rather friendly toward each other for we were all seafaring men and knew what it meant to the sailors when they could see the light and steer clear of the dangerous rocks.

But there was something strange in the air. Not terrible or fearful, but just a strange silence in the midst of the sea's roar, a peace we could not understand. From the tower we could see the ruins of the old chapel covered with snow. And the wind howled. We all felt it, but we thought that it was just the strangeness of the place . . . the newness of it.

So the first day passed. Then the days rolled by into weeks. Every two weeks the *Hesperus* arrived with mail and newspapers, supplies of oil and food. It would leave with one man who then enjoyed a vacation on the mainland. Two weeks on shore and six weeks on the island was the schedule for each man, leaving three men to tend the light.

But it was winter. Out of the arctic came violent storms, and mountainous waves lashed the huge rock, hungrily seeking to devour the tiny island and sending clouds of cold spray over the base of the lighthouse. The constant booming of the sea, the crash of the waves and their moan as they foamed and retreated relentlessly, emphasized their solitude and loneliness and tortured the men's nerves.

Trapped in their quarters, the men passed the dreary, monotonous days. After awhile there was little for each to say to the others, and they read and re-read their mail, newspapers, and books, or restlessly paced the small rooms at the tower's base.

On clear days they bundled up against the chill winds and tramped around the island, often pausing by the ruins where a saint three centuries before had found his sanctuary.

"Aye, that ruin was a strange place," Joseph Moore remembered. "We were old sailors and not much given to land legends. A good place on sunny days for a saint, rest his soul, but on stormy days—well, maybe then he could understand the wrath of God unleashed on the sea. But the old chapel was sorta peaceful, aye, sorta made you feel close to God."

So the days passed, and the men kept a log of the weather, adding now and then brief references to their little activities that broke the daily routine. Winter, with its gales and snow, was succeeded by spring, with its rain and fog.

At last summer came—days of peace and quiet when the sea was at rest and shining like a mirror. In the warm sunshine they spent the tranquil hours fishing or watching the eider ducks wing from surf to nest. Passing steamers often greeted them by tooting their fog horns.

Then fall came, and the return of rain and fog forecast the approaching winter. The men spoke less and less to each other. They withdrew into the solitude of their souls where thoughts are born that cannot be expressed. Then, with fierce winds from the frozen north, winter came once more.

Now the passing vessels no longer greeted them, but steered away from the threatening rocks. The days were chilly and gray, and the nights dark and lonely. Hour after dreary hour, they sat silently playing checkers or reading, listening to the wind and the sea.

On December 6, 1900, the tender *Hesperus* arrived and took off Joseph Moore for his two weeks' vacation. The men left behind to tend the light were Thomas Marshall, James Ducat, and Donald McArthur. Ducat had just ended his vacation.

"Looking ahead to shore leave?" the skipper asked, smiling.

"Aye," Moore answered. "It'll be good to be back on land for a space where you can see people, talk, and have a drink or two. 'Tis pretty lonely there sometimes."

The skipper nodded his head understandingly.

The two weeks passed all too quickly, and on December 21 Joseph Moore was again aboard the *Hesperus* ready to return for his six weeks' duty. During those two weeks the sea had been unusually calm for December, but a bad storm arose soon after the vessel left port.

For three days the tender rode the storm off the Scottish coast, then approached the Seven Hunters. But the seas were so violent that no landing was possible. For two more days and nights the vessel hovered several miles off Eilean Mor.

"Strange that we haven't seen the light the past two nights," the captain said. "Wonder if something is wrong."

"Aye," Moore replied, "I've been wondering too."

On the morning of December 26 the sea calmed to a glassy green and the ship drew near the east landing, her signal flags hoisted. The *Hesperus* blew its whistle.

But there was no sign of life from the lighthouse, no responding signal flags. Ordinarily the keepers could be seen coming down the steps to the dock, anxious for their mail and news from the outside world.

Puzzled, the captain ordered repeated blasts of the fog horn. The sounds wailed over the island and the watery wastes, but nothing stirred. The lighthouse stood bleak and silent against the winter sky.

The vessel's boat was lowered. Joseph Moore, carrying his ditty bag, climbed down to the boat, bewilderment in his pale blue eyes.

"There's certainly something wrong," said the captain. "I'm going in with you and look things over."

The captain, Moore, and six sailors rowed over to the dock. When the boat had been secured, the group, led by Moore, climbed the zig-zag steps cut into the rock up to the base of the lighthouse. As he reached the top, Moore shouted the names of his companions, but the only response was the echo of his own cries.

Everything in the living quarters was in order and the personal possessions of the keepers were intact. The clock had stopped, and the cold air told the searchers that there had been no fire in the stove for some time.

Moore climbed to the light. He found that the wicks had been cleaned and trimmed, the lenses polished, but the daytime cloth had not been placed over the lens. Meanwhile, the sailors searched the small island, including the chapel ruins and the rocks along the shore, but they found no clue to the vanished men.

And then Moore remembered the log. Perhaps there the mystery would be solved. With the captain at his side, Moore began reading the entries. The handwriting was Tom Marshall's.

"Dec. 12: Gale, north by north northwest. Sea lashed to fury. Stormbound. 9 P.M. Never seen such a storm. Waves very high. Tearing at lighthouse. Everything shipshape. Ducat irritable."

The two men exchanged puzzled glances. No storm had been reported that day. And Ducat, usually very good-natured, had just returned from his leave on shore. Why should he be irritable?

On the next page under the same date was another entry:

"12 P.M. Storm still raging. Wind steady. Stormbound. Cannot go out. Ship passed sounding fog horn. Could see lights of cabins. Ducat quiet. McArthur crying."

McArthur, a hardened, veteran seaman who had weathered the sea's worst blows, well known as a lusty, fearless brawler on land, crying! What could have been the mysterious, extraordinary situation that would make the strong McArthur weep?

"Dec. 13: Storm continued through night. Wind shifted west by north. Ducat quiet. McArthur praying."

Yesterday McArthur had wept. Today he was praying. Why? Moore turned to the next page.

"12 Noon. Gray daylight. Me, Ducat, and McArthur prayed."

The captain and Joseph Moore stared at each other in astonishment. Moore later reported that he had never known his com-

O-U-T—OUT!

panions to pray. Fear of the storm certainly was not the reason they had prayed at noon. All three of the men had lustily defied the most violent of storms on the open sea and returned again and again for more. The sea had been their home.

Moreover, on the dates recorded, no storm had been reported in the Outer Hebrides twenty miles distant, only moderate to heavy seas.

Then came the last and final entry in the puzzling log:

"Dec. 15: 1 P.M. Storm ended. Sea calm. God is over all."

So ends the log, eleven days before the *Hesperus* arrived. The storm that delayed the tender could not have been the storm referred to in the log. And what had happened on December 14, between the time when all three men prayed and the following day when the final entry had been made?

A board of inquiry was appointed. They arrived at Eilean Mor to find Moore and several sailors from the *Hesperus* caring for the light. Moore refused to stay any longer on the island. He was not anxious to find the "eternal peace" promised by the legend of St. Flannan.

Whatever happened to the missing men must have occurred on the 15th. The S.S. *Archer* reported that it passed the island on the night of December 15 and had a narrow escape from striking the rocks because no light was visible.

The investigators found that the only missing articles were the oilskins and seaboots of two of the men. They might have been swept into the sea, but what happened to the third man? Did he die in a futile effort to save the other two?

They also discovered that heavy waves had ripped off a railing and moved equipment stored 110 feet above the sea on a platform in the steps up to the lighthouse. But did this damage occur during the storm mentioned in the log or during the gale that delayed the arrival of the tender?

Had there been some curious freak storm that struck the island, but caused only heavy seas twenty miles away on the island of Lewis? The men could hardly have been swept away by this storm, if there had been one, for according to the log the storm had passed when the last entry was made. The storm was over and peace had come.

The board listened to the testimony of Joseph Moore and finally adjourned, puzzled, without a verdict. No additional information has come to light as the years have passed, and no theory of what happened has explained why rough seamen cried and prayed before they vanished. Could madness born of loneliness be the answer?

But the storm had ended, the sea was calm and God was over all at the end. Perhaps it was a peace we will never understand, a secret locked forever in the mute rocks of Eilean Mor, forever lost beneath the waves of the mighty Atlantic.[1]

There are apparently localized areas where ships—and now planes—have repeatedly vanished in numbers that altogether exceed the expectations of chance. There is one such in the Pacific now called the "Devil's Sea," that lies south of Japan, east of the Bonin Islands and Iwo Jima, and directly on the route between Japan and Guam.

After nine vessels disappeared in this area without trace between 1949 and 1954 with a loss of 215 lives, the Japanese authorities listed it as a special danger zone.

Only one radio signal was received from one of the lost ships. It consisted of one word—"sinking"—followed by silence.

There is, however, a factor here that must be taken into account. This is that the Devil's Sea is the scene of submarine volcanic activity that rims the Rampo Deep where the ocean floor drops to 34,600 feet—over six miles. In this region, two hundred miles south of Tokyo, in 1946 the crew of the British destroyer *Urania* witnessed the birth of a volcanic island, fifty feet in height and covering a square mile, though like other jack-in-the-box isles of ash, it was soon dissolved by waves, tides and currents.

In 1952 the Japanese survey ship *Kaiyo Maru* was blown up by an underwater volcanic explosion while off the Myojin Reef 320 miles south of Tokyo. Another survey ship, the *Shihyo Maru,* disappeared in the region in 1955.

It is unlikely, however, that volcanic activity accounts for all the disappearances of ships, and more especially of aircraft, in this area.[2]

March, 1957, is still known as the "nightmare month" of disasters in aviation annals. There were six accidents throughout the world, one taking the lives of Philippine President Ramon Magsaysay and twenty-four others on Cebu Island, and another near Ottawa claiming the lives of Canadian Air Vice Marshal R. C. Ripley and seven airmen. But three were near Japan, within or relatively close to the Devil's Sea region, and were total disappearances.

On March 12 a U.S. Air Force KB50 tanker with a crew of eight disappeared between Japan and Wake Island. No radio signals, no debris found. Only four days later, on March 16, a U.S. Navy JD1 Invader carrying a crew of five vanished on a flight from Japan to Okinawa. Again, no radio signals, no wreckage.

Then, on March 22, a C-97 U.S. Military Air Transport with sixty-seven aboard left Travis AFB on the U.S. west coast, crossed the Pacific and disappeared southeast of Japan. The last radio message from the pilot indicated all was well and the plane was about two hundred miles from Tokyo.

For nine days there was an extensive air-sea search, but no trace of the giant craft was found.

In a U.S. Air Force Intelligence report extract received in 1959 by the National Investigations Committee on Aerial Phenomena, a civilian organization with headquarters in Washington, concern was expressed over disappearances of aircraft south of Japan.

Classified as to details, the extract said that there had been repeated incidents in which multi-engined Air Force transports had vanished in the region.[3]

This might seem to imply a certain degree of secrecy but there is no reason so to suppose. That people, ships, and planes disappear is manifest. Most often nobody knows how or why. The Air Force is empowered with the defense of our country above land and, in part, on the seas and oceans; it is not their duty to speculate on the whereof or wherefore. Moreover, their intelligence is doubtless just as, if not more, baffled than that of the ordinary person. Planes do disappear without trace; and so who is to say why, how, or where they went—especially when they leave no remains. This is difficult enough but these disappearances sometimes have eerie connotations. Let us take, for instance, a singularly unpleasant incident of this nature that bugged the Navy.

It was a cloudy, damp day when Lieutenant (j.g.) Ernest D. Cody and Ensign Charles E. Adams of Airship Squadron 32 had their rendezvous with a fantastic fate. Rain fell intermittently from a low overcast as patches of fog drifted in from the sea.

The date was August 16 in the World War II year of 1942.

The two young naval aviators were assigned to patrol the California coast near San Francisco with a blimp, the Airship *L-8*, in search of enemy submarines. It was a daily, routine task. No Japanese submarines had been observed in the area and none were expected to be seen during the patrol.

Lieutenant Cody was an experienced blimp pilot with almost

five hundred flying hours to his credit. He had proved his ability in a special assignment four months earlier.

On April 11 he had guided the *L-8* through tricky air currents above the aircraft carrier *Hornet* which was steaming west on a classified mission. He and his co-pilot had lowered to the flight deck two boxes of navigational equipment left behind by the carrier. Later he learned that this equipment had been installed in the sixteen B-25 bombers that made the historic raid on Tokyo led by Lieutenant Colonel James H. Doolittle.

It was 6 A.M. when Lieutenant Cody and Ensign Adams left Treasure Island Naval Base. The blimp flew west over San Francisco Bay and the Golden Gate and out over the Pacific. Almost two hours later the control tower at Naval Air Station, Moffett Field, Alameda, received a message from the *L-8:*

"Investigating suspicious oil slick," Lieutenant Cody radioed. "Position about five miles east of Farallon Islands. Stand by!"

The report caused no excitement at the tower since oil slicks are common in that area.

Fifteen minutes passed. At 8:05 A.M. the tower attempted to contact the blimp, but there was no response. The air control officer ordered two OS2U Kingfisher search planes to investigate.

The ceiling, however, was so low that to avoid a possible collision with the blimp the search planes stayed above the clouds.

A Pan American Airways clipper sighted the airship south of the Golden Gate at 10:30 A.M. Ten minutes later one of the search planes reported seeing the blimp rise above the overcast at 2,000 feet, then descend into it again.

At 10:45 observers at Fort Funston watched the *L-8* drift in from the sea and hit the beach about a mile from the fort near the Coast Artillery Patrol Station. Two fishermen seized the tie lines and tried to hold the ship down, but a sudden gust of wind raised the blimp. The men were dragged over the sand for a hundred yards before they were forced to let go.

Questioned later by Navy investigators, the fishermen said there was no one aboard the *L-8* and the gondola door was open.

Next the blimp struck a cliff along the beach, knocking loose one of her three hundred pound depth bombs. At the same time, apparently, the impact opened up a slow leak in her gas-filled bag. With her weight lightened, the blimp rose and drifted southeast.

Thirty minutes later—at 11:15—its bag partly deflated, the *L-8* came to earth on a street in Daly City, just south of San Francisco. A naval salvage crew was rushed to the scene.

Everything in the gondola was in order. The radio was in operating condition. The parachutes and life raft were stowed in place. The classified document portfolio was undisturbed. Although the motors had stopped, one throttle was open, the other half-open, and the ignition switches were turned on.

But there was no trace of the pilots.

Since it was required that the crewmen wear their yellow life jackets when over water, they were also missing.

There was no water in the landing space beneath the gondola deck and the investigators agreed that the *L-8* had not touched the surface of the sea.

Whatever happened to Lieutenant Cody and Ensign Adams must have occurred during the fifteen minutes after their final radio message.

At the naval inquiry it was determined that two fishing boats, a Coast Guard patrol ship, and a Navy vessel were at the location of the oil slick. The crews watched the blimp circle the slick at about three hundred feet, and the fishing boats moved away to a safe distance in case the *L-8* began dropping depth bombs.

Witnesses aboard the four vessels testified that the blimp suddenly disappeared upward in the overcast. They did not see the airship again.

What happened to Lieutenant Cody and Ensign Adams?

Did they encounter an enemy submarine with gunners that forced the two men to jump and be taken prisoners?

It is not likely. Any surfacing submarine would probably have been spotted by at least one of the many surface craft in the general area. The classified portfolio was intact. Japanese war records have been checked and offer no clues.

A plausible theory is that one of the men may have fallen part way out while leaning out of the gondola. The other then hurried to his aid and during the struggle both fell into the sea.

If this had occurred over the oil slick, surely the crews of the two patrol vessels, only a few hundred yards away, would have noticed the men falling in their bright yellow life jackets. Moreover, a fall from this height would have made a noticeable splash. The life jackets would have kept the bodies afloat, or if torn from their bodies, would have drifted on the surface.

Of course, the accident may have happened elsewhere, but the

O-U-T—OUT!

171

position of the throttles does not support this theory. The pilot certainly would not leave one engine on full and the other half-way when he went to the rescue of his companion.

An intensive surface and air search turned up no trace of the life jackets or the bodies of the missing airmen. The mystery of Airship *L-8* remains unsolved in U.S. Navy records.[4]

Perhaps there may be a very simple explanation for this "disappearance" that has escaped not only our eye but also the perspicacious eye of the Navy but, frankly, we begin to perceive something not quite kosher! If something goes wrong with a mechanical device over the sea, bits and pieces should fall into the sea, and not all of them should sink immediately. If not people in "Mae Wests," then, at least, oil should come back up to the surface. But when nothing is found in a limited area crowded with shipping and close to shore one begins to wonder even more.

Why were almost all of the crew, and even a dog, on the fated *Ourang Medan* staring *at the sky*? Is the menace sometimes from above and not below?

This would seem to be at least possible when we come to investigate the most gruesome situation on the surface of our earth that is, as of now, known and confirmed. It has been called the "Bermuda Triangle." This we shall now proceed to discuss.

With a crew of thirty-nine, the tanker *Marine Sulphur Queen* began its final voyage on February 2, 1963, from Beaumont, Texas. Its announced destination was Norfolk, Virginia. Its actual destination was the unknown.

The ship transported molten sulphur in heavily insulated steel tanks that were kept at 265 degrees by steel coils. The ship's operators, the Marine Transport Corporation of New York, said hauling sulphur was no more dangerous than hauling other cargoes.

A routine radio message on the night of February 3 placed the 524-foot vessel near the Dry Tortugas in the Gulf of Mexico.

Overdue on February 6, a search was launched. Planes took off from Coast Guard stations from Key West to Norfolk, and all available cutters were placed in service patrolling the coast.

One search plane reported a "yellow substance" on the sea 240 miles southeast of Jacksonville. A check by surface craft revealed that the substance was only seaweed.

The search was abandoned on February 14. Five days later a Navy torpedo retriever found some debris and a life jacket believed from the tanker, in the Florida Straits, fourteen miles southeast of Key West. Nothing more has been found.[1]

The mysterious menace that haunts the Atlantic off the Florida coast had claimed another victim. It strikes again and again—swallowing a ship or a plane, or leaving behind a derelict with no life aboard.

On August 28, 1963, two KC-135 four-engine Strato-tanker jets left Homestead AFB, south of Miami, Florida, on a classified refueling mission over the Atlantic. The crews totaled eleven men. The weather was clear.

At noon the planes radioed their position as eight hundred miles northeast of Miami and three hundred miles west of Bermuda. According to an Air Force spokesman, "the planes were new, presumed in radio contact with each other and they weren't flying close together."

Then the planes vanished.

An extensive search was launched. Planes criss-crossed the area in formation, following a planned pattern of observation. Vessels churned the surface of the sea.

On the following day debris was found floating on the water about 260 miles southwest of Bermuda. No survivors or bodies were found.

The obvious explanation was that the tankers had collided in the air, but two days after the disappearance more debris was located—only it was found 160 miles from the first discovery. What happened remains a mystery.[2]

Two months earlier, on July 1, the sixty-three-foot fishing boat *Sno' Boy,* under U.S. registry, sailed from Kingston, Jamaica, for Northeast Cay, a small island eighty miles southeast of Jamaica. Forty persons were aboard.

When it was overdue, the U.S. Navy and Coast Guard launched a search. Several bits of debris believed to be from the vessel were observed. Finally, after ten days, the search was abandoned.[3]

On January 8, 1962, a KB-50 Air Force tanker rolled down a runway at Langley AFB, Virginia, became airborne and headed east, outward bound for the Azores. Major Robert Tawney was in command of the crew of eight men.

Shortly later the tower at Langley received weak radio signals from the plane. The only definite knowledge gained from the garbled signals was that the big tanker was in trouble. The signals faded into silence.

Again there was an extensive search, but there was no trace of wreckage or bodies. After 1,700 fruitless man-hours, the search was ended.[4]

During the past two decades alone, this sea mystery at our back door has claimed almost a thousand lives. But even this is only an inference. In this series of disasters, very few bodies have ever been recovered.

U.S. Navy, Air Force, and Coast Guard investigators have admitted they are baffled. The few clues to the phenomenon that we have only add to the mystery.

Draw a line from Florida to Bermuda, another from Bermuda to Puerto Rico, and a third line back to Florida through the Bahamas. Within this roughly triangular area, known as the

"Bermuda Triangle," most of the total vanishments have occurred. Others have happened in adjacent areas to the north and east in the Atlantic, south in the Caribbean, and west in the Gulf of Mexico.

This area is by no means isolated. Air Force spokesmen point out that the coasts of Florida and the Carolinas are well-populated as well as are the islands involved. Sea distances are relatively short. Day and night there is traffic over the sea and air lanes. The waters are well-patrolled by the Coast Guard, the Navy, and the Air Force.

Despite this situation, this relatively limited area is the scene of disappearances that total far beyond the laws of chance. Its history of mystery dates back to the enigmatic light observed by Columbus when he first approached his landfall in the Bahamas.

Over all the seas of earth, there is only one other localized area where mysterious disappearances have repeatedly occurred. This is the grim, but far more remote, "Devil's Sea" region in the Pacific south of Japan and east of the Bonin Islands. Here, too, in a limited area, the usual dangers that menace planes and ships fail to explain why it is seldom that wreckage or bodies are found.

The Bermuda Triangle underlines the fact that despite swift wings and the voice of radio, we still have a world large enough for men and their machines and ships to disappear without a trace. A mile is still a mile, and the miles can add up to a vast unknown—the same misty limbo of the lost feared by our forefathers.

Whatever this menace is that lurks within a triangle of tragedy, it was responsible for the most incredible mystery in the history of aviation—the story of the lost patrol.

Early on a Wednesday afternoon five TBM Avenger torpedo bombers lined up on runways at the Fort Lauderdale (Florida) Naval Air Station. It was a sunny day, and the skies were blue above the green surface of the Atlantic. The date was December 5, 1945.

Normally the Avengers carried a crew of three—a pilot, a gunner, and a radio operator, but one crewman failed to report on this day. The planes were manned by five pilots—four Navy men and one Marine.

The bombers had been carefully checked and fueled to capacity. The engines, controls, instruments, and compasses were in perfect condition, according to later testimony. Each plane carried a self-inflating life raft and each man was equipped with a life jacket. All fourteen men had flight experience ranging from thirteen months to six years.

At 2:02 P.M. the flight leader closed his canopy, gunned his engine, and the first plane roared down the runway. The others followed in quick succession, climbing up into the clear sky and heading east over the Atlantic at 215 mph.

It was a routine patrol flight. The navigation plan for the formation was to fly due east for 160 miles, then north for 40 miles, then back southwest to the air station, completing a triangle. The relatively short flight would require about two hours.

The first word from the patrol came to the base control tower at 3:45 P.M., but the strange message did not request the expected landing instructions.

"Calling tower, this is an emergency," the patrol leader said in a worried voice. "We seem to be off course. We cannot see land . . . repeat . . . we cannot see land."

"What is your position?" the tower radioed back.

"We're not sure of our position," came the reply. "We can't be sure just where we are. We seem to be lost."

Startled, the tower operators looked at one another. How was this possible? With ideal flight conditions, how could five planes manned by experienced crews be lost?

"Assume bearing due west," the tower instructed.

There was alarm in the flight leader's voice when he answered:

"We don't know which way is west," he said. "Everything is wrong . . . strange. We can't be sure of any direction. *Even the ocean doesn't look as it should!*"

In all reports of this mystery, the importance of this last remark by the flight leader has been overlooked. The implications of an ocean that didn't appear "as it should" are shocking . . . and chilling.

Let's suppose that the patrol had run into a magnetic storm that caused deviations in their compasses. The sun was still above the western horizon. The fliers could have ignored their compasses and flown west simply by visual observation of the sun.

Apparently not only the sea looked strange, but the sun was invisible.

During the next few minutes the tower operators listened in as the pilots talked to each other. It was obvious that they were

he R.C.M.P. motor-sailer *St. Roch,* which in 1940 (with a crew aboard) successfully navigated
e Northwest Passage.   *Royal Canadian Mounted Police*

he small, twin-screw motorship *Joyita,* found derelict and awash, thirty-seven days after leaving
ia, Samoa.   *Author's collection*

A BOAC Lancastrian airliner,
of the same type as the
ill-fated *Star Dust*.   *BOAC*

The cabin of airship *L-8* on a street of Daly City, California. The two men aboard the blimp ere gone, their whereabouts still unknown. *San Francisco Examiner*

The *Mary Celeste*. This obscure 282-ton brigantine is still the greatest mystery of all to the publ
New York Public Library

The Navy fuel ship, U.S.S. *Cyclops* vanished in 1918, and her disappearance is still shrouded i
silence.   *Official U.S. Navy Photo*

in sight of one another, but equally confused. The conversation progressed from bewilderment to fear, verging on hysteria.

Shortly after 4 P.M. the flight leader, for no apparent reason other than panic, suddenly turned over flight command to another pilot.

At 4:25 the new flight leader contacted the tower.

"We are not certain where we are," he said. "We think we must be about 225 miles northeast of base . . . it looks like we are. . . ." The message ended abruptly.

It was the last word from the doomed patrol.

Tower operators signaled a rescue alarm. Within a few minutes a huge Martin Mariner flying boat with full rescue and survival equipment and a crew of thirteen men was on its way.

The powerful Mariner, seventy-seven feet long with a wing span of 124 feet, was built to withstand rough landings at sea.

The tower tried to call the Avengers to tell them help was en route. There was no reply.

Several routine radio reports were received from the Mariner. About twenty minutes after it left the base, the tower called the flying boat to check its position. There was no answer. The call was repeated for five anxious minutes. The silence was ominous.

What was happening out there over the sea two hundred miles away?

By this time it was dusk. Alarmed, operations at Fort Lauderdale notified the Coast Guard at Miami. A Coast Guard rescue plane covered the flying boat's route and reached the last estimated position of the missing patrol. There was not a sign of the six planes—only the calm sea and empty horizons.

Navy and Coast Guard vessels joined the search. Through the long night they watched for possible signal flares from life rafts. But no lights broke through the darkness above the black sea.

At dawn the escort carrier *Solomons* moved into the area and dispatched its thirty planes in an aerial search. Within a few hours twenty-one vessels were combing the sea. Above the surface craft were three hundred planes flying in grid search pattern. The British Royal Air Force pressed every available plane into service from the nearby territorial islands. All during the day the sky and the sea were methodically criss-crossed over an ever-widening area.

The intensive search continued on the following day, not only between Florida and the Bahamas, but two hundred miles into the Gulf of Mexico. Twelve large land parties searched three hundred miles of shoreline from Miami Beach to St. Augustine. Low-flying planes checked beaches south to Key West and north to Jacksonville. But not a scrap of wreckage or debris was found. The sea refused to offer a single clue.

A red flare was reported near Melbourne by the pilot of a commercial airliner. And now the search was extended to the land.

Swamps were surveyed with jeeps, marsh buggies and on foot. Ground crews and low-flying planes carefully checked the Everglades.

Day after day the search continued until it had covered 280,000 square miles—one of the greatest air-sea surveys ever conducted. Even after the sea search ended, teams of men checked beaches for weeks in Florida and the Bahamas, examining debris cast up by tides and breakers. But no objects from the missing planes were ever found.

Military experts were mystified. How could six airplanes and twenty-seven men totally and completely vanish in such a relatively limited area?

Did the planes eventually run out of fuel? While the Avengers were not especially buoyant, Navy officials said they would remain afloat long enough for life rafts to be launched and the crewmen "shouldn't even get their feet wet." All of the missing men were trained in sea survival procedures and had "Mae West" life jackets. After similar ditchings pilots and crewmen had existed for days in open sea.

Each plane had its own radio facilities. Why was no S O S received from at least one of the planes, especially the Mariner?

Commander H. S. Roberts, executive officer at the base, suggested his fliers might have been blown off course by high winds. The Miami Weather Bureau reported that there had been gusts up to forty miles per hour in the general area where the patrol was last reported. These winds would not be strong enough to seriously affect flying.

It certainly was not logical to assume that all of the planes had collided in mid-air, killing all crew members simultaneously. Moreover, there would have been drifting wreckage.

A waterspout would affect only a low-flying plane. As a rule they can be observed at a distance and easily avoided. If a freak waterspout had struck the patrol, again there would have been debris.

And what about the Mariner? Did it meet the same fate as the patrol?

All of these theories disregard the puzzling circumstances reported by the flight leader—the curious observations and the strange inability to determine location.

On the night of the disappearances, the S.S. *Gaines Mills,* a merchant ship, notified the Navy that it had observed an explosion high in the sky at 7:30 P.M. No wreckage or oil slicks were found in the general area of the observation. The explosion, however, occurred over three hours after the last radio message from the patrol, and it is unlikely that there is a connection.

A Naval Board of Inquiry made an investigation. After listening to testimony and considering the evidence, the board members concluded that they "were not able to make even a good guess as to what happened."

"They vanished as completely as if they had flown to Mars," one officer said.

A study of this mystery reveals some possible clues.

If the patrol had flown west they would have reached Florida or the Florida Keys. If they had flown east they would have seen the Bahamas—Great Bahama is almost twenty-five miles long. Southeast were the Great Abaca and Andros Islands. Open areas were directly north and south, but on such a clear day some islands and the mainland should have been visible part of the time.

This indicates that the patrol planes were flying in a circle between Florida and the Bahamas. If so, the compasses on all five planes were thrown off erratically to the same degree. If the errors had been constant, they would have flown straight and seen land in some direction.

Something affected the compasses—and it may later have silenced the patrol's radios or prevented transmission of signals beyond a limited zone. The Mariner may have entered this zone. The rescue plane not only had the usual radio equipment, but a hand-cranked generator for emergency transmissions.

If we combine these speculations with the strange appearance of the sea, plus inability to see the sun, a possible theory may be some kind of atmospheric aberration—a phenomenon that might be called "a hole in the sky."

The exact nature of this aberration and why it would seem to be localized to semi-tropical waters within and near the Bermuda Triangle is, of course, not known at this time.

Officially, the Navy does not go along with this theory.

Captain E. W. Humphrey, coordinator of aviation safety, puts it this way: "It is not felt that an atmospheric aberration exists in this area, nor that one has existed in the past. Fleet aircraft carrier and patrol plane flight operations are conducted regularly in this same area without incident."

The fact that patrol operations are made without incident is no evidence against the phenomenon. It is obvious that it occurs only occasionally in the well-traveled triangle area, without warning, but frequently enough to be alarming.[5]

As for magnetic disturbances that can affect compasses, the U.S. Navy's "Project Magnet" is currently studying this phenomenon. Super Constellations, equipped with highly sensitive magnetometers, are covering much of the globe in an extensive geomagnetic survey. It is bringing up to date many measurements of the earth's magnetic field more than thirty years old.[6]

Another project, combining studies of magnetism with gravity, was authorized by the Canadian government in 1950. The late Wilbert B. Smith, an electronic expert residing at Ottawa, was in charge of the project which was terminated before his death. He claimed to have discovered regions of what he called "reduced binding" in the atmosphere with an instrument he devised.

Smith alleged that such regions had been found at locations where there had been unexplained plane crashes. They were described as roughly circular, up to 1,000 feet in diameter, and probably extending upward quite a distance. They appeared to be more common in the southern latitudes.

"We do not know if the regions of reduced binding move about or just fade away," Smith wrote. "However, we do know that when we looked for several of them after three or four months we could find no trace of them."

Smith believed that while many planes would not be affected by these regions, others, due to design or size, might experience turbulence that would disintegrate them. Project Magnet may well be investigating the theories of Smith as part of its research.[7]

Many commercial pilots who fly the triangle consider the aberration theory seriously. How else, they ask, can you explain what has been happening?

Let's take a look at what has happened.

In 1947 an American super-fortress vanished one hundred miles off Bermuda. There was an intensive air and surface search, but no wreckage was found.

Unofficially, some authorities theorised that "a tremendous current of rising air in a cumulo-nimbus cloud might have disintegrated the bomber." This would certainly be an "atmospheric aberration" producing the turbulence that has been known to destroy aircraft, especially jets, but turbulence followed by disintegration at sea invariably results in drifting debris.[8]

On January 30, 1948, the dark cloak of vanishment enveloped a commercial airliner.

The *Star Tiger* was a huge, four-engined Tudor IV owned by British-South American Airways. At 10:30 P.M. on the night of January 29 it radioed the control tower at Kindley Field, Bermuda, that it was four hundred miles northeast of the island.

"Weather and performance excellent," the pilot reported. "Expect to arrive on schedule."

That was the last message ever received from the airliner with its six crewmen and twenty-three passengers.

At dawn a search was launched. The U.S. Navy ordered ten surface vessels out. Over thirty military and civilian planes covered the region. But there was no wreckage, no bodies, no oil slicks.

Late on the following day bad weather set in, and by nightfall on the 31st the planes were recalled. The vessels continued their fruitless search for several more days.

Later, in London, there was an official court of investigation. The court concluded that the *Star Tiger* was "presumed lost at sea," since there was no actual evidence, and that the mishap must have had "some external cause."

Next came the DC-3 passenger plane, operated by Airborne Transport, Inc., and chartered for a pre-dawn flight from San Juan, Puerto Rico, to Miami.

It was December 28, 1948, when Captain Robert Linquist, of Fort Myers, Florida, maneuvered the big airliner above the San Juan Airport and headed for Florida, one thousand miles distant. The thirty-two passengers, including two babies, had been spending the Christmas holidays on the island. Ernest Hill, Jr., of Miami, was co-pilot. Miss Mary Burks, of Jersey City, the attractive dark-haired stewardess, served coffee and cookies.

Everyone was in a gay mood. Laughter and light conversation filled the cabin.

"What do you know?" Captain Linquist reported early on the flight. "We're all singing Christmas carols."

Several hours passed.

By this time most of the weary passengers had fallen asleep in the now-darkened cabin. Only a few scattered clouds drifted high in the sky below the bright stars. Below the smoothly humming plane, dim in the starlight, the Florida Keys began to slip by. They were almost home!

At 4:13 A.M. Captain Linquist made his last contact with the Miami control tower: "We're approaching field," he said. "Only fifty miles out to the south. All's well. Will stand by for landing instructions."

And then—seconds later—it happened!

It happened so swiftly that Captain Linquist and his co-pilot had no time to send an S O S. It happened so close to the mainland that the lights of Miami could be seen as a glow in the night sky ahead.

What is this doom that can strike a huge airliner so quickly—so close to home? What dread fate actually came to the men, women and infants aboard the DC-3?

The pilots were veterans—well acquainted with the area. The U.S. Weather Bureau said flying conditions were ideal—that there was no likelihood the plane had been forced down by bad weather.

The plane carried an emergency transmitter for automatically sending S O S signals—the snap of a switch would have turned it on. It carried life preservers for all passengers as well as ten-man life rafts.

Again there was a search. Forty-eight Coast Guard, Air Force, and Navy vessels joined in, carefully covering the area, fanning out from the plane's last reported position. In much of this region the sea is so shallow that any object the size of the airliner can be seen on the bottom through the clear water.

Again, planes crossed and criss-crossed the area, flying almost wing tip to wing tip. They watched for debris, for groups of sharks and barracuda. Eventually the searchers scanned 300,000 miles of sea and land, including the Caribbean and Gulf, the Keys and the Everglades. Nothing was ever found.

The Bermuda jinx struck again only twenty days later, on January 17, 1949. This time the victim was the *Ariel,* sister ship to the *Star Tiger* that had vanished just twelve days short of one year previously. It was checked at Bermuda, and fuel for an extra ten hours of flight was placed in the reserve tanks.

Under the command of trans-Atlantic veteran Captain J. C. McPhee, the four-engined airliner with its crew of seven and thirteen passengers left at 7:45 A.M. for the four-hour, one thousand-mile flight to Kingston, Jamaica.

It was the shortest hop on the *Ariel's* long trip from London to Santiago, Chile—but this hop was through the tragic triangle.

The skies were clear and the sea was calm. At 8:25 A.M. came the first and only message from the doomed craft:

"Captain McPhee of the *Ariel* reporting," it said. "We are approximately 180 miles south of Bermuda. Weather fair. All is well. I'm changing radio frequency to pick up Kingston."

Then the *Ariel* vanished into the thin air through which it flew.

At this time a large U.S. Navy task force was south of Bermuda on maneuvers. Now was the time to break the jinx—to discover what was happening to these disappearing planes.

Two aircraft carriers launched their scores of planes. North of Cuba the U.S.S. *Leyte* and *Kearsarge* led a group of three light cruisers and six destroyers. Between Jamaica and Cuba a cruiser, four destroyer minesweepers and auxiliary units were led by the 45,000-ton *Missouri*.

Coast Guard rescue planes left the mainland from Miami north to Massachusetts. At MacDill Field, Tampa, the Fifth U.S. Air Force Rescue Squadron became airborne. Several merchant ships swerved from their courses to join the search. From the islands came British planes and vessels.

This unprecedented search was inspired by two disappearances twenty days apart, the immediate availability of a large number of vessels and aircraft and as a gesture of friendship to the British.

There was only one possible clue. Before dawn on January 18 a U.S. bomber and a British BOAC plane reported observing "a strange light" on the sea about three hundred miles south of Bermuda. Several destroyers and seven planes were sent to the location. But nothing was found—no raft, no float with a light, no debris, no oil slick.

Despite this massive, widespread search—but concentrated along the plane's obvious route of less than a thousand miles in calm, clear weather—it was all in vain.

Why the planes of the British-South American Airways were especially plagued by disappearances is a mystery within a mystery. The company was merged a few years later with the British Overseas Airways Corporation (BOAC).[9]

Earlier, in 1947, one of its airliners, the *Lancastrian Star Dust,* was on the London-Santiago route. It didn't vanish in the Bermuda Triangle, but in Chile—leaving behind a classic enigma of the skyways.

The *Star Dust* was due to land at the Santiago Airport at 5:45 P.M. on August 2. At 5:41—just four minutes short of arrival— Captain R. J. Cook, the pilot, radioed his arrival time as scheduled. There was a brief pause—then came the word "Stendec" loud and clear.

The puzzled tower operator asked for a repeat. The strange word was twice repeated . . . then silence.

The *Star Dust* was never heard from again. There was the usual search by planes, cars, ski troops, and mountaineers. No wreckage was ever found.

Nor has anyone ever explained the meaning of the cryptic word "Stendec!"[10]

Following publication of an article I wrote on the Bermuda Triangle in *Argosy* magazine,* a number of letters were received from readers. Suggested explanations included all manner of wild things from interference by "flying saucers" or "something from outer space," to space-warps that caused the planes and ships to enter another dimension, and disintegrating rays from a 30,000-year-old Atlantean power plant which (according to the noted clairvoyant, the late Edgar Cayce) is fervently believed by some to be on the ocean bottom near the Bahamas!

However, one letter† was from a Mr. Dick Stern, of Atlanta, Georgia, who twice survived frightening experiences in the triangle. Mr. Stern wrote that during the last weeks of 1944 his bombing group left the United States for Italy where they were to replace the heavily battered groups from the Fifteenth; and then he goes on:

> Not more than 300 miles from Bermuda on a beautiful clear night, we were suddenly whipped over on our backs, found ourselves on the

---

* February, 1964.
† Published in *Argosy's* May, 1964, issue.

ceiling one moment and pinned down the next, as the ship was thrown about at an incredible rate of speed. Our pilot was a 240-pound strong man, and our co-pilot was six-feet-one and 200 pounds of hard muscle. I watched them pulling on the wheels with all their combined strength to avert a sure crash into the ocean, only a few hundred feet below. They miraculously pulled out of the dive so close to the water that the wind-generated whitecaps were clearly visible.

The entire incident took only a matter of seconds, perhaps less than one minute, but when we surveyed the crew, eleven frightened men had been reduced to quivering boys who unanimously agreed to resign from the Air Force.

We headed back to Bermuda, and no sooner had we landed than we jumped from the plane, almost to a man, kissed the ground and announced to one and all that we were now solid infantrymen. We were told that of the seven planes which had taken off in our "box," only two had returned and nothing was ever heard from the others. No wreckage was sighted, there had been no radio contact. And yet, it was a clear starry night.

We subsequently regained our composure after a few weeks in Bermuda, while the Air Force conducted a thorough, if somewhat futile, search and investigation. Then we flew without incident to our ultimate destination.

Three years ago, my wife and I were returning from London by plane via a route which took us to Bermuda, then to Nassau and on to Miami where we lived.

After leaving Bermuda on what appeared to be a clear day with only a thunderstorm playing on the distant horizon, I was discussing the area with the pilot and my wife was relating the above incident. At almost the same moment, we were thrown into a tremendous shock treatment that dropped the plane (a Bristol Britannia) with such force that the food we were eating was thrown to the ceiling. Fortunately, we had our seat belts fastened or we would have hit the ceiling in the same manner.

After a harrowing fifteen minutes of up and down, and no storm in our immediate vicinity, we managed to clear the area.

Phenomenon? Perhaps. Frightening? You bet!

The turbulence twice experienced by Dick Stern may well account for some of the disappearances and be one aspect of atmospheric aberrations in this region. In fact, it may be the violent climax of all aberrations that cause vanishments.

It seems evident, however, in the messages from the lost patrol that there are other factors than mere turbulence in some of these cases. The compasses on the planes were affected, the sea didn't look "as it should," and apparently the sun couldn't be seen.

My own opinion is that within and near the triangle (perhaps, also, in the "Devil's Sea" and more rarely elsewhere) occasional aberrations of an unusual type occur in the air and on the surface of the ocean. These aberrations might cause magnetic, possibly gravitational, effects; in which case they might for all practical purposes be referred to as "space-warps," and cause deadly turbulence ending in total disintegration of planes and ships, for the latter are by no means immune.

In March, 1950, north of the triangle, an American Globemaster disappeared on a flight to Ireland.

Less than three months later the jinx struck a vessel.

The S.S. *Sandra* was a freighter, 350 feet in length, radio-equipped. From Savannah, Georgia, in June, 1950, she sailed for Puerto Cabello, Venezuela, with three hundred tons of insecticide. Heading south, she passed Jacksonville and St. Augustine along the well-traveled coastal shipping lane.

Then she disappeared as completely as if she had never existed —in the tropic dusk, in peaceful weather—just off the Florida coast.

There was another futile search by air and sea. Nothing was ever found floating on the surface. No debris or bodies were ever washed up on the beaches by waves or tides.[11]

A British York transport, with thirty-three passengers and a crew of six, vanished over the Atlantic north of the triangle on a trooping flight to Jamaica on February 2, 1953. In this case there was an S O S sent—which ended abruptly without explanation. A court of inquiry in London reported: "Cause unascertainable."[12]

In October, 1954, a U.S. Navy Super-Constellation disappeared, again north of the triangle area. There were forty-two people aboard, some of them Navy wives and children. Although the plane had two transmitters, no radio signals were received. There was no trace of debris or bodies, though hundreds of planes and vessels searched for days.

Commander Andrew Bright, head of the Navy's Aviation Safety Section, admitted the service had no explanation for the disappearance.

Another Navy patrol bomber flew into oblivion near Bermuda on November 9, 1956. No radio signals were received.

Meanwhile, the triangle hoodoo was not neglecting surface

vessels. In September, 1955, the yacht *Connemara IV*, of New York registry, was found abandoned four hundred miles south-west of Bermuda.

Al Snyder, internationally famous jockey, and two friends left Miami on March 5, 1948, to go fishing. They anchored their cabin cruiser near Sandy Key and left in a small skiff to fish in the sur-rounding shallow waters.

But they never returned.

The Coast Guard and volunteer skippers of fishing boats began the search. They were joined later by over a thousand men, a hundred boats and fifty military and private planes. The skiff was finally found lodged beside a small unnamed island near Rabbit Key, sixty miles north of the cabin cruiser.

Snyder's wife and his racing friends offered rewards totaling $15,000 for rescue of the men or recovery of their bodies. Even a blimp was chartered to join the helicopters and planes.

But Snyder and his companions were never seen again.[13]

Actually the disappearance of vessels and ships in good condi-tion found mysteriously abandoned in or near the triangle goes back for over a century. It is only recently, in the air age, that these occurrences have increased with the addition of vanishing aircraft.

On abandonments, my own incomplete records go back to 1840 when the *Rosalie,* a large French ship bound for Havana, was found in or near the triangle. Most of her sails were set, cargo intact, everything shipshape, but the only living thing aboard was a half-starved canary in a cage.[14]

The German bark *Freya* sailed from Manzanillo, Cuba, on October 3, 1902, for Chile. Seventeen days later she was found partly dismasted, listing badly and nobody aboard. Weather re-ports showed that there had been only light winds in the region.

Whatever happened must have occurred soon after the vessel left Cuba. The anchor was still hanging free at her bow and the date on a calendar in the captain's cabin was October 4.[15]

In April, 1932, the Greek schooner *Embiricos,* while sailing fifty miles south of Bermuda, found the two-masted *John and Mary* of New York registry, her sails furled, the hull freshly painted, but not a soul aboard.

A curious case of apparent resurrection occurred late in 1935. When the S.S. *Aztec* arrived in her home port of Bristol from the West Indies, the crew reported they had found the yacht *La*

Dahama drifting off Bermuda, crewless, her skylights smashed, and her masts trailing overboard.

Then came the extraordinary news from Italy that the liner *Rex* had rescued the crew of the yacht and that men and women aboard the *Rex* had actually watched the *La Dahama* plunge beneath the waves.

If the *La Dahama* was a ghost ship, she was certainly a substantial one since a group of sailors from the *Aztec* had boarded her and examined her from bow to stern.[16]

In February, 1940, the U.S. Coast Guard found the yacht *Gloria Colite*, of St. Vincent, British West Indies, two hundred miles south of Mobile, Alabama, in the Gulf of Mexico. Everything was in order. Seas were calm. There was "no indication as to the cause of the abandonment."[17]

Fourteen months before the disappearance of the Navy patrol from Fort Lauderdale, the Cuban freighter *Rubicon* was sighted by a Navy blimp off the coast of Florida. When a Coast Guard cutter from Miami arrived, the crew found the only living thing aboard was a dog.

The vessel was in excellent condition with the personal possessions of the crew intact. A lifeboat was missing and a broken hawser was hanging down from the bow.[18]

Total disappearances of vessels have been far more frequent than mystery derelicts, beginning with the schooner *Bella* in 1854.

The British frigate *Atalanta*, a training ship with 290 cadets and sailors aboard, left Bermuda for England in January, 1880, and vanished. A beautiful, stoutly built vessel, she apparently went down in a storm that arose soon after she left port, but no identifiable debris was ever found despite an extensive search.

An outstanding disappearance within the Bermuda Triangle occurred in 1918. This was the U.S.S. *Cyclops*, a U.S. Navy supply ship, five hundred feet in length with a 19,000-ton displacement.

When she sailed from Barbados, British West Indies, on March 4, bound for Norfolk, she had 309 people aboard and a cargo of 10,800 tons of manganese. The weather was fair. No radio messages were ever received. No trace of wreckage was found.

After many months, the Navy ended its investigation with this statement: "The disappearance of this ship has been one of the most baffling mysteries in the annals of the Navy, all attempts to locate her having proved unsuccessful. Many theories have been advanced, but none that satisfactorily accounts for her disappearance."[19]

Seven years later the cargo ship S.S. *Cotopaxi*—Charleston to Havana—vanished. And a year later, in 1926, the freighter *Suduffco* sailed south from Port Newark into the limbo of the lost with her crew of twenty-nine men.

The sea guards well her secrets.

On December 8, 1963, Pan American World Airways Clipper 214 left Puerto Rico, crossed the Bermuda Triangle without incident, and landed at Baltimore where it discharged passengers. Then, with eighty-one remaining passengers and crew members, it took off on the last leg of its flight to Philadelphia.

Near Elkton, Maryland, the 120-ton Boeing 707 jet was flying through a thunderstorm when something happened. The captain or, more likely, the co-pilot, radioed the Federal Aviation Agency's approach control tower at Philadelphia.

On the following day a group of investigators and newsmen listened in grim silence as a tape recording reproduced the final message from the doomed plane:

"Clipper 214 . . . Mayday, Mayday . . . out of control . . . down we go."

The control officer replied: "Clipper 214, did you call Philadelphia?"

Back came the last words of a man hurtling to his death—spoken as calmly as if he were requesting a routine landing clearance:

"Clipper 214 . . . we're going down in flames."

The center's answer also was strangely calm: "Clipper 214, Roger, message has been received."

Seconds later the debris of the huge airliner and the bodies of the passengers were scattered over a mile long area. Alan S. Boyd, Civil Aeronautics Board Chairman, said the destruction was so complete that no mockup of the wreckage would be attempted.

Several witnesses said it appeared lightning had struck the jet and the plane had exploded. Asked if there was any evidence that lightning could destroy an airliner, Boyd replied: "Not to my knowledge."

The pilot's last radio contact made no mention of lightning and it is unlikely that he knew the cause of the disaster. All pilots know the importance of giving clues to causes in the interest of air safety.

Deputy Director Robert Allen, of the CAB's Bureau of Safety, said there was probably an explosion, "but what type I don't know."

With no evidence of a lightning strike other than the quite possibly inaccurate accounts of some witnesses, the investigators were more inclined to believe that extreme turbulence may have caused structural failure. Fire and an explosion frequently follow a mid-air breakup, causing witnesses to believe that the blast preceded disintegration. There have been several cases of swept-wing jets being stalled by extreme turbulence. A stall in a jet can cause loss of pilot control and even structural failure during the recovery attempt, according to CAB officials.[1]

Whatever caused this particular crash, the same factors are present that have cropped up in several other unexplained air disasters—a flash of light usually attributed to lightning if a storm is in progress, explosion and flames, and often disintegration in the air. Since these effects can result from known causes, it is additional observations in certain accidents that have brought out the more mysterious factors.

In the Bermuda Triangle we have had disappearances of planes and ships and missing crews. Common sense tells us that more than one explanation is required to cover all these occurrences, and that the well-known dangers of air and sea have claimed some of these victims. Yet a mysterious cause seems to remain, one that may be world-wide but particularly haunting the triangle, and all available evidence points to its being an atmospheric phenomenon.

Again, common sense tells us that there may be more than one type of atmospheric aberration that can cause trouble. Such disturbances could range from severe magnetic storms to releases of energy capable of causing total destruction or combustion of large material objects. At this early stage of our knowledge of obscure or even unknown natural laws and phenomena, we can only seek possible relationships in occurrences, and then theorize.

While it may be true that most of us are fascinated by mysteries, it appears that solutions are demanded with even greater fervor. Mysteries may be exaggerated by tellers of tales, but known facts are often stretched to greater, sometimes incredible, lengths to achieve at least tentative explanations.

At the same time, we must recognize that in an apparently limitless universe, extending into nobody knows how many dimensions, all phenomena cannot be neatly classified. The realm of the unknown will ever "surround" us, and it is a realm without end.

According to many reports, separated by time and space, a vast array of objects, substances, and energies have dropped down from the heights of the atmospheric sea above us. Some of these are the amusing oddities used as fillers on inside newspaper pages; but others have reaped a grim toll of property destruction and human life.

There have been reported showers of fish, frogs, seeds, snails, snakes, spiders, and even flesh and blood. Inorganic substances have included great hunks of ice, slag, sulphur, charcoal, various metals, punk, gelatinous materials, so-called "angel hair," and fire. It is fire and fireballs that menace life and property.

Our use of the term fireballs does not refer to meteors that flame out of existence many miles above the earth's surface in a matter of seconds and only rarely reach the lower atmosphere. Nor does it refer to ball lightning* as a rare phenomenon during an electrical storm, although our fireballs are sometimes called ball lightning and there may be a relationship.

The fireballs we refer to invariably drop from unknown heights regardless of weather conditions as spheroids of some kind of illuminated gas or condensed energy. They apparently become detached from a layer of balanced force, becoming visible as they descend into a denser atmospheric medium and then disintegrate. They may dissipate slowly or rapidly, but in the end they expire with a blast of radiant energy and intense heat. Far above us is a seething sea of electromagnetic energy that man is only beginning to explore—belts of radiation bombarded by cosmic rays and penetrated by interstellar impulses. Is this the spawning ground of these fantastic fires? Once the existence of these fireballs is scientifically proved, we may have solutions to many of the fantastic flames that have long puzzled man—from the weird lights that have mystified navigators to the several recorded cases of human bodies that have seemingly burst into flames for no apparent reason.

Reverting to occurrences within or near the Bermuda Triangle, there was mystery in the simultaneous fiery crash of four Air

---

* Nobody knows what this is, or even if it exists or "happens" at all. It is a convenient and much over-used "explanation" for several as yet unexplained natural phenomena.

National Guard Thunderjets near Lawrenceville, Georgia, on December 6, 1953. The planes, returning from Miami, Florida, all plunged from about 11,500 feet in flames, killing the pilots.

Dobbins Air Base officials said all of the men were experienced fliers and three of them made up a stunt team specializing in acrobatic flying. The weather was cloudy with occasional rain, but this should not have been a detriment to experienced pilots.

Just before the crash, base tower operators heard one of the pilots say, "We can't miss it," followed by silence.[2]

On February 7, 1955, a huge fireball flamed across the Caribbean and South Florida. It was observed by hundreds of persons, by the pilots of two planes over the Atlantic between Miami and Nassau and the crew of a ship near Cuba. Several motorists near Miami said they swerved to keep from being hit.

One pilot, Captain Black of Eastern Airlines, was quoted as follows in an Associated Press Dispatch of February 8: "I thought it was coming in the window of my plane. I was over Fort Pierce at the time. It looked like a ball of fire 10 to 15 feet in diameter. I took my plane up about a thousand feet to keep from being hit, but I felt a little foolish when I got to Miami and learned that a pilot flying over Key West did the same thing."

The press reports indicated that the fireball was a meteor, but Senior Captain William B. Nash, of Pan American Airways, sent the following information to *Orbit,* a magazine formerly published by L. H. Stringfield at Cincinnati, Ohio: *

> Very odd meteor—I did a little checking, and found that a PAA airplane crew with Captain Charles Elmore in command saw three bright white lights due south of their DC6B as they crossed Biscayne Bay 1200 feet high on a west heading to the airport enroute from Nassau. The lights were 15 degrees higher than the aircraft. They were much brighter than aircraft flares and larger. They appeared to hover with the front two connected by a line of light between them. Suddenly they blinked out.
>
> The tower saw them too—couldn't identify them. The time was 8:35 P.M. The lights had fuzzy edges and were round. Clear night, no inversion, too bright for reflections. Four persons on Biscayne Bay reported odd lights moving at sea about 8:05 to 8:15 P.M. Many persons and pilots saw a very bright streaking object at 7:55 P.M. (see UP and AP reports). Airplanes at Ft. Pierce, Vero Beach, Havana and

---

* See vol. 11, no. 1.

over Andros Island in the Bahamas reported a bright green object as big as the moon with a long white tail. No sound reported.

The times of sightings varied over a forty minute period from 7:55 to 8:35. Some meteorologist who didn't see it tagged it a meteor. The PAA pilots say that what they saw was no meteor. A Marine pilot over Andros Island said it landed gradually on Andros.

If one of these fireballs landed on Andros there is no record of it, but something in the following November flashed out of the sky, gouged a hole the size of a boxcar on the farm of W. R. Wacaser in east Hillsborough County, Florida, and burned for forty days!

Officers from MacDill AFB stated that the object was not a missile, there was no radioactivity, and they suggested the hole was probably caused by lightning. They could not explain why the fire burned so long.[3]

There was mystery, too, in the crash of an airliner at Jacksonville, Florida, on December 21, 1955. This was brought out by Damon Runyon, Jr., Miami *Daily News* staff writer, who by-lined the story on January 26–27, 1956.

"A post-mortem on an Eastern Air Lines Constellation showed the pilot was ducking 'something' when he crashed at Jacksonville Airport, killing all 17 aboard," Runyon wrote. "But what the 'thing' was remained a mystery in what observers called the most confusing testimony in memory at a CAB investigation."

CAB officials said the Miami-to-New York airliner was operating normally on an instrument approach in foggy weather. At the inquiry an aeronautical engineer said the plane was traveling at a speed of 140 knots when it crashed, although the engines had been cut off. Normal speed for such a landing is 115 knots. "It appeared a pull-up maneuver was in progress at the time of the impact," he said. He added that the plane crashed with the nose slightly down and banked to the right.

Other expert observers testified that apparently the pilot had seen something that caused him to make the maneuver. However, William McKinney, who was observing the airliner on radar as it was attempting to land, insisted he saw no other planes in the landing pattern. And George Van Epps, CAB air safety investigator, said a check disclosed there was no known military aircraft in the area at the time of the crash.

On the other hand, a Miami truck driver testified he saw what appeared to be two jets shoot in front of the airliner, one following behind the other at approximately two hundred feet separation and at an approximate altitude of two hundred feet.

"Each aircraft's silhouette had a red and white flashing light . . . immediately following this occurrence, I observed through my windshield a big flash," he said. The driver added there was no "obstruction in horizontal visibility" but that he noted a low overcast. No stars were visible.

On January 24, 1957, United Press reported that two B-47 Stratojet bombers collided in flight south of Cuba, and three of the crewmen were rescued. Sister planes of the downed craft reported upon their return to Homestead AFB, Florida, that they saw a "huge bolt of fire" and then flames shot out in "many directions." One of the rescue planes on the scene radioed that it observed an unknown object turning south of the Isle of Pines. This "object" was never identified.

Six weeks later, on March 9, 1957, a Pan American World Airways DC-6 en route from New York to San Juan, Puerto Rico, nearly collided in flight with a mysterious luminous object off the Florida coast near Jacksonville.

Captain Matthew Van Winkle pulled back on the controls and shot his plane upwards almost at a ninety degree angle to avoid the object. A stewardess and a woman passenger were hurt and later hospitalized, and three other passengers were shaken up.

An INS dispatch* quotes one passenger as stating that a strong light "like a hundred suns" filled the cabin of the plane. Another described the object as a "big fire ball advancing with tremendous speed with a roaring sound."

If the collision had occurred, would this plane have been added to our list of lost airliners?

Sometimes fireball observations are accompanied by mysterious skyquakes.

On the evening of April 4, 1956, a seventy-mile strip of the Florida west coast was shaken by a series of explosions in the sky. The Sarasota *Herald-Tribune* offices were flooded with phone calls from 9:10 P.M. until after 11.

A pilot of J. and J. Aircraft, Inc., reported he was flying to Sarasota from Miami, cruising at about 8,500 feet just north of

---

*March 9, 1957.

Immokalee, when he saw two flashes of light southwest of Sarasota. He thought the flashes were from a squall, but a weather check showed the area to be clear.

A civil defense supervisor at Englewood reported he saw two flashes in the Gulf—the second brighter than the first. He added that a few minutes after he saw the second flash there appeared what looked like "a meteor flash across the sky and stop. It did not hit the water."[4]

Skyquakes have repeatedly occurred in Florida and in the triangle area as well as in other parts of the world. They are definitely not sonic booms *and their repeated occurrence in limited areas* argues against the bolide (exploding meteor) explanation.

Mysterious luminous objects in the sky are often reported. Many cases that never reach the public are published in *Notices to Mariners,* issued by the U.S. Navy Hydrographic Office, which lists them as "celestial phenomena" (observed at sea). During the period of frequent UFO (unidentified flying objects) reports, from 1947 to 1960, there were hundreds of observations in the triangle region. As early as 1952 Florida was described as "saucer-ridden."

There is doubtless more than one explanation for UFO's, and certainly one is fireballs, whatever their origin and nature may be. If our theory is correct, and since most of the earth's surface is covered with water, there should be many reports of fireballs of an unknown type at sea—and there are!

A few examples:

In coastal waters off Ensenada, California, on September 2, 1954, a Honduran freighter reported a "strange fireball which skipped along the surface of the sea, then vanished." It left a trail of white smoke, paralleling the ship's course. The Coast Guard searched the area but found nothing that would explain the observation.

H. G. Rovner, of Philadelphia, in an account published in the Philadelphia *Bulletin,* December 12, 1954, tells of being at sea (apparently in the Atlantic) in 1946, when he saw a fireball one morning. It was observed by other crew members, including the captain.

"As it sailed over our heads," Rovner writes, "we noticed it was a monster meteor about 200 feet long, with a tail burning fiercely and sputtering fire . . . the object was in horizontal flight, it was flaming red, it flew at mast height, and it did not crash in the ocean but flew into the horizon.

"It was a beautiful sight, even though it scared us out of our wits. The captain remarked if it had hit us there would have been no trace of crew or ship."

At midnight on February 24, 1885, somewhere in the Pacific between Yokohama and Victoria, the crew of the bark *Innerwich* saw the sky turning fiery red. All at once a large mass of fire appeared over the vessel, then fell into the sea.

A huge wave rushed toward the ship with a deafening noise. The bark "was struck aback and a roaring white sea passed ahead." According to the account in *Science*,* the captain, "an old experienced mariner, declared that the awfulness of the sight was beyond description."

The British steamer *Siberian* near Cape Race on November 12, 1887, observed an enormous ball of fire. It *rose* from the surface of the sea to a height of fifty feet, advanced close to the ship, then moved away. According to reports in *Thunder and Lightning*, by Camille Flammarion, and the American *Meteorological Journal*,* the ball was visible for five minutes and moved against the wind before retreating.

The late Charles Fort, in his *Book of the Damned*, tells of a curious observation reported by Sir W. S. Harris at the meeting of the British Association of Science in 1848. It was a vessel toward which had whirled two balls of fire described as rolling millstones of flame.

"When they came near, an awful crash took place: the topmasts were shivered to pieces," the account states. A strong sulphurous odor was also reported.[5]

Obviously such fireballs can set vessels aflame and there are cases of fires of unknown origin on ships at sea. In April, 1938, a "serious fire of mysterious origin" afflicted the British *Anglo-Indian,* sister ship of the *Anglo-Australian*. The sea was "like a millpond" when the freighter *Anglo-Australian* disappeared near the Azores in March, 1938, with a crew of thirty-nine. On March 14 she radioed that she was off Fayal and all was well. She was never heard from again.

---

* Vol. 5, p. 242.
* Vol. 6, p. 443.

About a month later the fire of unknown origin damaged her sister ship.[6]

We do not know if there is a connection between strange lights in the sky, skyquakes, and the loss of airliners. What we do seek are possible relationships in phenomena.

Also, the theory of atmospheric aberrations is a generalized term that can cover many possibilities—all of them speculative at this stage of our knowledge. Atmospheric aberrations may range from conditions that stop the operations of engines, thus causing mass crashes of aircraft, to exploding centers of energy that can completely destroy a plane or vessel.

Likewise, the term "fireball" covers a wide variety of fiery phenomena ranging from mammoth meteorites to the sprays of light known as St. Elmo's Fire. Under some conditions even the tiny flares of St. Elmo's Fire can be a menace since this phenomenon is blamed for the destruction of the zeppelin *Von Hindenburg* at Lakehurst, N.J., in 1937.

Fireballs and lightning, especially ball lightning, are responsible for many curious, often mysterious, happenings. Bolts of lightning have transported fragile objects like mirrors without damage, emptied inkstands, stripped persons naked, and in one case (cited by Flammarion) destroyed the pubic hair of a young girl without otherwise harming her!

Ball lightning has been known to condense, pass through a keyhole, and expand again. In one case a ball entered a house and exploded, killing a kitten on a girl's lap but not hurting the girl. Sometimes they travel as rapidly as a bolt, but occasionally they drift about as if guided intelligently before disintegrating.[7]

Then there is a more sinister form of fireball that apparently can appear regardless of weather conditions, kill or injure human beings and animals, and cause serious damage to property. There are literally thousands of cases on record that offer grim evidence of the fury of this type of fireball. Since, year after year, they apparently are responsible for the premature cremation of human beings, striking automobiles with a heat so intense that the metal is fused and melted, and starting "inexplicable" building and brush fires, we can assume that they may also be responsible for air and sea disasters.

It may have been a fireball that struck a plane in the China Sea on April 11, 1955, and carried eleven communists to their death. An AP report filed in Bombay, India, quoted the surviving crew members as stating that the crash "was preceded by a muffled explosion. This was followed by fire emanating from an extraneous source wholly unconnected with the structure of the aircraft." It was, of course, assumed that "lightning or some other meteorological freak had caused the crash."

The size of these fireballs may vary considerably. It was a "queer" fire on the port main wing of a Wellesley bomber that caused it to crash in England on May 19, 1938, killing one man. As reported in the London *Daily Telegraph*, the experts at the inquest and inquiry admitted they could not explain how the fire started since it was not near the engine.[8]

Although it did not result in an accident, press dispatches on July 27, 1957, told of a ball of fire that burned a hole in the tail of an American Airlines plane while it was flying over Knoxville, Tennessee, during a storm.

A spokesman for the airline said he believed it was caused by static electricity, but he also stated that all aircraft have short wires which are designed to carry static electricity away from the body of the plane.

On February 13, 1955, a Belgian airliner carrying twenty-nine persons vanished a few minutes after radioing Rome's Ciampino Airport that it was preparing for a routine landing. Early press reports stated that the pilot said he had seen a "fireball" in the sky. A minute later he opened his transmitter and started sending another message, which broke off suddenly.

Later news stories ignored the fireball report, but on February 14 the French African radio station at Brazzaville said that due to a "mysterious orange spot in the sky" the departure of the Italian Prime Minister and Foreign Minister, who were planning to leave Rome for London on another flight, had been delayed. The source for this report was not announced.

Nine officers and men were killed when a U.S. Army bomber crashed on a farm near Delaware, Illinois, on June 10, 1938. On the following day a Chicago *Daily News* account quoted a woman witness as stating that there had been a sudden "crash in mid-air" followed by a big flash of light and a blaze that lit up the sky. *Then* came a violent explosion, and the plane plunged to earth.

There are a number of cases in which planes apparently collide with invisible objects in the air before crashing. All reports of fireballs state that they seem to drop down from above. We suggest that usually the energy that is contained in these balls is invisible, and it becomes visible within the limited range of human sight as it approaches the earth's surface.

The very rarity of fireballs of this nature indicates that they have been dislodged from their usual and invisible medium in the atmospheric sea above us. As they descend they become momentarily visible and die violently with a dissipation of energies.

In the words of the English writer Eric Frank Russell, who refers to cases of this type in *Fate* Magazine, December, 1950, "what becomes visible after it has fallen downstairs must obviously have been upstairs even though undetected."

On July 24, 1938, *Pester Lloyd* (Budapest) reported the crash of a Polish airliner near the Romano-Polish border that killed fourteen persons, including the Japanese military attache in Warsaw. The report stated the crash was "inexplicable" and that the plane appeared to collide in the air with something that was invisible.

A British BOAC Comet jetliner took off from the Calcutta Airdrome on May 2, 1953, and five minutes later, before it reached the sea, it suddenly disintegrated. Forty-three persons aboard were killed and the wreckage fell over a five mile area. Tower observers and witnesses said there was no other aircraft near the plane.

On May 20 J. H. Lett, of the British Ministry of Civil Aviation, told United Press that a study of the parts indicated that the airliner was struck "in the air by a fairly heavy body." He added that a preliminary investigation did not indicate that there was structural failure due to poor construction or workmanship.

Also ruled out was lightning, a bomb or fuel explosion, and collision with another plane. At the Royal Aircraft Research Center at Farnborough where the parts were reassembled, Dr. P. B. Walker, chief of the structure department, said that examination of the starboard and port main wings and the tailplane gave the impression that "they had all been torn off by a giant."

Another investigator suggested that a wing may have torn off after metal fatigue and struck the side and tailplane of the liner. This, however, would hardly account for the total disintegration of the plane in the absence of a fuel explosion.[9]

There are a number of cases of planes disintegrating in the air, and the total destruction makes it almost impossible to determine the cause. An example is the explosion of a twin jet Night

Intruder on December 9, 1953, in the sky over Bel Air, Maryland, where the wreckage was "widely scattered."

In France, the *Echo de Paris*, June 23, 1938, reported that seven airmen were killed when their Potez twin-engined plane flew to pieces in mid-air near Tours. Residents were awakened by a crash overhead, followed by the noise of falling debris. Oddly enough, five aviators had lost their lives in the same mysterious manner in the same district only a few months before.

Less than two months later, *Reynold's News*, on August 14, 1938, told of a Royal Air Force flying boat that suddenly disappeared in a "terrific column of water and smoke" while flying a few feet above the surface of the sea off Felixstowe, England. A boatman near the scene said it was "the most amazing crash I have ever seen." (He failed to state how many crashes he *had* seen).[10]

Is there some occasional aberration that can affect the engines of aircraft? And would this explain some of the mass crashes that have occurred over land?

In 1950 three Air Force planes took off from a field near Washington, D.C., and without colliding, all three fell into Chesapeake Bay. The one surviving pilot, according to press reports, said his engine stopped for no apparent reason. On June 8, 1951, four jets simultaneously crashed near Richmond, Indiana, killing three of the pilots. The published explanation was that ice may have formed over the intakes, but other pilots said the planes were not high enough for this to happen.

The usual explanation for such occurrences is that the planes simultaneously ran out of fuel. But this would hardly explain the crash of four Meteor jets at Waterbeach, England, in 1953, since the accidents happened a few minutes after they had been serviced and had taken off.

And then there are the clouds that may be visible manifestations of strange aberrations:

In March, 1952, British Wing Commander J. Baldwin, World War II ace, was flying with several other planes on a short reconnaissance flight along the Korean coast. He flew his jet into a cloud and neither he nor his plane was ever seen again. (At about the time of his disappearance a U.S. aircraft carrier reported seeing an unidentified object in the sky off the coast.[11])

On the afternoon of July 10, 1930, five Kansas City businessmen took off from the Municipal Airport at Corpus Christi, Texas, to return home. They left behind them a sixth man, Frederick H. Dierks, who had been a member of their group but who had decided to remain in Texas. Minutes later the plane crashed on the flats five miles from Aransas Pass.

> The plane made a perfect takeoff, Dierks told newsmen. The sky was clear, and I watched until it was fully 4,000 feet up. Ahead several miles I could see an exceedingly dark cloud. I watched the plane until it disappeared into this dark cloud. A few minutes later I heard that there had been an accident.
>
> Farmers who had gathered at the scene of the accident told me the story of what happened. Some of them had noticed the plane disappear into the black cloud. All of a sudden, the plane came crashing out of the cloud. One wing was off, or partly so. Before the ship was half way to the ground the gasoline tanks separated from the remainder of the plane.
>
> I don't suppose anyone will ever know positively what happened up there in that black cloud, but it seemed to be the impression of nearly all who saw the accident that the plane had been struck by lightning.

Some of the witnesses said they heard an explosion. As the plane fell, they saw the wings break away from the fuselage. There had been scattered showers in the area all day, but with the exception of the black cloud the sky was clear at the scene of the crash. W. C. Maus, manager of the airport, "discounted the lightning theory since there was no sign of an explosion or fire about the wreckage," according to an AP story on the accident. Maus suggested that the plane flew into the dark cloud at high speed, and that when it emerged the pilot pulled back on the stick so fast that the wings crumpled. The pilot, however, was experienced, and it is unlikely that simply emerging from a cloud would cause him to have such a violent reaction.[12]

Only eleven days after this crash, a similar accident occurred at Meopham, Kent, England, when a rented Junkers plane fell, killing six prominent persons. Again, there was an explosion in the air.

The fuselage of the plane came down near the village green, and parts of the machine were scattered over the green, a witness said. One wing landed about a mile away from the green, the engine a quarter of a mile away, and the tail 300 yards away. As far as I could see, the plane came to pieces in mid-air.

"It fell out of a cloud, and I saw one wing and the tail floating clear. The fuselage crashed more heavily, directly to the ground."

The following day London newspapers said the accident was "one of the most mysterious crashes in the history of aviation." There was no evidence of fire or explosion, and it was said that the sound heard by witnesses must have been caused by the wings tearing off.

The plane had left the Junkers factory in Germany only seven months before and had been flown about a hundred hours. The investigation revealed no evidence of structural defects nor negligence by the airline that had rented the plane. Factory officials pointed out that hundreds of planes of the same type had had up to ten years of operation, including trans-Atlantic flights, without complaint.

The investigation finally ended in January, 1931, with the theory that the tailplane had folded on the elevators due to buffeting by air currents.[18]

There are other cases of this type involving clouds and aerial disintegration, but the above are sufficiently representative. But, what was the "aberration" that doomed an F-89 Interceptor jet over Lake Superior?

Early on the evening of November 23, 1953, U.S. Air Force radar operators picked up the blip of an unknown object over the Soo Locks at Sault Sainte Marie, Michigan. This was a restricted area. A jet from Kinross Field was sent to investigate. Lieutenant Felix Moncla, Jr., twenty-six, was the pilot. In the rear cockpit was Lieutenant R. R. Wilson, twenty-two, the radar observer. The plane was equipped with two rubber rafts and each man wore a life jacket.

The unknown object, at first thought to be a Canadian airliner that had strayed off course, moved out across Whitefish Bay and over Lake Superior. The jet, flying at over five hundred miles per hour, pursued the object for nine minutes to a point seventy miles off Keweenaw Point. Suddenly the ground observers saw the blip of the unknown object merge with that of the F-89 and the single blip moved off the radar screen. Apparently there had been a collision.

Search planes with flares were sent to the location. All night they roared through the darkness over the icy water. On the following day boats joined in the search as American and Canadian fliers checked a hundred mile area.

But no trace was ever found of the jet, the unknown object, or the missing men.

Canadian authorities said no planes were in the vicinity of the blip and no planes were missing. A check of airliner speed and the time plus distance involved proved that the object could not have been an airliner.

The original story was released at Traux AFB, Madison, Wisconsin, and carried by Associated Press on an early wire. Later, the story was killed when Air Force Intelligence decided to classify the report. It is *still* classified. Pressed for an explanation, an Air Force spokesman said the radar operators had made a mistake. But the operators were doubtless experienced, highly trained men.

It really doesn't matter. The Air Force is probably still puzzled. We can ignore the blip and simply say the F-89 vanished—for an unknown reason—for it has happened to planes time and time again.[14]

The complications and time involved in a major aircraft disaster investigation are well illustrated in the following case:

On the evening of November 8, 1957, Pan American Clipper 944 left San Francisco International Airport for a flight to Honolulu. It swung up far above the patches of fog drifting in from the sea and headed west out over the Pacific, its running lights blinking in the darkness.

Thirty-six passengers were aboard. Captain Gordon H. Brown, a veteran of trans-Pacific crossings, was in command. The crew of eight also included First Officer William P. Wygant and Second Officer William H. Fontenberry.

The plane was a Boeing 377 Strato-Cruiser. Its flight path specified a speed of 226 knots at an altitude of 10,000 feet. Routine position reports were made. Four hours and thirty-nine minutes after it left California it reported to Ocean Station *November,* where a radar fix established that the clipper was ten miles east of the vessel.

Thirty-four minutes later came the last message from the doomed airliner—another routine position report. The clipper was listed as "unreported" after no additional position reports were received.

Weather conditions were favorable in the area. The air temperature was well above freezing over the sea described as "unusually calm." Other pilots reported that there was no precipitation, lightning, or turbulence.

During the early morning hours of November 9 a search was launched. Coast Guard surface vessels and Air Force planes left Hawaii, scanning the darkness for flames or flares. As dawn brought light over the watery wastes, the search was intensified. The aircraft carrier U.S.S. *Philippine Sea* sent its planes to join in the hunt. But day after day passed with no trace of the clipper being found.

Finally, on the sixth day, planes from the aircraft carrier discovered bodies and some wreckage ninety miles north of the clipper's designated flight path, and the *Philippine Sea* proceeded to the scene.

CAB investigators, pathologists and Pan American officials were flown to the aircraft carrier. A total of nineteen bodies were recovered, fourteen of them wearing life jackets.

This was all the public was told at the time. As in most similar disasters, civilian and military, information was "classified" until a final report of the investigation was made. Some investigations require a period of years and public interest has vanished when the report is announced. In some military accidents no report at all is made to the general public.

The CAB report on this disaster was finally released in 1961 and published in *Aviation Week* magazine. It is a lengthy and exhaustive account of studies that covered several years. It states: "External examination of the bodies was made, carefully noting all external injuries. There was no evidence of foul play found on any of the recovered bodies. . . . Further, the lack of extensive crash-induced mutilation, together with the general condition of the bodies, suggested that the water impact, although severe, was not sufficiently great to cause complete disintegration of the aircraft."

Pathological examination indicated that at least ten of the nineteen victims had died from drowning. There was some evidence of toxication from carbon monoxide, but the evidence was not conclusive.

Several wrist watches were stopped at the probable time of impact (at 1:27 A.M.) twenty-three minutes after the clipper made its final position report. The point of impact was 105 miles west of the last reported position and ninety miles off course to the north. Why the airliner was some thirty degrees off its route is unknown.

"Two pertinent conclusions regarding the final position of the flight are evident," the report continues. "Consideration of the distance flown from the last reported position to the impact point, and of the time required to traverse that distance, shows that the flight did not turn back toward Ocean Station *November*. Also, the ditching to the north of the planned route indicates that appreciable lateral distance, not on course and away from the ocean station, was traversed after the start of the emergency.

"It is difficult to understand why the captain would have elected to continue away from *November* had he been able to do otherwise. Weather was not a factor, and it is not believed that the shipping lanes to the north offered any inducement to turn in that direction. Conversely, *November,* a fixed ocean station equipped with radio homing and radar devices and rescue equipment, was in close proximity with trained personnel readily available."

This brought up another mystery. If the clipper was in a state of emergency while traveling ninety miles off course, and certainly long enough in any case for some passengers to put on life jackets, why were no radio messages received?

Clipper 944 was equipped with two high frequency radio transmitting and receiving systems. It was also equipped with SELCAL, located on the control pedestal where both pilots could use it. SELCAL generates pre-set codes which are transmitted on a voice communication frequency without pilot monitoring.

Since it seemed incredible that at least one of the officers aboard would not have attempted to send a signal, CAB officials made an intensive investigation of this possibility.

There were forty-four other airline flights to Hawaii the night and early morning of the disaster. A check disclosed that not one of them had received any communication from the clipper. Communications with Pan American planes in flight are handled by ARINC (Aeronautical Radio, Inc.). CAB investigators listened to ARINC tape recordings for the frequency over which a possible undetected emergency message might have been sent.

At first nothing was apparent, but repeated playbacks revealed some extremely weak transmissions which were "subject to varied and conflicting interpretations." For three months, using the finest special monitoring equipment and Pan American communications personnel with experience in talking to the missing crewmen, this part of the inquiry was then further pursued. But in the end, "despite this comprehensive research, the Board could not definitely establish that any emergency transmissions came from Clipper 944."

Only on wreckage floating above the water was there any evidence of fire. This indicated that any fire must have occurred after the impact. CAB found no evidence of an in-flight explosion in the fuselage.

In checking cargo manifests, a shipment of sodium sulfide, a volatile chemical, was found. However, it had been packed according to strict regulations.

A check of the crew revealed that all members were experienced and had excellent records. Nothing unusual was found in the clipper's maintenance background, although the Board was not satisfied with the thoroughness of some maintenance reports.

One of the conclusions of the Board was that exposure of the crew to carbon monoxide was indicated, "but incapacitation could not be definitely established."

The report continued: "A . . . probable source of CO (carbon monoxide) would be an unusual occurrence in a power package which could have initiated a chain of events leading to the introduction of carbon monoxide in the fuselage. Such an unusual occurrence could be a failure which would release part of a propeller blade or the entire propeller, or a failed turbo-supercharger disk. It is likely that such an occurence would be accompanied by serious flight control problems and possibly fire.

"If a propelled object, such as a propeller, came through the fuselage, it could easily start a fire, knock out some radio equipment, make emergency smoke evacuation procedures ineffective, and destroy the crew's oxygen supply. Such an occurrence fits the known circumstances better than any other possibilities."

Other conclusions of the Board are as follows:

Shortly after the last routine report an emergency of an undetermined nature occurred. This was followed by a descent from 10,000 feet. No emergency message was received from the aircraft.

Some preparation for ditching was accomplished. The aircraft broke up on impact, followed by a surface fire. Weather was not a factor. There was no evidence of foul play or sabotage. Irregularities of maintenance procedures disclosed during the investigation could not be linked to the accident.

Finally the Board states that it has "insufficient evidence at this time to determine the cause of the accident."

Regarding the carbon monoxide theory, it should be pointed out that the evidence indicates that at least some of the passengers drowned. If the gas had been limited mainly to the pilots' compartment, the severe headache and grogginess that usually precede unconsciousness should have given sufficient warning for a radio message to be sent at least automatically. We can only guess what happened while the clipper drifted ninety miles off course.

Aviation Week headlined its story on the CAB report: "Pan Am Crash Cause Remains Unknown."[15]

And so it is—still a mystery—and one that will probably never be solved.

Did the U.S. Navy in a classified experiment during wartime secrecy apply Dr. Albert Einstein's "Unified Field" theory and successfully cause a warship and its crew to become invisible?

Were the experiments abandoned when sailors involved continued to be accompanied by "force fields" after leaving the vessel that caused them to suffer occasional attacks of invisibility, immobility, and even insanity?

At one time during the experiments was the warship unaccountably teleported from Philadelphia to its berth near Norfolk?

The story that raises these fantastic questions began in 1955 when *The Case for the UFO's*, the first of four books on "unidentified flying objects" written by the late Morris K. Jessup, was published by The Citadel Press, New York.

Dr. Jessup brought to this controversial subject the background of an extraordinary career. He had been an instructor in astronomy and mathematics at the University of Michigan and at Drake University. After receiving his Ph.D. degree in astro-physics, he erected and operated the largest refracting telescope in the Southern Hemisphere, in South Africa, for the University of Michigan. There his research program resulted in the discovery of numerous double-stars now catalogued by the Royal Astronomical Society.

Later he studied the sources of crude rubber along the headwaters of the Amazon for the U.S. Department of Agriculture. His interests now turned to exploration, and he participated in archeological studies of Maya ruins in the jungles of Central America for the Carnegie Institute of Washington. He also engaged in independent explorations of Inca remains in Peru and early cultures on the high plateau of Mexico.

Jessup's book, *The Case for the UFO's*, discussed the more mysterious phenomena in the fields of astronomy, meteorology, and the history of these sciences, as well as the problems of space travel. He believed that the use of rockets limited the distances we could reach and that man would have to discover the nature and application of gravity before he could navigate in outer space.

On January 13, 1956, Jessup received a strange letter from a Carlos Miguel Allende, who also used the Americanized version of his name, Carl M. Allen. The letter had been mailed from Texas, but gave a home address in Pennsylvania.

Its composition was awkward, with capitalization in the middle of sentences, errors in punctuation, misspelled words and frequent underlining. After commenting on several subjects discussed in Jessup's book, it gave details about an alleged secret naval experiment in October, 1943, in which a ship was rendered invisible with disastrous results to the crew. The writer indicated he was in the service at the time and was a witness.

Jessup's first reaction was that the letter was either a hoax or the rantings of a crackpot. The very nature of UFO investigation attracts twisted and unstable minds.

On the other hand, perhaps the writer was giving an exaggerated account of an actual occurrence. There were many classified experiments made during World War II. In 1943 research was in progress that led to the creation of the atomic bomb. It had been inspired by Einstein's letter to President Roosevelt. The "Unified Field" theory of this famed scientist could also have been the basis for other not so successful experimentation.

Jessup sent a postcard to the Pennsylvania address and requested additional information and evidence to support the allegations. Slightly over four months later he received a second letter.

This time Allende added a few details and offered to be questioned under the influence of hypnosis or "truth serum" so that he could recall dates, names of other witnesses and their service serial numbers. He suggested that the testimony of these witnesses would confirm his own account. But this plan of investigation would have been impractical and too costly in time and money.

Meanwhile, in Washington, another occurrence had taken place. Jessup learned about it when he responded to an invitation to visit the Office of Naval Research (ONR). There he was handed a paperback copy of his book.

"This book was sent to us through the mail anonymously," one of the officers explained. "Apparently it was passed back and forth among at least three persons who made notations. Look it over, Mr. Jessup, and tell us if you have any idea who wrote those comments."

Jessup spun the pages. Several hundred comments written in three different colors of ink appeared at the top, bottom and edges of the printed text. The notations applied to passages in the book that were underlined. There were discussions between the writers, questions and answers, and additions to earlier notes. The book was well worn from use.

Now Jessup began reading the comments with growing bewilderment. They implied intimate knowledge of UFO's, their methods of propulsion, and the origin and background of the beings operating them. Many of the comments were "teasers," hinting at a store of alien information, bizarre and fantastic.

Why, Jessup wondered, was the Navy interested in this book? It was a good example of the type of material that is tossed into wastebaskets. Was the annotated book an elaborate hoax or the product of deranged minds?

Then Jessup noticed a passage that seemed to answer his question. It referred to the secret naval experiment in 1943. As he continued reading, he found other references to the invisible ship. Moreover, they were written in the same style and used the same terms and wording as in the letters he had received earlier.

There could be little doubt that Carlos Allende was one of the writers in the annotated book.

"I feel certain that I have two letters from one of the commentators," Jessup told the officer.

"Thank you, Mr. Jessup," he replied. "It is important that we see those letters. You may be interested in knowing that your book along with all the notes is going to be reproduced in a limited edition for circulation among some of our top people. We'll see that you get a copy."

Jessup left the office, puzzled. He turned the two letters over to ONR a day or so later.

The annotated book was reproduced by the Varo Manufacturing Company of Garland, Texas. Due to the peculiar writing style, grammar and proper placing of text and the comments by the three writers so each could be easily identified, the typing was a slow, laborious task. It is not certain whether ONR or the Varo Corporation—an electronics firm engaged in classified space age work—assumed the cost of the project.

At least twenty-five copies of the large mimeographed book were produced. It contained close to two hundred pages, printed on standard 8½ x 11 letter-head-sized paper, bound with plastic covers. The book included the two letters received by Jessup from Allende.

Some obvious questions will be answered in the introduction to the Varo edition, which reads as follows:

Notations that imply intimate knowledge of UFO's, their means of motion, their origin, background, history, and habits of beings occupying UFO's provide an interesting subject for investigation. Such notations were found in a copy of the paperback edition of M. K. Jessup's *Case for the UFO's.* Because of the importance which we attach to the possibility of discovering clues to the nature of gravity, no possible item, however disreputable from the point of view of classical science, should be overlooked.

The annotated copy, addressed to Admiral N. Furth, Chief, Office of Naval Research, Washington, 25, D.C., came in a manila envelope postmarked Seminole, Texas, 1955. Written across the face of the envelope in ink was "Happy Easter." In July or August of that year the book appeared in the incoming correspondence of Major Darrell L. Ritter, U.S.M.C. Aeronautical Project Office in ONR. When Captain Sidney Sherby reported aboard at ONR he obtained the book from Major Ritter. Captain Sherby and Commander George W. Hoover, Special Projects Officer, ONR, indicated direct interest in some of the material therein.

Varo Mfg. Co., Garland, Texas, offered to re-publish the book together with all notations in a very limited edition as a prelude to consideration of further pursuit of this unconventional material.

Miss Michael Ann Dunn has undertaken the task of rewriting* this book including all notes, interjections, underscoring, and etc. By form, position, color and footnotes as much of the meaning and relationships of the original annotated copy is retained as possible. No attempt has been made, with ultra violet light or other methods, to read material which has been crossed out by one of the correspondents.

It appears that these notes were written by three persons. The use of three distinct colors of ink—blue, blue-violet, and blue-green—and the difference in handwriting lead to this conclusion. Hereafter, they will be referred to as Mr. A, Mr. B, and Jemi.

It was assumed that the third person was Jemi because of the direct use of "Jemi" in salutations and references to that name by Mr. A and Mr. B throughout the book. There are many, some of which appear on pages 2, 81, 122, 126 in the original book.† It is possible, of course, that it is merely a salutation.

---

* It was not *rewritten* but *retyped,* conforming word for word with the printed editions.

† That is, the original marked copy of the Citadel Press edition.

(Here follows a paragraph giving evidence from some of the notes that two of the men may have been twins.)

It is probable that these men are Gypsies. In the closing pages of the book Mr. B says ". . . only a Gypsy will tell another of that catastrophe. And we are a discredited people, ages ago. Hah! Yet man wonders where 'we' come from. . . ." On page 130 Mr. A says ". . . ours is way of life, time proven and happy. We have nothing, own nothing except our music & philosophy & are happy." On page 76 Mr. B says, "Show this to a Brother Gypsy. . . ." On page 158 the reference to the word "we" by Mr. A could refer to the "discredited people."

Charles G. Leland in his book *English Gypsies and Their Language* states that the Gypsies call each other brother and sister, and are not in the habit of admitting to their fellowship people of a different blood and with whom they have no sympathy. This could explain the usage of the term in the closing notes "My Dear Brothers" and perhaps the repeated reference to "vain humankind."

This book was apparently passed through the hands of these men several or many times. This conclusion is drawn from the fact that there are discussions between two or all three of the men, questions answered, and places where parts of a note have been marked through, underlined, or added to by one or both of the other men. Some have been deleted by marking through.

Shortly after publication of his book, Mr. Jessup received a letter from a Carlos Miguel Allende. (A copy of this letter and the one that followed appear in the appendix.) Mr. Jessup said that he "had felt from the first that this man was the one who mailed the book to the Navy. . . ." Consideration of the handwriting, style, content and phraseology of both the notes and letter show a distinct possibility that the letter was written by Mr. A. This conclusion comes from the notes by Mr. A on pages 130, 117, and 150. These references to Farraday, hobnail or cleated shoes, and catching fire are nearly the same as the ones in the letter.

The letter was received by Mr. Jessup in Miami, on Friday, Jan. 13, 1956. It was postmarked Gainesville, Texas, and mailed in an envelope of the Turner Hotel, Gainesville. It is copied as nearly verbatim as possible.

Mr. Jessup received a second letter from Mr. Allende postmarked Du Bois, Pennsylvania, May 25, 1956. Due to peculiar spelling and other idiosyncrasies there can be little doubt that Mr. A and Carlos Allende are the same person.

These men have been careless in their spelling, capitalization, punctuation and sentence structure; though consistency indicates adherence to custom, perhaps dictated by their original language. The notes are arranged as close to the original as possible.

It might seem that the underscore in the book was in the form of a code or that if read separately it would have a meaning of its own. Superficial examination has failed to disclose such a code. The underscored text usually refers to the notes by the same man.

(Here follow several paragraphs explaining the composition of the reprint so the reader can distinguish between original text and the handwritten notes.)

It might be helpful for you to know a little about the nature of the notes before you begin reading this book. The notes refer to two types of people living in space. Specifically, the "stasis neutral" and *undersea* [italics mine—author] are mentioned as habitats. They seem to live in both interchangeably. The building of undersea cities is mentioned. Many different kinds of ships are used as transportation. These two peoples, races or whatever they may be called, are referred to over and over again. They are called the L-M's and S-M's. The L-M's seem to be peaceful; the S-M's are not. It seems that the annotations are inclined toward the L-M's as they speak more kindly of them than the S-M's.

Terms such as: mothership, home-fleet, Great ark, great bombardment, great return, great war, little-men, force-fields, deep freezes, undersea building, measure markers, scout ships, magnetic and gravity fields, inlay work, clear-talk, telepathing, burning "coat," nodes, vortices, magnetic "net," and many others are used quite naturally by these men. They explain how, why, and what happens to people, ships and planes that have disappeared. They explain the origin of odd storms and clouds, objects falling from the sky, strange marks and footprints, and other things which we have not solved.

These men seem to feel that it is too late for man to obtain space flight. They feel that mankind could not cope with "those mind wrecking conditions that sea and space contain" for man is too egotistical, values too much the material, wars over mere parcels of this planet, is too filled with jealousy, and lacks true brotherhood.

How much truth is there in this? That cannot be answered. It is evident that these men provide some very intriguing explanations; explanations that may be worth consideration.

Thus ends the introduction to the Varo edition of Jessup's book with its weird and puzzling comments.* Bound with the

---

* There is no signature to this introduction but, as it was not written by Jessup, and was, of course, not in the original printed editions, we can assume only that it was composed at ONR.

book are the two letters sent by Allende (or Mr. A) to Jessup. They gave a home address of R.D. 1, Box 223, New Kensington, Pa.

Since both letters are very long, somewhat repetitive, and difficult to read, I will summarize their contents.

In his first letter Allende referred to Jessup's plea that further research be made into Einstein's Unified Field theory, stating it was not necessary. "It may interest you to know," he wrote, "that the good doctor was not so much influenced by mathematics in his retraction of that work, as he . . . was by humantics. His later computations . . . upon cycles of human civilization and progress compared to the growth of man's general over-all character were enough to horrify him. Thus we are told today that the theory was 'incomplete.' "

Allende then states that it is complete, and that the "results of my friend Dr. Franklin Reno were used. . . . Yet the Navy fears to use this result . . . (which) stands today as proof that the Unified Field theory to a certain extent is correct." Allende refers to the experiments of Michael Faraday, then writes:

The "result" was complete invisibility of a ship, destroyer type, and all its crew, while at sea (Oct. 1943). The field was effective in an oblate spheroidal shape, extending one hundred yards (more or less) out from each beam of the ship. Any person within that sphere became vague in form, but he too observed those persons aboard that ship as though they too were of the same state, yet were walking upon nothing. Any person without that sphere could see nothing save the clearly defined shape of the ship's hull in the water, providing of course, that that person was just close enough to see, yet, just barely outside of that field.

Allende continues: "Half of the officers and crew of that ship are at present mad as hatters. A few are, even yet, confined to certain areas where they may receive trained scientific aid when they either 'go blank' or 'go blank and get stuck.' Going blank (is) an after effect of the man having been within the field too much . . . when also they 'get stuck' . . . the man cannot move of his own volition unless two or more of those within the field go and touch him, quickly, else he 'freezes.' " (The writer called this act the "laying on of hands.")

If a man freezes, his position must be marked out carefully and then the field is cut-off. Everyone but that "frozen" man is able to move; to appreciate *apparent* solidity again. Then the newest member of the crew must approach the spot, where he will find the "frozen" man's face or bare skin, that is not covered by usual uniform clothing. Some times it takes only an hour or so, sometimes all night and all day long, and worse it once took six months, to get the man "unfrozen." This "deep freeze" was not psychological. It is the result of a hyper-field that is set up within the field of the body, while the "scorch" field is turned on and this at length or upon an old hand.

Allende alleged that a highly complicated piece of equipment had to be constructed to "unfreeze" those who became "true froze" or "deep freeze" subjects. A "deep freeze" victim usually went insane if his condition continued for more than a day. He adds that "frozen men" are not aware of time as we know it.

"The first 'deep freeze' as I said took six months to rectify," Allende wrote. "It also took over five million dollars worth of electronic equipment and a special ship berth. . . . You will hear phrases from these men such as 'caught in the flow' (or the push) or 'stuck in the green' or 'stuck in molasses.' . . . These refer to some of the decade-later after effects of force-field work."

Allende says to "go blank" is to become temporarily invisible, while the other terms refer to the sensations when entering a "plain freeze" or a "deep freeze."

He continues: "There are only a very few of the original experimental D-E's crew left by now, sir. Most went insane, one just walked through his quarter's wall in sight of his wife and child and two other crew members (was never seen again), and two 'went into the flame,' i.e., they 'froze' and caught fire while carrying common small-boat compasses. One man carried the compass and caught fire, the other came for the 'laying on of hands' as he was nearest, but he too took fire. The faith in 'hand laying' died when this happened and men's minds went by the score. The experiment was a complete success. The men were complete failures."

According to Allende, there was a short report in a Philadelphia newspaper sometime in 1944–46 "describing the sailors' actions after their initial voyage." The men, apparently in a semi-visible condition, entered a tavern near the Navy Yard, shocking the waitresses. The skeptical reporter wrote a "tongue-in-cheek" story.

Allende implies he witnessed the October, 1943, experiment from an observer vessel, the S.S. *Andrew Furnseth,* a "Matson Lines Liberty ship out of Norfolk." Others aboard that he re-members were a Richard "Splicey" Price, of Roanoke, Virginia,

Chief Mate Mowsely and a man named "Connally," from New England. Following his signature, Allende wrote Z416175—which may have been his service number.

In a lengthy postscript Allende says the Navy, obviously, did not know in advance that the "hyper-field" that made the ship invisible would affect the men after they left the ship. He expresses the opinion that something about the compass triggered the fire that killed two of the men. And when "one or two of their men, visible-within-the-field-to-all-the-others, just walked into nothingness; and nothing could be felt of them, either when the field was turned on or off . . . more fears were amassed" and the experiments were stopped.

"I wish to mention," Allende wrote, "that somehow, also, the experimental ship disappeared from its Philadelphia dock and only a very few minutes later appeared at its other dock in the Norfolk, Newport News, Portsmouth area. This was distinctly and clearly identified as being that place, but the ship again disappeared and went back to its Philadelphia dock in only a very few minutes or less. This was also noted in the newspapers, but I forget what paper I read it in or when it happened. Probably late in the experiments, may have been in 1956 after experiments were discontinued, I cannot say for sure."

Allende believes that many of the more serious after-effects of the experiment could have been prevented by a more careful selection of personnel and a more cautious program. He adds that there should have been a more careful watch over such items as rings, identification bracelets, watches, belt buckles, and especially hob-nailed or cleated shoes.

In his second letter Allende said that under the influence of hypnosis and/or sodium pentothal he could assist Jessup in any investigation by remembering names, addresses, and service numbers of his shipmates, plus the dates that the newspaper stories he referred to were published. He suggested that once the names and home towns of some of the men involved were known, they (and perhaps the waitresses in the tavern incident) could be tracked down, induced to undergo hypnosis and be questioned.

Allende concludes his letter as follows: "I am a star-gazer, Mr. Jessup. I make no bones about this and the fact that I feel that if handled properly, i.e. presented to people and science in the proper psychologically effective manner, I feel sure that man will go where he now dreams of being—to the stars via the form of transport that the Navy accidentally stumbled upon (to their embarrassment) when their experimental ship took off and popped-up a minute or so later on several hundred sea travel-trip miles away at another of its berths in the Chesapeake Bay area. I read of this in another newspaper and only by hypnosis could any man remember all the details of which paper, date of occurrence, etc., you see? Perhaps already the Navy has used this accident of transport to build your UFO's. It is a logical advance from any standpoint. What do you think?"

At this point, one big question will haunt the reader's mind. Why did certain Navy officers and/or Varo corporation officials regard the annotated book (and Allende letters) so seriously that they called in Jessup for questioning, then went to the trouble and great expense of having the entire book, notes and letters typed, reproduced and distributed to various key persons?

The Varo edition introduction says it was "because of the importance which we attach to the possibility of discovering clues to the nature of gravity." Yet the references to gravity in the notes are vague, non-technical, and offer no illustrations or mathematical formulae from which experiments could be developed.

Why were Allende's curious letters added to the book? Was the Navy interested because they disclosed some information, possibly exaggerated, of a top secret naval experiment? And, since the Varo books were never classified, did officials believe that the puzzling comments about UFO's and races in space would serve as a smoke-screen of doubt over references to the invisible and teleported ship?

There was certainly *something* in the notes and letters that justified the time and cost of producing the Varo edition. What was it? It is far from obvious to an uninformed reader of the book.

Eventually several copies of the Varo book drifted into civilian hands. Two booklets of limited circulation have published the Allende letters, plus the introduction and preface of the Varo edition. One is *M. K. Jessup and the Allende Letters*, by Riley Crabb;[1] the other, *The Strange Case of Dr. M. K. Jessup*, by Gray Barker.[2] Crabb's Varo copy disappeared in 1960 when he mailed it to his California home from Washington.*

---

* The writer has had access to photostatic copies of appropriate sections of Jessup's own, annotated, copy of the Varo edition, which is unique in that it contains his counter-comments, and is the only such copy in existence.

Did Navy investigators ever locate Allende? We do not know. Jessup once told a friend that he understood they failed to find him.

Did Jessup ever have further contact with Allende? We do not know. From some source, however, he apparently did secure some additional information. He told friends that a man went to the Navy and said, in effect: "You want camouflage, gentlemen! Give me a ship and I'll show you perfect camouflage." When this man went aboard the experimental ship, he was carrying a black box.

If this is true, was the man "Dr. Franklin Reno"? If not, who was he?

Barker says he knows a close friend of Jessup's who is said to have documents "which might solve the mystery." This unidentified friend told Barker that on an unspecified date he tried to locate Allende at the rural New Kensington, Pa., address. The farmhouse was vacant.

Neighbors said a man known to them only as "Carlos" or "Carl" had formerly roomed there with an elderly couple. He had disappeared and later the couple had left. One morning a truck pulled up, loaded all the furniture in the house, and drove away, its destination unknown.

It is unlikely that our story has any connection with Jessup's tragic death. However, during the months that preceded his passing, his close friends report that he seemed very tense and nervous. He gave his own Varo edition copy and personal notes on the Allende mystery to one friend in particular "to be held in trust." Then he went to Florida.

Several weeks later, on the evening of April 20, 1959, the body of fifty-nine-year-old Dr. M. K. Jessup was found in his station wagon in Dade County Park, near Coral Gables, Florida. A hose attached to the vehicle's exhaust pipe led into the closed car. There were no marks of possible violence on the body. No notes were found.

The death certificate lists the cause as suicide.

Mysteries are fascinating. But more important, they are occurrences or phenomena on the frontiers of our knowledge. They are indications of learning yet to come. If we speculate about them, we may catch glimpses of wilderness trails that the sciences of tomorrow will pave into highways.

To the cave man, practically everything was a mystery. We have made some progress. We have a long way to go. The road ahead is as endless as time and the starry mainland beyond.

Today we witness the beginning of the space age. Yet, close to home and within ourselves lie a million mysteries. There are still vast areas on the earth's surface that remain unexplored. Very little is known about our planet's interior or the depths of its oceans. As for our inner selves, our ignorance is abysmal.

At this early stage, to try to pigeonhole (or deny) all phenomena, to reduce the universe to a pocket-size nugget of knowledge, is to assume the role of an intellectual clown. This is a time for broad views, daring theories, and open-mindedness.

The mysteries in this book fall into two categories—those for which explanations may lie in powers and abilities latent within ourselves, and those that are physical puzzles. The first would include the "wild talent" of Bottineau who foretold ship arrivals and the premonitions and visions that led to rescues and saved lives.

Many of us will agree that human minds can attain knowledge through sources other than the five basic senses. We can conceive of a mental reservoir or medium into which thought concepts flow as impulses, are transmitted, and then unite with similar projections like birds of a feather. And like the visual and auditory impulses received by our television sets, they overcome barriers of time and space—and, perhaps, to a far greater extent. Thus what we call supernormal information might be acquired.

But most of our riddles are in the second category.

We have the disappearances of crews from ships. Obviously some of these occurrences can be explained by possible piracy, mass murders or fright-induced abandonments. Others are more puzzling. Could some of these crews have been kidnaped by extra-terrestrials?

To those who have investigated this question, the evidence that there is interplanetary or interstellar traffic is impressive. We may be ignored for the same reason that savages on a jungle-clad isle are ignored by passing merchant vessels. After all, we *are* warring primitives. Still, occasional visitors from the void may pick up some of us for exhibition in their zoos!

Again, we have the total disappearance of vessels and aircraft. And again, there are well-known reasons—storms, fires, malfunction of structure or equipment—for many of these vanishments. But others are more bewildering.

There was British Wing Commander J. Baldwin who flew into a cloud and never came out. There was the F-89 Interceptor jet that was absorbed or destroyed by something that appeared as a blip on radar. There are the unexplained disintegrations of planes in mid-air.

We have discussed fireballs and flames from the sky and suggested that occasionally masses may drop from the seething seas of electro-magnetic energy that exist above us—from the grim, recently-discovered Van Allen belts.

And there are Wilbert Smith's circles of gravitational "reduced binding" still to be confirmed or publicly announced as confirmed. These strange clouds and atmospheric aberrations—what are they?

In 1951 Jesse M. Caldwell, a middle-aged civilian employee at Chanute AFB, Rantoul, Illinois, received public attention with his uncanny ability to predict airplane crashes. In March of that year he correctly predicted three crashes, in one giving not only the date but the place where a Douglas Globemaster came down over the North Atlantic.

As a test, the Chicago *Daily News* sent a reporter to interview him. Caldwell said April 4 and 8 would be "critical days" for aircraft. The newspaper withheld its story until after those days had passed, and then released the story when it found Caldwell was right both times. On April 4 a Navy plane was lost in the Gulf of Mexico. On April 8 two crashes caused the death of twenty-two persons.

Caldwell said his theory, which applied only to crashes caused by failure of the electrical system on planes, was based on magnetic effects. When the sun and moon are in certain relative positions to the earth, their magnetic fields intensify the earth's magnetism which, in turn, affects electrical systems in the atmosphere.

Magnetic effects were apparently a factor in the case of the lost patrol—that incredible vanishing of five torpedo bombers from Fort Lauderdale and the flying boat that flew to their rescue. They were lost and obviously their compasses had failed. Then the sea didn't look as it should, and for some unknown reason they couldn't see the sun and simply fly west. Then they vanished.

This brings us to the alleged naval experiment of 1943—and if this experiment was not performed, the time will come when it will be. If it has occurred naturally or spontaneously, once we understand the laws involved we can induce it experimentally.

Our mysterious Carlos Allende said the experiment was based on an application of Einstein's "unified field" theory. Einstein, in his special theory of relativity, amalgamated space and time into space-time; and in his general theory of relativity absorbed the gravitational field into space-time. The unified field theory went a step further by including the electromagnetic field into his concept of a single, unified background to all fundamental laws.

Mathematical formulae, yes, but the atomic and hydrogen bomb projects were developed from mathematical formulae. And since the days of Bolyai, Lobatchewsky, and Gauss over a century ago, higher mathematics has pointed to dimensions and realms beyond our ken.

The implications of space-time are well-known. As Minkowski said: "From henceforth space in itself and time in itself sink to mere shadows, and only a kind of union of the two preserves an independent existence."

These implications have been applied to outer space. Time slows down for an object moving near the speed of light. A man on the object ages more slowly. L. R. Shepherd, a British physicist, calculates that astronauts traveling at 99 per cent the speed of light could go to the star Procyon (10.4 light years away) and back in twenty-one years. Yet, to the astronauts it would seem that only three years had passed. Meanwhile, on the earth, everyone would be twenty-one years older.

This theory is confirmed by the *mu*-meson, a particle which considerably increases its life span when it approaches the speed of light in a cloud chamber.

Space-time has resulted in some astonishing speculations. In

1931 Dr. Gilbert Lewis of the University of California, upon receiving the 1930 Gold Medal of the Society of Arts and Sciences, read a paper in which he expressed his theory that time moves in two directions—backward and forward. He stated that there is no positive future or past, but that one exerts a "pull" on the other. He illustrated this by suggesting that events of today could have been among the factors which caused Caesar about two thousand years ago to cross the Rubicon.

Thus space-time continua may exist around us on the earth interpenetrating our known world. The ancient Hindu philosophers, who sought knowledge from within themselves, tell us of the "Akashic Records"—that in the "ethers" surrounding earth are retained all the scenes of the planet's history at any point on the surface. That such knowledge might be obtained by introspective practices is indicated by the astonishing expansion of consciousness induced by certain psychedelic drugs, especially LSD-25.

Writing in *Cosmopolitan* magazine (January, 1960), Eugene D. Fleming suggests the existence of a "psychic ether, something like a TV tape on which is recorded everything that happens." He tells of two young Englishwomen who were spending a holiday in Dieppe, France, in August, 1951. During early morning hours they heard a re-enactment of the World War II raid in which almost a thousand Canadian soldiers were killed, although they could not see anything in the darkness. They had enough presense of mind to take notes on the time the battle started, its heights of intensity, and when it ended. A later check by the Society for Psychical Research in London revealed their report was correct.

Their experience illustrates the human factor. No one else in their hotel heard the battle. Something in their minds established a rapport. But this is not always true. Hundreds witnessed three re-enactments of the Battle of Edge Hill in England.

There are thousands of cases in parapsychological annals of persons witnessing scenes from the past. Some are tragedies and emotionally-charged events. But others are visions of quiet ghosts going about their daily activities and glimpses of earlier, more carefree, days.

And there are many cases of phantom aircraft. Airports, for example, in the vicinity of Davenport, Iowa, were plagued by one early in 1957 (*Fate,* May, 1957, p. 13).

Another interesting observation was reported in *Coronet*

(April, 1943). A Lieutenant Grayson, early in 1940, was flying night patrol near Dover when he noticed a plane with an unfamiliar silhouette. He gave chase, but the plane kept well ahead. Finally, in brilliant moonlight, he got a clear view of the stranger. It was an ancient biplane. Its wings bore the iron cross symbol of the Kaiser's Germany. On the fuselage was the Flying Circus insignia of Baron Manfred von Richthofen, Germany's Red Knight, who was shot down in 1918.

Individuals, buildings, ships, islands, cities, and landscapes have been "ghosts." Do they co-exist in what—in our limited perception—we call reality? Our senses are limited. Animals possess different concepts of reality than man. Dogs hear sounds beyond our range. Cats can see deeper into the infra-red spectrum. There are, doubtless, thousands of vibrations and radiations around us of which we have no knowledge.

We do not know what lies beyond the atom—between matter and energy. The controversy about the existence of ether continues. And now we have the new concept of a negative universe that may be interpenetrating our positive universe—an entirely different type of space made up of reversed electrical charges (positrons and anti-protons), as first suggested by Nobel prize-winner Dr. P. A. M. Dirac. We have much to learn about the nature of matter.

But in our mysteries, a pattern emerges: "Reduced binding" or aberrations may be the first manifestations of an electromagnetic and/or gravitational vortex that, first, renders ships and planes and other objects invisible, and second, creates the conditions that make teleportation possible. If this teleportation is not to another point on the earth's surface, it must be into another space-time continuum, co-existing with our own.

We have asked if ghost ships are real, tangible objects? In their own continuum they certainly are, but when we can see and hear them, have they entered our own continuum? Did the crews of the *Marlborough* and other floating morgues die when the ships entered vortexes, and the vessels later reappear in our own realm? If the *Marlborough* (Chapter 8) and *Baychimo* (Chapter 9) were boarded, could men have also boarded the M.S. *Tricoleur* or the *Lady Luvibund* (Chapter 7) when they appeared in response to some cosmic or time cycle? Did the men from the *Ellen Austin* and other vanished crews (Chapter 9) board a derelict only to disappear with it into another dimension or continuum?

It's an interesting theory that would explain many riddles. These continua, realms, planes (or "Akashic Records") may be closer to us than we suspect. Many of our enigmas that have such diverse interpretations may be the result of interaction between these realms and our limited concept of reality. And since the human mind obviously plays a part in some of these occurrences, to understand their nature will be an important advance in understanding ourselves.

In the years to come, we should know.

BIBLIOGRAPHICAL NOTES

Chapter 1 / Over the Horizon

(1) E. P. Dutton and Co., New York, 1943; revised edition, 1957. (2) An excellent review of the work of Dr. Harold S. Burr and his associates will be found in *MD* (medical news magazine for physicians), June, 1959, under the title "Current of Life." (3) "The Subtle Tides of Life," by Rutherford Platt, *Readers Digest,* April, 1963. (4) Charles Fort, famed collector of bizarre and amazing data who died in 1932. His book *Wild Talents* was published the year he died, Claude Kendall, publisher. All four of his books are now available in *The Books of Charles Fort* (Henry Holt and Co., New York, 1941). (5) *Oddities: A Book of Unexplained Facts* by Rupert T. Gould (Philip Allan and Co., London, 1928). (6) *Letters on Natural Magic* was published in 1832 by J. and J. Harper, New York. It is very scarce. (7) Reported from a press clipping by Curtis Fuller, publisher, *Fate* magazine, December, 1954.

Chapter 2 / Vanishing Islands

(1) Robert Casey, *Easter Island,* Bobbs-Merrill Co., Indianapolis, Ind., 1931. (2) The search for Davis Land (and Sarah Ann Island) is also covered in *The Problem of Lemuria,* by Lewis Spence, David McKay Co., Philadelphia, 1933. (3) See "Peekaboo Islands of the Pacific," by Karl Versteeg, Department of Geology, College of Wooster, *American Weekly,* July 7, 1946; condensed in *Science Digest,* October, 1946. (4) *Ibid.* (5) AP dispatch, September 24, 1955. (6) For an account of the situation in California, see the author's article, "California's Coming Earthquake," in *Science Digest,* December, 1963. (7) Karl Versteeg, *op. cit.* (8) *Oddities: A Book of Unexplained Facts,* by Lieutenant Commander Rupert T. Gould, R.N. (Ret.) (Philip Allan and Co., London, 1928), p. 193. (9) *Islands of Adventure,* by Karl Baarslag (Farrar and Rinehart, New York, 1940). (10) *Ibid.* (11) Gould (*op. cit.,* p. 197) tells us that the subsidence of a volcanic island off the southwest corner of Iceland was the cause of the extinction of a famous bird—the Great Auk. These rare birds had their last colony on Garefowls Rock, 15 miles from land and the rock's sides were so high and steep that their aukery was practically inaccessible to man. The rock island sank in a volcanic eruption in 1830, and the birds were forced to move to the island of Eldey, nearer the coast and more accessible. "Here," Gould writes, "in obedience to that law of (museum) supply and demand which enacts that the rarer a species becomes the more rapidly it shall be exterminated, their numbers were rapidly depleted by the hardy

Icelanders, who dared not only the perils of a six-mile voyage, but also the grave risk of getting quite a sharp nip in the slack of their trousers before they could safely knock their formidable quarry on the head. Rabbit-shooting itself could scarcely offer more thrills and dangers. It was on Eldey, in 1844, that the last pair of Great Auks were murdered by two heroes named Jon Brandsson and Sigurur Islefsson, both natives of Iceland. It is permissible to hope that by now they are experiencing a much hotter climate." (12) See "Nature's Strangest Hoax," by Ralph H. Major, Jr., *Coronet* magazine, July, 1951. (13) *Ibid.* (14) Curtis Fuller's column "I See by the Papers," *Fate*, May, 1962. (15) Quoted by Russell W. Gibbons in his article "Vanishing Islands of the Arctic," *Fate*, December, 1957. Gibbons, who has written many articles on the Polar regions, is a Fellow of the American Geographical Society, an Associate of the Arctic Institute, and a Member of the American Polar Society. (16) The story of these floating islands will be found in *Skyways* magazine, January, 1952, and *Readers Digest*, February, 1952. (17) Interesting accounts of other vanished islands, considered mythical, will be found in *Traveller's Tales: A Book of Marvels*, by H. C. Adams (New York, 1927).

Chapter 3 / Bottles, Casks, and Caskets

(1) The preceding cases are taken from two articles: "Bottled Mailmen of the Seas," by Thorp McClusky and Albert A. Brandt, *Coronet*, December, 1950; and "Bottles in the Briny," by Ken Ferguson, *Coronet*, June, 1959. (2) *The Books of Charles Fort*, p. 636. (3) *Mysteries and Adventures Along the Atlantic Coast*, by Edward Rowe Snow (Dodd, Mead and Co., New York, 1948), p. 173. (4) Ken Ferguson, *op. cit.* (5) Edward Rowe Snow, *op. cit.* (6) See note 1. A very puzzling incident was reported by United Press, August 4, 1942. On May 9, Walter Jewett of Nantucket, Massachusetts, and a companion threw a bottle into the Atlantic off Tuckernuck with a note bearing their names and addresses. Two months later, on July 12, Jewett received a letter from Cape Flattery, Washington, stating that the bottle had been found by a diver engaged in salvaging an airplane that was wrecked in the Pacific 15 miles off shore. (7) "Bottle Notes Help U.S. to Map Oceans," by Charles Hillinger, Los Angeles *Times*, May 10, 1964. (8) McClusky and Brandt, *op. cit.* (9) The Clearwater (Florida) *Sun*, March 31, 1946. (10) *Fate*, September, 1955, p. 85. (11) Ken Ferguson, *op. cit.* (12) In addition to Sir Johnston Forbes-Robertson's *A Player Under Three Reigns* (Little, Brown & Co., Boston, 1925), see *The Days I Knew*, by Lily Langtry. More detailed accounts will be found in *Believe It or Not Omnibus*, by Robert Ripley (Simon and Schuster, New York, 1934), and "The Man Who Came Home," by Albert A. Brandt, *Fate*, June, 1952.

Chapter 4 / The Watchers and the Avengers

(1) "Captain Johnson's Incredible Catch," by Norman Carlisle, *Coronet*, January, 1960. (2) "Miracles at Sea," by Harvey Berman, *Fate*, March,

1958; *Stranger Than Science,* by Frank Edwards (Lyle Stuart, Publisher, New York, 1959), p. 81. (3) "Miracle in Mid-Atlantic," by Jerry Klein, *Coronet,* December, 1954. (4) "Double Play at Sea," by Jay Patnick, *Coronet,* April, 1952. (5) *Fate,* June, 1959, p. 81. (6) UPI dispatch, November 21, 1956. (7) UPI dispatch, October 30, 1962. (8) *Fate,* June, 1956, p. 6. (9) Quoted by Dr. Nandor Fodor, *Encyclopaedia of Psychic Science* (Arthurs Press, Ltd., London, 1934), p. 298. (10) *Fate,* March, 1953; *Strangest of All,* Frank Edwards (Lyle Stuart, Publisher, New York, 1956), p. 128. (11) "Was God the Skipper," by Henry Galus, *Fate,* April-May, 1952. (12) "The Night the Captain Died," by Stanley S. Jacobs, *Coronet,* February, 1952; letter from Claire Spofford, of San Francisco, a personal friend of the late Captain Baufman (Jacobs spells his last name "Baughman"), *Fate,* December, 1952. (13) *Fate,* September, 1952. (14) One of the best detailed accounts of this amazing occurrence will be found in *Mysteries of the Sea* by Robert de la Croix (American edition, John Day Co., New York, 1956). Other accounts of the revenge of the *Frigorifique* will be found in *True* magazine, July, 1961, and *Coronet,* January, 1959.

Chapter 5 / The Jinxed and the Damned

(1) *Stranger Than Science,* by Frank Edwards. (2) *Mammoth Believe It or Not* by Robert Ripley (Simon and Schuster, New York, 1955). (3) San Francisco and Portland, Oregon, newspapers, July 12, 1962 ff. (4) Mobile, Alabama, newspapers, March 19, 1956 ff. (5) *Fate,* June, 1952. (6) *Ibid.,* December, 1960; November, 1961. (7) *Ships and How They Sailed the Seven Seas,* by Hendrik Willem Van Loon (Somerset Books, Inc., New York, 1935). (8) *The Great Iron Ship,* by James Dugan (Harper and Brothers, New York, 1953). (9) The story of the *Charles Haskell* is taken from a column of true psychic news events written under the pseudonym of "Count Cagliostro" in the former *Ghost Stories* magazine, May, 1930. The late Fulton Oursler conducted this column for a time. (10) *Tomorrow* magazine (London, England), Winter, 1963.

Chapter 6 / The Haunts and the Horrors

(1) Percy B. Prior's article appears in "Count Cagliostro's" column, *Ghost Stories,* August-September, 1931. (2) *Forgotten Mysteries* by R. DeWitt Miller (Cloud, Inc., Chicago, 1947). (3) *The Invisible World,* by Hereward Carrington (Bernard Ackerman, Inc., New York, 1946). (4) "Count Cagliostro's" column, *Ghost Stories,* March, 1930. (5) The story of the *Ivan Vassili* will be found in R. DeWitt Miller's *Forgotten Mysteries; Coronet,* December, 1942; and *American Weekly,* April 14, 1940.

Chapter 7 / Fiery Phantoms and Noisy Specters

(1) The observation by the S.S. *Fort Salisbury* was originally published in the English magazine *Zoologist.* My notes are taken from *The Books of*

Charles Fort, p. 642. (2) Seattle, Washington, and Vancouver, British Columbia, newspapers, November 3, 1957 ff. (3) R. DeWitt Miller's *Forgotten Mysteries;* Sylvan Muldoon's *Psychic Experiences of Famous People* (Aries Press, Chicago, 1947). (4) Miss Elizabeth Dickens also blames a confusion of terminology. She points out that the word "wrecking" also signifies salvage; "and in that sense the islanders have always been wreckers, receiving by prearrangement with the ship-owners a share of the value recovered" (John Kobler). (5) *Great Storms and Famous Shipwrecks of the New England Coast,* by Edward Rowe Snow (Yankee Publishing Co., Boston, 1943). (6) de la Croix, *op. cit.* (7) AP dispatch, December 8, 1953; *Fate,* November, 1949. (8) *Fate,* June, 1955. (9) *Ibid.,* January, 1955. (10) Howard H. Brisbane's report was published in *Fate,* April, 1962.

Chapter 8 / Floating Morgues

(1) Robert Ripley, *Believe It or Not Omnibus,* p. 159. (2) Other accounts of the *Octavius* will be found in Edwards' *Stranger Than Science* and in *Fate,* February, 1953. (3) Richard L. Neuberger wrote an excellent story of the cruise of the *St. Roch.* It appeared in *Coronet* magazine, February, 1945. (4) Lewis Thompson, well known for his detailed stories of true murder cases, turned to the sea in telling of the ghastly discovery of the bark *Josepha.* His article appeared in *True Mystery* magazine, February, 1955. (5) Reported by John Hix in his syndicated newspaper feature *Strange as It Seems* in 1946. (6) *Fate,* June, 1952. (7) *National Geographic Society News Bulletin,* October 8, 1934. (8) *Case for the UFO,* by M. K. Jessup (The Citadel Press, New York, 1955); *Strangest of All,* by Frank Edwards; *Fate,* June, 1953.

Chapter 9 / The Wanderers and the Homers

(1) *National Geographic Society News Bulletin,* October 8, 1934. (2) UPI dispatch as published in the Washington, D.C., *Times-Herald,* February 11, 1953; other accounts in *Strangest of All* by Frank Edwards, and *Fate,* June, 1953. (3) *The Stargazer Talks* (Geoffrey Bles, London, 1944) is a book based on talks over the British Broadcasting System by Lt. Comdr. Gould, formerly a member of the BBC Brains Trust. (4) In addition to Edward R. Snow, other writers who tell of the *James B. Chester* include Gould, Edwards, and R. DeWitt Miller. (5) *Tomorrow* magazine, Winter, 1963. (6) AP dispatch, July 14, 1941. (7) Gould, *The Stargazer Talks* (see note 3). (8) Other accounts of the *Seabird* will be found in R. DeWitt Miller's *Forgotten Mysteries;* Edwards' *Strangest of All;* and *Coronet,* December, 1952. (9) *Fate,* October, 1955. (10) *The Devil's Tramping Ground,* by John Harden (University of North Carolina Press, Chapel Hill, 1949). (11) Quoted by Edward R. Snow in *Mysteries and Adventures Along the Atlantic Coast.* Snow made a careful, detailed investigation of the case.

Chapter 10 / **The Classic Drifter**

(1) The allegations of some writers that a half-eaten meal was on a table and that an unfinished letter was in the mate's cabin are not supported by court testimony. (2) *The Stargazer Talks*. (3) *New Light on the Mary Celeste* (Haldeman-Julius Publications, Girard, Kansas, 1947); *Strange Mysteries of Time and Space* (The Citadel Press, New York, 1959). (4) *Mysteries of the Sea: A Book of Strange Tales* (Frederick A. Stokes Co., New York, n.d.). (5) Both of the preceding cases are cited by Gould. (6) The later history of the *Celeste* is reported by Snow. Tom Mahoney presents a detailed account of the insurance fraud in *True Police Yearbook* (Vol. 1, No. 4).

Chapter 11 / **The Most Famous Derelict**

(1) Some accounts state that Capt. Gerald Douglas did not send a boarding party to the *Joyita*, but merely reported her location. Robin Maugham indicates that he did. (2) *Life*, December 12, 1955. (3) AP dispatch, November 21. (4) I have heard that the *Arakarimoa* was found wrecked and abandoned several months after her disappearance but have been unable to confirm this. (5) *Orbit*, March 2, 1956. Harold Fulton of New Zealand sent the New Zealand *Herald* clippings to Leonard H. Stringfield, editor and publisher of the *Orbit*. (6) Leslie Hobbs in *Life*, December 12, 1955; Robert Lund in *Sea Stories* magazine, Summer, 1964. (7) Quoted from the official Commission of Inquiry report. (8) Quoted by Stephen Noakes in his article "Ghost Ship of the South Seas," *Modern Man Quarterly*, Winter 1957–58 issue. (9) See UP dispatch, April 14, and AP dispatch, April 13, 1956. (10) UP dispatch, July 12, 1956. (11) The statement that the ship struck a horseshoe reef is contained in a letter from Jeanne Booth Johnson of Maui, Hawaii, a personal friend of the late Thomas Miller, and published in *Fate*, March, 1959.

Chapter 12 / **O-U-T—Out!**

(1) A number of writers, including Harold T. Wilkins and Frank Edwards, have told the story of the Seven Hunters Lighthouse. One of the best accounts is by Edward Rowe Snow, *Mysteries and Adventures Along the Atlantic Coast*. All of these writers, however, had no knowledge of the strange entries in the log. This is found in an article by Ernest Fallon, who derived his information from English sources, published in *True Strange Stories* magazine back in August, 1929. (2) Information on the "Devil's Sea" region will be found in Wilkins' *Strange Mysteries of Time and Space*, p. 158. (3) See *Flying Saucers: Top Secret*, by Maj. Donald E. Keyhoe (G. P. Putnam's Sons, New York, 1960), p. 272 ff. (4) San Francisco newspapers, August 17, 1942 ff. Other accounts of the *L-8* blimp mystery will be found in *Stranger Than Science*, by Frank Edwards; *Saga* magazine, February, 1964, and *Fate* magazine, November 1959.

Chapter 13 / The Triangle of Death

(1) All press services carried reports of the *Marine Sulphur Queen's* disappearance in February, 1963. What will probably be the final word on this mystery came on April 14, 1964, when Adm. E. J. Roland, Coast Guard commandant, and a special Coast Guard board of inquiry, announced that no solution to the mysterious disappearance of the tanker had been found. According to a UPI dispatch and the New York *Times* News Service, the ship was a T-2 tanker built during World War II. The board recommended that no other oil tanker should be modified in the same manner as the *Sulphur Queen* to carry liquid sulphur. (2) UPI dispatches, August 30, 1963 ff. (3) UPI dispatches, July 5 and 10, 1963. (4) AP and UPI reports, January 10, 1962 ff. (5) One of the best detailed accounts of this case is "The Mystery of the Lost Patrol," by Allan W. Eckart, *American Legion Magazine,* April, 1962. Also see *The Flying Saucer Conspiracy,* by Maj. Donald E. Keyhoe (Henry Holt and Co., New York, 1955); *Stranger Than Science,* by Frank Edwards; and the various round-ups of triangle disappearances cited in following notes. (6) "Project Magnet" is explained in a folder issued by the U.S. Navy Hydrographic Office, Washington 25, D.C., now known as the U.S. Naval Oceanographic Office. In a letter from this office dated April 6, 1964, and signed by George R. Lorentzen, the following statement is made: "Project Magnet is not classified and we have not observed peculiar magnetic forces coming from above in the Key West-Caribbean area." This denial was in response to an article in the U.F.O. *Investigator* (September, 1963), published by the National Investigations Committee on Aerial Phenomena, Washington 6, D.C. (NICAP). Maj. Donald E. Keyhoe is executive director of this organization. The article, which linked these observations of "peculiar magnetic forces" with the lost patrol, was based on an interview between a civilian scientist connected with Project Magnet and Robert C. Beck, a Los Angeles electronics company president and former Lockheed flight test engineer. (7) The late Wilbert B. Smith was internationally known for his work in radio communications with the Canadian Government Department of Transport. Project Magnet began in Canada in December, 1950, when the Department of Transport authorized Smith to use its laboratory and field facilities for his gravitational studies. The project ended late in 1954, and the U.S. Navy adopted the same project name in its survey to measure the earth's magnetic field. Smith died December 27, 1962, at Hull, Quebec. His article on "reduced bindings" in the atmosphere was published in the *Journal of the Ottawa UFO Club,* Spring, 1963, issue, Box 2280, Postal Station D, Ottawa, Ontario, Canada. (8) *Flying Saucers on the Attack,* by Harold T. Wilkins (The Citadel Press, New York, 1954), p. 140. (9) In addition to press reports at the time of the disappearances of the *Star Tiger,* the chartered DC-3, and the *Ariel,* accounts will also be found in "Sea Mystery at our Back Door," by George X. Sand, *Fate,* October, 1952, and an AP feature

round-up of Bermuda triangle disappearances by E. V. W. Jones released at Miami, Florida, on September 16, 1950. (10) *Strange Mysteries of Time and Space,* by Harold T. Wilkins, p. 156; and *The Case for the UFO,* by M. K. Jessup (The Citadel Press, New York, 1955), p. 165. (11) Disappearance of the S.S. *Sandra* is discussed in the articles listed in note 9. (12) *The Case for the UFO,* p. 165. (13) Information on four preceding cases taken from press reports at time of occurrences. Disappearance of Al Snyder and companions discussed in *Fate* article, October, 1952. (14) *The Books of Charles Fort,* p. 635. (15) *Ibid.,* p. 642. (16) "Ships that Pass in the Night," by C. V. Tench, *Tomorrow* magazine, Winter, 1963. (17) INS dispatch, February 5, 1940. (18) INS dispatch, October 22, 1944. (19) The disappearance of the U.S.S. *Cyclops* is discussed in practically all articles and books on missing ships. AP had a feature story on the mystery released at Boston on March 2, 1958. Two books, *Posted Missing* and *Sea Dogs of Today,* by Alan J. Villiers (Henry Holt and Co., New York, 1931), present excellent accounts of missing ships.

Chapter 14 / Flames from the Sky

(1) UPI dispatch, December 10, 1963. (2) Press Reports, December 7, 1953 ff. (3) A feature story on this occurrence appeared in the Ft. Lauderdale *Sunday News,* April 1, 1956. (4) The Sarasota *Herald-Tribune,* April 5, 1956 ff. Also *Orbit,* May 4, 1956. (5) *The Books of Charles Fort,* p. 273 ff. (6) Reported by the English writer Eric Frank Russell in his article "Invisible Death," *Fate,* December, 1950. (7) For details on these curious cases see Camille Flammarion's *Death and Its Mystery* (The Century Co., New York, 1922), vol. II, p. 268 ff. (8) Preceding cases cited by Eric Frank Russell. (9) In addition to press reports at the time, see a discussion of this case in *The Flying Saucer Conspiracy,* p. 290. (10) Preceding cases cited by Eric Frank Russell. (11) *Flying Saucers on the Attack,* p. 288. *The Case for the UFO,* p. 164. (12) AP dispatches, July 11, 1930 ff. (13) "UFO's and Unnatural Clouds," by Frank Reid, *Saucer News* (P.O. Box 163, Fort Lee, N.J.), August-September, 1956. (14) Before the F-89 disappearance was classified, the AP report appeared in early editions of the Chicago *Tribune,* November 23, 1953; the Sault Ste. Marie *Evening News,* November 23 and 24, 1953. See *The Flying Saucer Conspiracy,* p. 13 ff. (15) I am indebted to Max B. Miller, a Los Angeles writer, for his comprehensive account of this case based on press reports and articles in *Aviation Week* magazine. His article "What Happened November 9, 1957," appeared in *Saucer News,* September, 1961.

Chapter 15 / Is There An Answer?

(1) *M. K. Jessup and the Allende Letters,* by Riley Crabb (BSRA Publications, P.O. Box 548, Vista, Calif., 1962). (2) *The Strange Case of Dr. M. K. Jessup,* by Gray Barker (Saucerian Books, Clarksburg, W. Va., 1963).

INDEX

INDEX

A former newspaperman, Vincent H. Gaddis is a freelance writer who specializes in exploring the borderlands where fact emerges from myth and legend. He has written numerous articles for national publications. This is his first book on his favorite subject: mysteries. He has been a part-time professional magician since boyhood and is a member of the International Brotherhood of Magicians. Gaddis, a native of Ohio, lives in Escondido, California. His wife, the former Margaret Paine Rea, is the author of five Crime Club novels written under the name of M. P. Rea. Mr. and Mrs. Gaddis have one daughter.